McGRAW-HILL

Microsoft *97*
Excel

Timothy J. O'Leary
Arizona State University

Linda I. O'Leary

Boston, Massachusetts   Burr Ridge, Illinois   Dubuque, Iowa
Madison, Wisconsin   New York, New York   San Francisco, California   St. Louis, Missouri

Irwin/McGraw-Hill

A Division of The **McGraw·Hill** Companies

Microsoft Excel 97

Copyright © 1998 by The McGraw-Hill Companies, Inc. All rights reserved. Printed in the United States of America. Except as permitted under the United States Copyright Act of 1976, no part of this publication may be reproduced or distributed in any form or by any means, or stored in a data base or retrieval system, without the prior written permission of the publisher.

This book is printed on acid-free paper.

domestic   5 6 7 8 9 0 BAN BAN 9 0 0 9
international   5 6 7 8 9 0 BAN BAN 9 0 0 9

ISBN 0-07-228254-1

The Sponsoring Editor was Rhonda Sands.
The Developmental Editor was Kristin Hepburn.
The Editorial Assistant was Kyle Thomes.
The Marketing Manager was James Rogers.
The Production Supervisor was Richard DeVitto.
The cover was designed by Lorna Lo.
Project management was by Elaine Brett, Fritz/Brett Associates.
Composition was by Pat Rogondino, Rogondino & Associates.
The typeface was ITC Clearface.
Banta Co. was the printer and binder.

Library of Congress Cataloging Card Number 97-72181

Information has been obtained by The McGraw-Hill Companies, Inc. from sources believed to be reliable. However, because of the possibility of human or mechanical error by our sources, The McGraw-Hill Companies, Inc. or others, The McGraw-Hill Companies, Inc. does not guarantee the accuracy, adequacy, or completeness of any information and is not responsible for any errors or omissions or the results obtained from use of such information.

International Edition
Copyright © 1998. Exclusive rights by The McGraw-Hill Companies, Inc., for manufacture and export. This book cannot be re-exported from the country to which it is consigned by The McGraw-Hill Companies, Inc. The International Edition is not available in North America.

When ordering this title, use ISBN 0-07-115474-4.

http://www.mhhe.com

Contents

ssiv

Spreadsheet Overview

I n contrast to a word processor, which manipulates text, an electronic spreadsheet manipulates numerical data. The first electronic spreadsheet software program, VisiCalc, was offered on the market in 1979. Since then the electronic spreadsheet program has evolved into a powerful business tool that has revolutionized the business world.

Definition of Electronic Spreadsheets

The electronic spreadsheet, or worksheet, is an automated version of the accountant's ledger. Like the accountant's ledger, it consists of rows and columns of numerical data. Unlike the accountant's ledger, which is created on paper using a pencil and a calculator, the electronic spreadsheet is created using a computer system and an electronic spreadsheet application software program.

The electronic spreadsheet eliminates the paper, pencil, and eraser. With a few keystrokes, the user can quickly change, correct, and update the data. Even more impressive is the spreadsheet's ability to perform calculations from very simple sums to the most complex financial and mathematical formulas. The calculator is replaced by the electronic spreadsheet. Analysis of data in the spreadsheet has become a routine business procedure. Once requiring hours of labor and/or costly accountants' fees, data analysis is now available almost instantly using electronic spreadsheets.

Nearly any job that uses rows and columns of numbers can be performed using an electronic spreadsheet. Typical uses of electronic spreadsheets are for budgets and financial planning in both business and personal situations.

Advantages of Using an Electronic Spreadsheet

An electronic spreadsheet application helps you create well-designed spreadsheets that produce accurate results. The application not only makes it faster to create the spreadsheet, but produces a professional-appearing result. The advantages are in the ability of the spreadsheet program to quickly edit and format data, perform calculations, create graphs, and print the spreadsheet.

The data entered in an electronic spreadsheet can be edited and revised using the program commands. Numeric or text data is entered into the worksheet in a location called a cell. These entries can then be erased, moved, copied, or edited. Formulas can be entered that perform calculations using data contained in specified cells. The results of the calculations are displayed in the cell containing the formula.

The design and appearance of the spreadsheet can be enhanced in many ways. There are several commands that control the format or display of a numeric entry in a cell. For instance, numeric entries can be displayed with dollar signs or with a set number of decimal places. Text or label entries in a cell can be displayed centered or left- or right-aligned to improve the spreadsheet's appearance. You can further enhance the appearance of the spreadsheet by changing the type style and size and by adding special effects such as bold, italics, borders, boxes, drop shadows, and shading around selected cells. Columns and rows can be inserted and deleted. The cell width can be changed to accommodate entries of varying lengths.

You can play with the values in the worksheet, to see the effect of changing specific values on the worksheet. This is called what-if or sensitivity analysis. Questions that once were too expensive to ask or took too long to answer can now be answered almost instantly and with little cost. Planning that was once partially based on instinct has been replaced to a great extent with facts. However, any financial planning resulting from the data in a worksheet is only as accurate as that data and the logic behind the calculations.

Electronic spreadsheet programs also have the ability to produce a visual display of the data in the form of graphs or charts. As the values in the worksheet change, a graph referencing those values automatically reflects the new values. These graphs are a tool for visualizing the effects of changing values in a worksheet. Many spreadsheet programs let you include a graph with the spreadsheet data. This way you can display and print it with the data it represents. You can also enhance the appearance of a graph by using different type styles and sizes, adding three-dimensional effects, and including text and objects such as lines and arrows.

Another feature of many spreadsheet programs is the ability to open and use multiple spreadsheet files at the same time. Additionally, you can create multiple spreadsheets within a file, called 3-D spreadsheets. Even more important is the ability to link spreadsheets so that when data in one file changes, it automatically updates the linked data in another file.

Electronic Spreadsheet Terminology

Alignment: The position of an entry within the cell space.

Cell: The space created by the intersection of a horizontal row and a vertical column. It can contain a label (text), value (number), or formula.

Columns: The vertical blocks of cells in the spreadsheet identified by letters.

File linking: A spreadsheet feature that creates a connection between two files in order to share data.

Format: The styles applied to a cell that control how entries in the spreadsheet are displayed (currency, percent, number of decimal places, and so on).

Formula: An entry that performs a calculation.

Function: A built-in or preprogrammed formula.

Graph: The visual representation of ranges of data in the worksheet. Also called a chart. Some graph types are line, bar, stacked-bar, and pie.

Label: An entry that consists of text and numeric characters.

Rows: The horizontal blocks of cells in the worksheet identified by numbers.

Value: An entry that is a number or the result of a formula or function.

What-if analysis: A process of evaluating the effects of changing one or more values in formulas to help in decision making and planning.

Case Study for Labs 1–6

As a recent college graduate, you have accepted your first job as a management trainee for The Sports Company. The program requires that you work in several areas of the company. In this series of labs, you are working in a retail store as an assistant to the store manager.

In Labs 1 and 2 you will create an operating budget for the retail store. You will learn how to use the worksheet program to enter descriptive text, numbers, formulas, and functions. You will also learn how to format the worksheet to improve its appearance.

Lab 3 demonstrates how to freeze row and column titles and split windows to manage large worksheets. You will open and work with multiple workbook files and create a workbook containing multiple worksheets. It also shows you how to perform what-if analysis. Finally, in this lab you learn how to link workbook files.

In Lab 4 you decide you want to analyze the sales data by sport at the store. To better visualize the changes in sales over time, you learn how to create several charts of the data.

In Lab 5 you will create a worksheet template to be used to track the monthly new charge card enrollments and employee bonuses. While working on this project, you learn about the IF function, naming ranges, and using worksheet protection.

Lab 6 demonstrates how an Excel chart can be incorporated into a Word document. The differences between linking and embedding are demonstrated.

Before You Begin

To the Student

The following assumptions have been made:

- The Microsoft Excel 97 program has been properly installed on the hard disk of your computer system.

- The data disk contains in the root directory the data files that are needed to complete the series of Excel 97 labs and practice exercises. These files are supplied by your instructor.

- You have completed the Windows 95 Labs or you are already familiar with how to use a mouse and Windows 95.

To the Instructor

The following assumptions about the setup of the Excel 97 program have been made:

- When the worksheet window is maximized, the number of rows and columns that are displayed varies with the computer system display settings established in Windows. These labs assume a standard VGA display setting (640 X 480), which displays columns A through I and rows 1 through 18. The text and figures reflect this setup.

- The Standard and Formatting toolbars are displayed whenever a worksheet is opened.

- The Tip of the Day is not displayed at Startup.

- The Office Assistant is on.

- The Solver application has been installed.

Office Shortcut Bar

The Microsoft Office Shortcut Bar (shown below) may be displayed automatically on the Windows 95 desktop. Commonly it appears in the upper right section of the desktop; however, it may appear in other locations, depending upon your setup. Because the Shortcut Bar can be customized, it may display different buttons than those shown below.

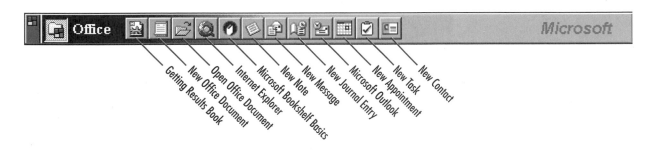

The Office Shortcut Bar makes it easy to open existing documents or to create new documents using one of the Microsoft Office applications. It can also be used to send e-mail, add a task to a to-do list, schedule appointments using Outlook, or add contacts or notes.

Instructional Conventions

This text uses the following instructional conventions:

- Steps that you are to perform are preceded with a bullet (■) and are in blue type.

- Command sequences you are to issue appear following the word "Choose." Each menu command selection is separated by a /. If the command can be selected by typing a letter of the command, the letter will appear bold and underlined.

- Commands that can be initiated using a button and the mouse appear following the word "Click." The menu equivalent and keyboard shortcut appear in a margin note when the action is first introduced.

- Anything you are to type appears in bold text.

Creating a Worksheet: Part 1

CASE STUDY

The Sports Company is a chain of sporting goods shops located in large metropolitan areas across the United States. The stores are warehouse oriented, discounting the retail price of most items 15 percent. They stock sporting goods products for the major sports: team sports, racquet sports, aerobics, golf, and winter sports.

As a recent college graduate, you have accepted your first job in a management training program for The Sports Company. The training program emphasis is on computer applications in the area of retail man-

S. Name
10/10/98   1999 First Half Budget

	JAN	FEB	MAR	APR	MAY	JUN	TOTAL
SALES							
Clothing	140000	135000	175000	210000	185000	185000	1030000
Hard Goc	94000	89000	120000	145000	125000	125000	
Total Sales							
EXPENSES							
Advertising							
Cost of Goods							
Salary	30000	30000	30000	30000	30000	30000	
Lease	19000	19000	19000	19000	19000	19000	
Miscellar	16000	16000	16000	16000	16000	16000	
Overheac	22000	22000	22000	22000	22000	22000	
Total Expenses							
INCOME							

agement. The program requires that you work in several areas of the company, beginning in a retail store as an assistant to the store manager.

The software tool you will learn about in this series of labs is the spreadsheet application, Microsoft Excel 97. Its purpose is to store, manipulate, and display numeric data. During the next six labs, you will use Excel to create several spreadsheets for The Sports Company that will help with budget projections and sales analysis.

In this lab you will learn how to enter and edit descriptive row and column headings, enter numbers and formulas, copy data, and align entries as you create a six-month budget for the store, as shown on the previous page.

Concept Overview

The following concepts will be introduced in this lab:

1. Worksheet Design	A well-designed worksheet produces accurate results, and is clearly understood, adaptable, and efficient.
2. Types of Entries	The information or data you enter in a cell can be text, numbers, or formulas.
3. Copy and Move Cell Contents	The contents of worksheet cells can be copied or moved to new locations in the worksheet.
4. Range	A selection consisting of two or more cells on a worksheet is a range.
5. Formulas	A formula is an entry that performs a calculation.
6. Automatic Recalculation	Excel automatically recalculates formulas whenever a change occurs in a referenced cell.
7. Format	Formats control how information is displayed in a cell and are used to improve the appearance of the worksheet data.
8. Alignment	Alignment settings allow you to change the horizontal and vertical placement and the orientation of an entry in a cell.
9. Dates	Excel automatically recognizes certain types of data input, such as dates and times, and formats the entry as appropriate.

Part 1

Loading Excel 97

You will use Excel 97 to create the budget for The Sports Company for the first six months of 1999. To start Excel 97,

- ■ If necessary, turn on your computer.

- ■ Click **Start**.

- ■ Choose **P**rograms Microsoft Excel .

If a Shortcut to Excel button Microsoft Excel is displayed on your desktop, you can double-click on the button to start the program.

If the Microsoft Office suite is on your system and the Office Shortcut Bar is displayed, you can load Excel by clicking the New Office Document button and selecting Blank Workbook.

SPREADSHEET

After a few moments the Excel application window is displayed. Your screen should be similar to Figure 1-1.

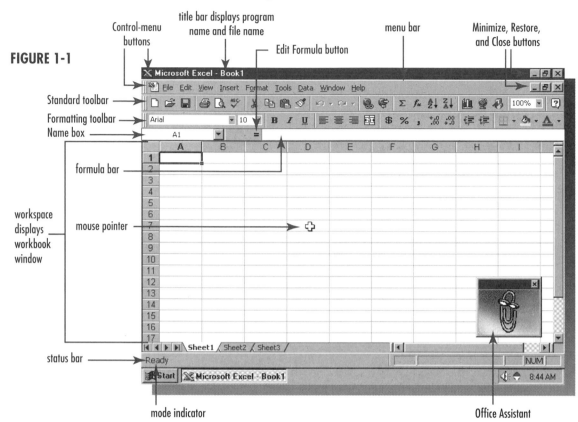

FIGURE 1-1

Control-menu buttons

title bar displays program name and file name

Edit Formula button

menu bar

Minimize, Restore, and Close buttons

Standard toolbar

Formatting toolbar

Name box

formula bar

workspace displays workbook window

mouse pointer

status bar

mode indicator

Office Assistant

If necessary, maximize the Excel application window.

If the title bar does not display the file name, the workbook window is not maximized. Maximize the workbook window by clicking on the workbook window Maximize ▢ button.

As you can see, many of the features in the Excel application window are common to the Windows 95 environment. Among those features are a title bar, menu bar, control menus, Minimize and Restore buttons, toolbars, scroll bars, document windows, and mouse compatibility. You can move and size Excel windows, select commands, use Help, and switch between files and programs just as in Windows and other Windows-based applications. Your knowledge of how to use Windows makes using Excel much easier. The Excel window includes all these features, plus some additional features that are specific to Excel.

The Excel window title bar displays the program name, Microsoft Excel, followed by the file name Book1, the default name of the file displayed in the workbook window. The left end of the title bar contains the Excel application window Control-menu icon ✖, and the right end displays the Minimize ▬, Restore ▣, and Close ✖ buttons. They perform the same functions and operate in the same way as in Windows 95.

The menu bar below the title bar displays the Excel program menu. The left end of the menu bar displays the workbook window Control-menu icon ▣, and the right end displays the workbook window Minimize ▣, Restore ▣, and Close ☒ buttons.

The two toolbars below the menu bar contain buttons that are mouse short-cuts for many of the menu items. The upper toolbar is the **Standard toolbar**, and the bottom is the **Formatting toolbar**. There are 13 different toolbars in Excel, and they operate just like Windows 95 toolbars. You will learn more about Excel toolbars shortly.

Below the toolbars is the formula bar. The **formula bar** displays entries as they are made and edited in the workbook window. The **Name box**, located at the left end of the formula bar, provides information about the selected item. The ▣ Edit Formula button is used to create or edit a cell formula.

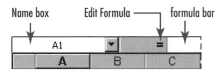

The largest area of the Excel window is the **workspace**. The workspace is where different windows are displayed. Currently there is only one window open, and it occupies the entire workspace. The window displays a workbook. A **workbook** is an Excel file that stores the information you enter using the program. Excel calls a window that displays a workbook file a **workbook window**. You can have several workbook files open at once, each displayed in their own workbook window in the workspace. You will learn about the different parts of the workbook window shortly.

The status bar at the bottom of the Excel window displays information about various Excel settings. The left side of the status bar displays the current mode or state the Excel program is in. The current mode is Ready. When "Ready" is displayed, you can move around the workbook, enter data, use the function keys, or choose a command. As you are using the program, the status bar will display the current mode. The modes will be discussed as they appear throughout the labs.

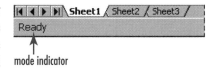

The mouse pointer probably appears as a ⊹ or ↖ on your screen. As in Windows 95, the mouse pointer changes shape depending upon the task you are performing or where the pointer is located on the window.

Finally, your screen may display the Office Assistant. You will learn about this feature shortly.

The Workbook Window

The workbook window displays a new blank workbook file containing three blank sheets. A sheet is used to display different types of information, such as financial data or charts. Whenever you open a new workbook, it displays a worksheet.

A **worksheet,** also commonly referred to as a **spreadsheet,** is a rectangular grid of **rows** and **columns** used to enter data. It is always part of a workbook and

The default workbook opens with three worksheets. The number of sheets in a workbook is limited only by the available memory on your computer.

is the primary type of sheet you will use in Excel. The parts of the worksheet are shown in Figure 1-2, below.

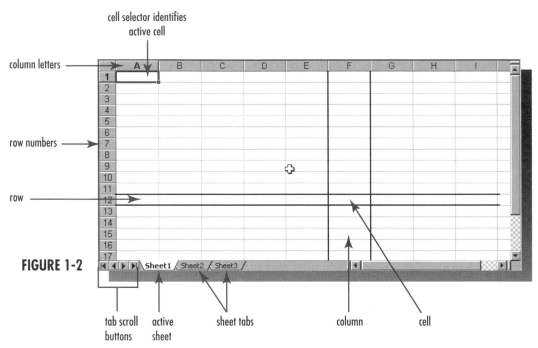

column letters

row numbers

row

cell selector identifies active cell

FIGURE 1-2

tab scroll buttons

active sheet

sheet tabs

column

cell

Do not be concerned if your workbook window displays more column letters and row numbers than in Figure 1-2. This is a function of your computer monitor.

The **row numbers** along the left side and the **column letters** across the top of the workbook window identify each worksheet row and column. The intersection of a row and column creates a **cell**. Notice the heavy border, called the **cell selector**, surrounding the cell located at the intersection of column A and row 1. The cell selector identifies the **active cell**, which is the cell your next entry or procedure affects. In addition, the row number and column letter appear bold to further identify the location of the active cell. Finally, the Name box displays the **reference**, consisting of the column letter and row number of the active cell. The reference of the active cell is A1.

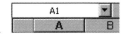

Each sheet in a workbook is named. The default names are Sheet1, Sheet2, and so on, displayed on **sheet tabs** at the bottom of the workbook window. The name of the **active sheet**, which is the sheet you can work in, appears bold. The currently displayed worksheet in the workspace, Sheet1, is the active sheet.

The sheet tab area also contains **tab scroll buttons**, which are used to scroll tabs right or left when there are more worksheet tabs than there is available space. You will learn about these features throughout the labs.

Using Toolbars

By default the Standard toolbar and the Formatting toolbar, shown below, are automatically displayed.

move handles

Standard toolbar

Formatting toolbar

The Standard toolbar contains buttons that are used to complete the most frequently used menu commands. The buttons in the Formatting toolbar are used to change the format or design of the worksheet. Many of the buttons are the same as those you have seen in toolbars in other Windows 95 applications. Many, however, are specific to the Excel 97 application. Any buttons that are dimmed indicate they are not available for use.

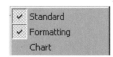

■ To quickly identify the toolbar buttons, point to each button in both toolbars to display the button name in the Screen Tip.

Although many of the toolbars open automatically as different tasks are performed, you can also open toolbars whenever you want using the toolbar Shortcut menu. Clicking on a toolbar from the menu will display it onscreen. Likewise, clicking on a checked toolbar will remove the toolbar from the screen.

■ To open the toolbar Shortcut menu, right-click on the toolbar.

■ Press Esc to clear the Shortcut menu.

> The menu equivalent is **V**iew/**T**oolbars.

> You can also click outside the Shortcut menu to clear it.

Using the Office Assistant

Note: If you are already familiar with this feature, skip this section.

The **Office Assistant** is used to get Help on features that are specific to the Office application you are using. The Assistant can display tips that point out how to more effectively use the features or keyboard shortcuts in the program. A tip is available when a yellow light bulb 💡 appears in the Assistant; click the light bulb to see the tip. It can also automatically display Help suggestions based on your actions. In addition, you can activate the Assistant at any time to ask for Help on any topic. To activate it,

> If your Office Assistant is not displayed, click 🔲 or press F1 .

> The Office Assistant feature is common to all Office 97 programs.

> Your Assistant may be different than the one displayed in this text.

> You can also access Help using the Help menu.

■ Click 📎 Office Assistant.

A yellow balloon displays a prompt and a text box in which you can type the topic on which you want help. Then you click the Search button to display a topic list related to your question. In addition, the Tips option button displays the most recent tip and lets you scroll through tips that the Office Assistant has recently displayed. The Options button is used to configure the Office Assistant to provide different levels of help or display a different Assistant.

■   Click (● Tips) and read the tip that appears in the box.

the information displayed in the Tip box
changes depending on what you are doing

closes the
Assistant

Your tip may be different than shown here.

Tip of the day: Point to Macro on the Tools menu, and click Macros to record your actions in Visual Basic for Applications. You can then examine the recorded macro to learn about Visual Basic.

Back   Next   ● Close

■   To clear the tip, click (● Close).

You can leave the Office Assistant open or you can close it and activate it when needed. This text will not display the Assistant open.

■   If you want to hide the Assistant, click [✗] in the Assistant's window.

Moving Around the Worksheet

You can use the directional keys in the numeric keypad or, if you have an extended keyboard, you can use the separate directional keypad area.

If you are using the numeric keypad area, make sure the Num Lock feature is off. "NUM" is displayed in the status bar when it is on.

Either the mouse or the keyboard can be used to move the cell selector from one cell to another in the worksheet. To move using a mouse, simply point to the cell you want to move to and click the mouse button. Depending upon what you are doing, using the mouse to move may not be as convenient as using the keyboard, in which case the directional keys can be used. To use the mouse, then the keyboard to move the cell selector,

■   Click cell B3.

■   Press [→] (3 times).

■   Press [↓] (4 times).

Your worksheet should be similar to Figure 1-3.

Name box displays reference
of active cell

cell selector identifies
active cell

FIGURE 1-3

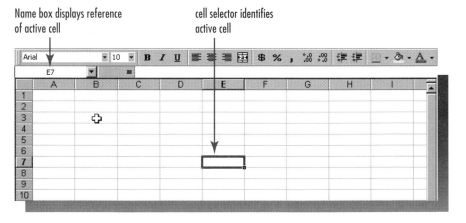

The cell selector is now in cell E7, making this cell the active cell. To return quickly to the upper left corner, cell A1, of the worksheet,

- Press [Ctrl] + [Home].

Scrolling the Worksheet

The worksheet is much larger than the part you are viewing in the window. The worksheet actually extends many columns to the right and many rows down. An Excel worksheet has 256 columns and 65,536 rows. For example, to see the rows immediately below row 17,

- Press [Page Down].

Your worksheet should be similar to Figure 1-4.

> The column letter and row number containing the cell selector appear raised.

> [Page Up] moves up a window on the worksheet.

FIGURE 1-4

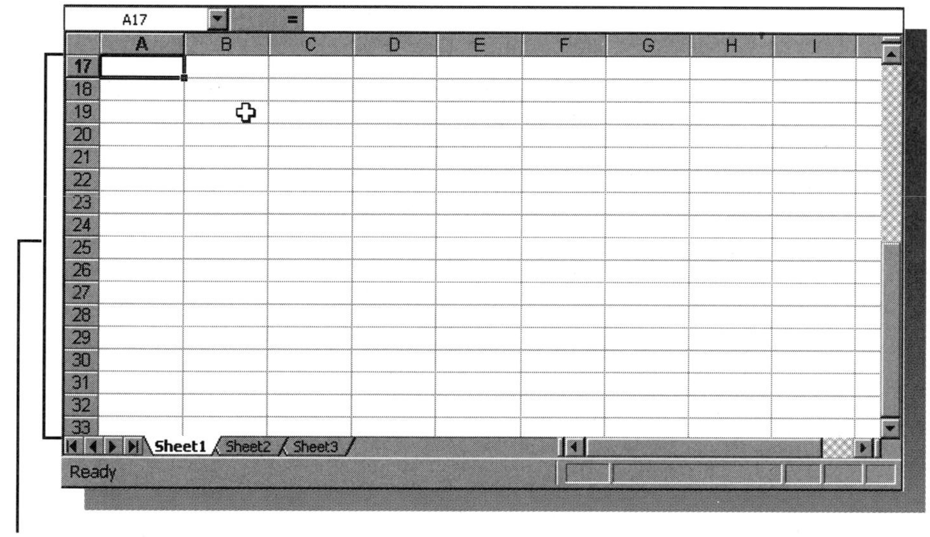

pressing [Page Down] displays next full window down in worksheet

The worksheet has scrolled upward in the window and is positioned over rows 17 through 33 of the worksheet. Columns A through I have remained the same.

Either the keyboard or the mouse can be used to quickly scroll a worksheet to see an area that is not currently in view. Again, both methods are useful depending upon what you are doing. The keys and mouse procedures shown in the table that follows can be used to move around the worksheet. In addition, if you hold down the arrow keys, the [Alt] + [Page Down] or [Alt] + [Page Up] keys, or the [Page Up] or [Page Down] keys, you can quickly scroll through the worksheet. As you scroll the worksheet using the keyboard, the cell selector moves to the new location. When you use the mouse and the scroll bar, however, the cell selector does not move until you click on a cell that is visible in the window.

Keys	Action
Arrow keys (← ↑ → ↓)	Moves cell selector one cell in direction of arrow
Alt + Page Down	Moves cell selector right one full window
Alt + Page Up	Moves cell selector left one full window
Page Down	Moves cell selector down one full window
Page Up	Moves cell selector up one full window
Ctrl + Home	Moves cell selector to cell in upper left corner of worksheet
Home	Moves cell selector to beginning of row
End →	Moves cell selector to last-used cell in row
End ↓	Moves cell selector to last-used cell in column

Mouse	Action
Click cell	Moves cell selector to selected cell
Click scroll arrow	Scrolls worksheet one row/column in direction of arrow
Click above/below scroll box	Scrolls worksheet one full window up/down
Click right/left of scroll box	Scrolls worksheet one full window right/left
Drag scroll box	Scrolls worksheet multiple windows up/down or right/left

Notice as you drag the scroll box that a Scroll Tip appears showing the column or row location.   Row: 12

■   Practice moving the cell selector around the worksheet using each of the keys and mouse procedures presented in the table above.

■   Move to A1.

You can use the mouse or the keyboard with most of the exercises in these labs. As you use both the mouse and the keyboard, you will find that it is more efficient to use one or the other in specific situations.

Designing Worksheets

Now that you are familiar with the parts of the worksheet, you will begin creating the budget for the first six months for The Sports Company. The first step to creating a worksheet is to develop the worksheet design.

Concept 1: Worksheet Design

A well-designed worksheet produces accurate results, and is clearly understood, adaptable, and efficient. To achieve a well-designed worksheet, a worksheet plan must be developed. There are four steps in this planning process.

1. Specify purpose   As your first step, you must decide exactly what you want the worksheet to do. This means clearly identifying the data that will be input and the output that is desired.

2. Design and build   You can design the worksheet on paper or directly in Excel for Windows. Your design should include a worksheet title and row and column headings that identify the input and output. Sample data is used to help generate the formulas needed to produce the output.

3. Test   Once your design is complete, you are ready to test the worksheet for errors. Several sets of real or sample data are used as the input, and the resulting output is verified. The input data should include a full range of possible values for each data item to ensure the worksheet can function successfully under all possible conditions.

4. Document   Well-designed worksheets typically include documentation to ensure that whoever uses the worksheet will be able to clearly understand its objectives and procedures.

As the complexity of the worksheet increases, the importance of following the design process increases. Even for simple worksheets like the one you will create in this lab, the design process is important.

After reviewing past budgets and consulting with the store manager, you have designed the basic layout for the six-month budget for the retail store as shown below.

Six Month Budget				
Sales	January	February	•••	Total
_____	$100,000	$125,000	•••	$225,000
_____	xx,xxx	xxx,xxx		xxx,xxx
Total Sales	$ xxx,xxx	$ xxx,xxx		$ xxx,xxx
Expenses				
_____	$ _____	_____		_____
_____	_____	_____		_____
⋮	_____	_____		_____
Total Expenses	$ _____	_____		_____
Income	$(Total Sales – Total Expenses)			_____

Entering Data

As you can see, the budget contains both descriptive text entries and numeric data. These are the two types of entries you can make in a worksheet.

Concept 2: Types of Entries

The information or data you enter in a cell can be text, numbers, or formulas. **Text** entries can contain any combination of letters, numbers, spaces, and any other special characters. **Number** entries can include only the digits 0 to 9, and any of the special characters, + − ( ) , . / $ % E e. Number entries are used in calculations. An entry that begins with an equal sign (=) is a **formula**. Formula entries perform calculations using numbers or data contained in other cells. The resulting value is a **variable** value because it can change if the data it depends on changes. In contrast, a number entry is a **constant** value. It does not begin with an equal sign and does not change unless you change it directly by typing in another entry.

First you will enter the worksheet headings. Row and column **headings** are entries that are used to create the structure of the worksheet and describe other worksheet entries. Generally, headings are text entries. The column headings in this worksheet consist of the six months (January through June) and a total (sum of entries over six months) located in columns B through H. To enter data in a worksheet, you must first select the cell where you want the entry displayed. The column heading for January will be entered in cell B2.

- Move to B2.

- Type **J**.

Your worksheet should be similar to Figure 1-5.

FIGURE 1-5

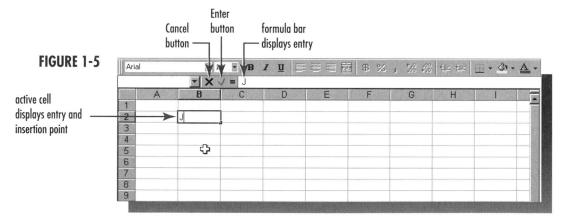

Several changes have occurred in the window. As you type, the entry is displayed both in the active cell and in the formula bar. An insertion point appears in the active cell and marks your location in the entry. Two new buttons, Cancel ⊠ and Enter ☑, appear in the formula bar. They can be used by the mouse to complete your entry or cancel it.

Notice also that the mode displayed in the status bar has changed from "Ready" to "Enter." This notifies you that the current mode of operation in the worksheet is entering data. To continue entering the heading,

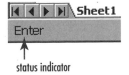

status indicator

■   Type **anuary**.

Although the entry is displayed in both the active cell and the formula bar, you need to press the ⟨←Enter⟩ key or click ☑ to complete your entry. If you press ⟨Esc⟩ or click ☒, the entry is cleared and nothing appears in the cell. Since your hands are already on the keyboard, it is quicker to press ⟨←Enter⟩ than it is to use the mouse to click ☑.

■   Press ⟨←Enter⟩.

Your worksheet should be similar to Figure 1-6.

text entries are
left-aligned in cell space

cell selector moves down to next
cell after ⟨←Enter⟩ is pressed

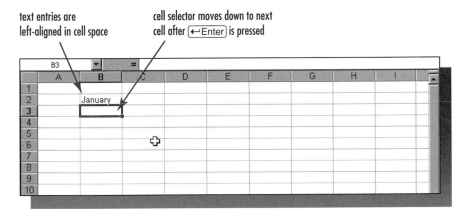

FIGURE 1-6

> If you made an error while typing the entry, use ⟨Backspace⟩ to erase the characters back to the error. Then retype the entry correctly.

The entry "January" is displayed in cell B2, and the mode has returned to Ready. Notice that the entry is positioned to the left side of the cell space. The positioning of cell entries in the cell space is called alignment. By default text entries are displayed left-aligned. You will learn more about this feature later in the lab.

Clearing an Entry

After looking at the entry, you decide you want the column headings to be in row 3 rather than in row 2. This will leave more space above the column headings for a worksheet title.

The ⟨Delete⟩ key can be used to clear the contents from a cell. To remove the entry from cell B2 and enter it in cell B3,

■   Move to B2.

■   Press ⟨Delete⟩.

■   Move to B3.

■   Type **January**.

■   Click ☑.

> Pressing ⟨←Enter⟩ also moves the cell selector down one cell.

> Pressing ⟨⇧Shift⟩ + ⟨←Enter⟩ to complete an entry moves the cell selector up a cell, and ⟨Ctrl⟩ + ⟨←Enter⟩ completes the entry without moving the cell selector.

> The menu equivalent is **E**dit/**C**lear/**C**ontents. Clear Contents is also an option on the Shortcut menu.

The cell selector remains in the active cell when you use 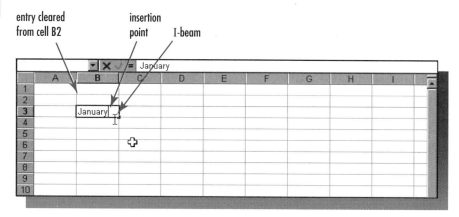 to complete an entry. Also notice, because the cell selector is positioned on a cell containing an entry, the contents of the cell are displayed in the formula bar.

Editing an Entry

You would like to change the heading from January to JAN. An entry in a cell can be entirely changed in the Ready mode or partially changed or edited in the Edit mode. To use the Ready mode, you move the cell selector to the cell you want to change and retype the entry the way you want it to appear. As soon as a new character is entered, the existing entry is cleared.

Generally, however, if you need to change only a part of an entry, it is quicker to use the Edit mode. To change to Edit mode, double-click on the cell whose contents you want to edit.

■   Double-click B3.

Your worksheet should be similar to Figure 1-7.

Pressing the F2 key will also change to Edit mode.

The mouse pointer must be when you double-click on the cell.

entry cleared
from cell B2

insertion
point   I-beam

FIGURE 1-7

The status bar shows the new mode of operation is Edit. The insertion point appears in the entry, and the mouse pointer changes to an I-beam ⏐ when positioned on the cell. The mouse pointer can now be used to move the insertion point in the entry by positioning the I-beam and clicking.

In addition, in the Edit mode, the following keys can be used to move the insertion point:

Excel automatically corrects common spelling errors as you type.

Key	Action
Home	Moves insertion point to beginning of entry
End	Moves insertion point to end of entry
→	Moves insertion point one character right
←	Moves insertion point one character left

Once the insertion point is appropriately positioned, you can edit the entry by removing the incorrect characters and typing the correct characters. The ⌈Delete⌋ key erases characters at the insertion point, and the ⌈←Backspace⌋ key erases characters to the left of the insertion point. To change this entry to JAN,

■   If necessary, move the insertion point to the end of the entry.

■   Press ⌈←Backspace⌋ (4 times).

■   Press ⌈Home⌋.

■   Press ⌈Caps Lock⌋.

■   Press ⌈→⌋.

■   Press ⌈Insert⌋.

■   Type **AN**.

■   Press ⌈←Enter⌋.

■   Press ⌈Caps Lock⌋.

the insertion point is a highlight when overwrite is on

Jan

⌈Ctrl⌋ + ⌈Delete⌋ will delete everything to the right of the insertion point.

The ⌈Caps Lock⌋ key produces uppercase characters when on.

The ⌈Insert⌋ key acts as a toggle to switch between inserting and overwriting text.

Overwrite is automatically turned off when you leave Edit mode or if you press ⌈Insert⌋ again.

The new heading JAN is entered into cell B3, replacing January. As you can see, editing will be particularly useful with long or complicated entries.

Next you will enter the month heading for February in cell C3. You can also complete an entry by moving to any other worksheet cell. To try this,

■   Move to C3.

■   Type **February**.

■   Press ⌈→⌋ or click D3.

■   Using Edit mode, change February to FEB.

■   Complete the column headings by entering MAR, APR, MAY, JUN, and TOTAL in cells D3 through H3.

■   When you are done, turn off ⌈Caps Lock⌋.

Above the column headings, in row 2, you want to enter a title for the worksheet.

■   Move to C2.

■   Type **1999 First Half Budget**.

■   Press ⌈←Enter⌋.

Your worksheet should be similar to Figure 1-8.

FIGURE 1-8

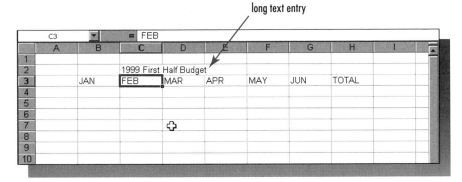

When a text entry is longer than the cell's column width, Excel will display as much of the entry as it can. If the cell to the right is empty, the whole entry will be displayed. If the cell to the right contains an entry, the overlapping part of the entry is not displayed.

Next the row headings need to be entered into column A of the worksheet. The row headings and what they represent are shown below:

Heading	Represents
SALES	Category head for all items that are a result of sales
Clothing	Income from clothing sales
Hard Goods	Income from equipment, machines, and miscellaneous sales
Total Sales	Sum of clothing and hard goods sales
EXPENSES	Category head for all items that are a result of expenses
Advertising	Monthly advertising costs (4 percent of total sales)
Cost of Goods	Cost of items sold (58 percent of total sales)
Salary	Personnel expenses
Lease	Monthly lease expense
Miscellaneous	Monthly expenses for phone, electricity, water, trash removal, and so on
Overhead	Monthly payment to corporate headquarters
Total Expenses	Sum of advertising, cost of goods, salary, lease, miscellaneous, and overhead expenses
INCOME	Total Sales minus Total Expenses

■ Complete the row headings for the SALES portion of the worksheet by entering the following headings in the indicated cells:

Remember to press ⟨←Enter⟩ or an arrow key to complete the last entry.

Cell	Heading
A4	**SALES**
A5	**Clothing**
A6	**Hard Goods**
A7	**Total Sales**

Your worksheet should be similar to Figure 1-9.

column headings describe contents of columns

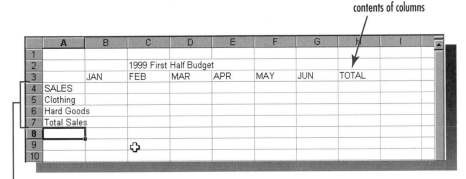

FIGURE 1-9

row headings describe contents of rows

Entering Numbers

Next you will enter the expected clothing sales numbers for January through June into cells B5 through G5. As you learned earlier, number entries can include the digits 0 to 9 and any of these special characters: + − ( ), . / $ % E e. When entering numbers, it is not necessary to type the comma to separate thousands or the currency ($) symbol. You will learn about adding these symbols later.

Refer to Concept 2: Types of Entries.

To enter the expected clothing sales for January,

■ Move to B5.

■ Type **140000**.

■ Press →.

You can use the number keys above the alphabetic keys or the numeric keypad area to enter numbers. If you use the numeric keypad, the ⟨Num Lock⟩ key must be on.

Your worksheet should be similar to Figure 1-10.

FIGURE 1-10

numeric entries are
right-aligned in the space

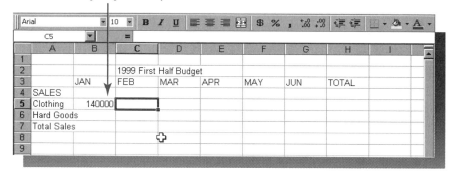

■   In the same manner, using the numbers shown below, enter the clothing sales numbers for February through June and the hard goods sales for the six months in row 6 in the specified cells:

Cell	Number
C5	135000
D5	200000
E5	210000
F5	185000
G5	185000

Cell	Number
B6	94000
C6	89000
D6	120000
E6	145000
F6	125000
G6	125000

Notice that the entry in cell A6 is no longer completely displayed. It is a long text entry, and because the cell to the right (B6) now contains an entry, the overlapping part of the entry is not displayed.

■   Move to A6.

Your worksheet should be similar to Figure 1-11.

display of long text entry in A6 is interrupted because the cell to the right contains an entry

entry is fully displayed in the formula bar

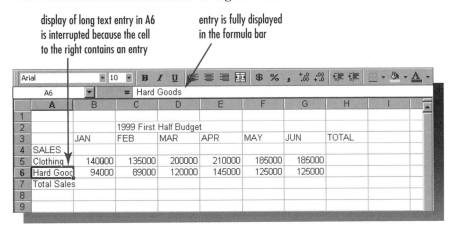

FIGURE 1-11

In Lab 2 you will learn how to change the width of a column so the entire entry can be displayed.

Closing and Opening a Workbook

The rest of the row headings and several of the expense numbers for the month of January have already been entered and saved on your data disk in a file called January Data. Before opening this workbook file, you will close the current workbook.

■   Choose **F**ile/**C**lose.

A dialog box is displayed asking if you want to save the contents of the current workbook to disk. Since the file you will open next contains the same information, you do not need to save it.

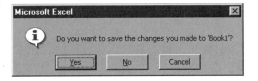

You can also click ⌧ to close the workbook file.

If Office Assistant is displayed, the message appears in a balloon instead of the dialog box.

■   Click   No   .

The workbook window is cleared from memory, and the Excel window displays an empty workspace.

    You are now ready to open the file named January Data. As in all Windows 95 applications, the Open command on the File menu is used to open files. In addition, the toolbar shortcut can be used instead of the menu command.

■   Put your data disk in the A drive (or the appropriate drive for your system).

■   Click 📂 Open.

If you want to save your work, choose Yes. Then follow the directions on page SS36–37 to save the workbook as Lab 1 Budget to the drive containing your data disk.

The menu equivalent is **F**ile/**O**pen or Ctrl + **O**.

The Open dialog box on your screen should be similar to Figure 1-12.

FIGURE 1-12

specifies the location where
Excel will look for files

file list area displays
Excel file names in
specified location

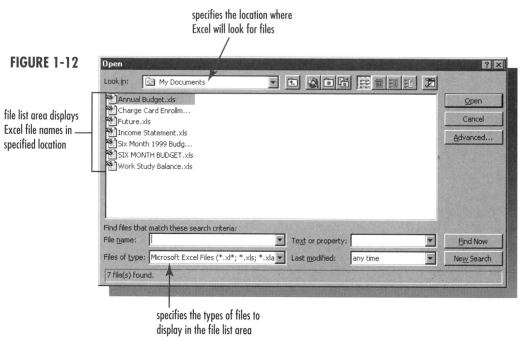

specifies the types of files to
display in the file list area

This dialog box is used to specify the name and location of the file to open. You may need to change the location shown in the Look In drop-down list box to the drive containing your data disk. If necessary,

- Select Look **i**n.

- Select ⬜ 3½ Floppy (A:) (or the drive containing your data disk).

Now the file list area of the dialog box displays the names of the Excel files on your data disk. The file you want to open is January Data. The file name extension .xls identifies this file as an Excel workbook file. If there are other types of files on your data disk, they are not listed. This is because the Files of Type list box shows the currently selected type is Excel files.

- Select January Data.

- Click [Open].

The new workbook file is loaded and displayed in the workbook window.

- Move to A18.

If your drive is already correctly specified in the Look In list box, skip this step.

If an error message is displayed, check that your disk is properly inserted in the drive.

If your screen does not display file extensions, your Windows 95 program has this option deactivated.

If necessary, scroll the list box until the file name January Data is visible. If the file name is not displayed, ask your instructor for help.

You can double-click on the file name to both select it and choose [Open].

Your screen should be similar to Figure 1-13.

file name

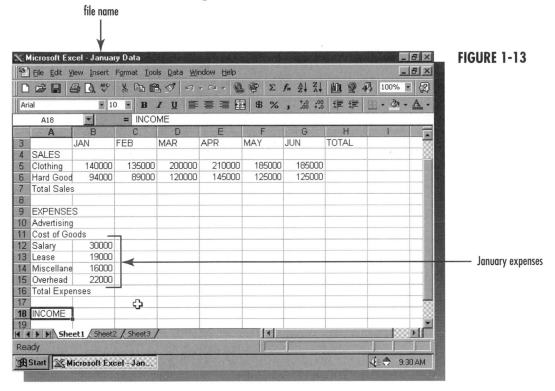

FIGURE 1-13

January expenses

The opened workbook, January Data, contains the expense row headings and numbers for salary, lease, miscellaneous, and overhead for the month of January.

Note: If you are stopping at the end of Part 1, follow the instructions on page SS40 to exit the program. When you begin Part 2, load Excel and open the January Data file.

Part 2

Copying Data

Next you want to enter the estimated expenses for salary, lease, miscellaneous, and overhead for February through June. They are the same as the January expense numbers.

When you entered the sales numbers for January through June, you entered them individually into each cell because the numbers changed from month to month. However, the number in cell B12 is the same number that needs to be entered in cells C12 through G12. You could type the same amount into each month, or you can copy the number in B12 into the other cells.

Concept 3: Copy and Move Cell Contents

The Clipboard is a temporary storage area in your computer's memory.

The contents of worksheet cells can be moved by cutting them and then pasting them in a new location in the worksheet. They can also be duplicated (copied) and pasted. When you cut or copy cell contents, the contents are stored in the Clipboard. Then when they are pasted to the new location, the Clipboard contents are copied into the selected cells. Be careful when pasting to the new location because any existing entries will be replaced.

There are several methods you can use to copy entries in a worksheet. One method is to use the Copy and Paste commands on the Edit menu or their toolbar shortcuts. To use the Copy command, you first must select the cell or cells containing the data to be copied. This is called the **copy area** or **source**.

To copy the value in cell B12,

- Move to B12.

The menu equivalent is **E**dit/**C**opy and the shortcut key is Ctrl + C. Copy is also an option on the Shortcut menu.

- Click 📋 Copy.

Your screen should be similar to Figure 1-14.

Copy button

FIGURE 1-14

The moving border indicates the source has been copied to the Clipboard

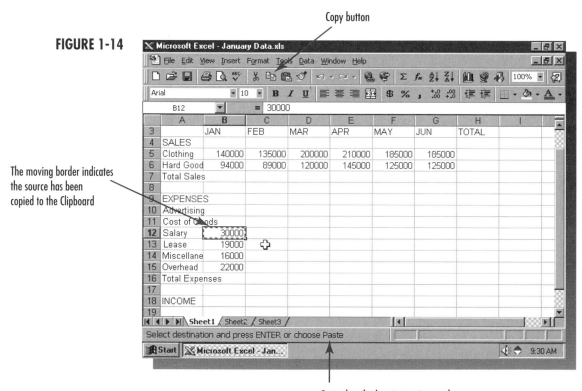

Status bar displays instructions on how to complete the command

The instructions displayed in the status bar tell you to select a **destination**, also called the **paste area**, where you want the contents copied. To specify cell C12 as the destination,

- Move to C12.

- Click 📋 Paste.

Your worksheet should be similar to Figure 1-15.

While the moving border is still displayed, you can also simply press ←Enter to paste. However, because using this method clears the contents of the Clipboard immediately, it can only be used once. You can cancel the moving border by pressing Esc.

The menu equivalent is **E**dit/**P**aste and the shortcut key is Ctrl + V. Paste is also an option on the Shortcut menu.

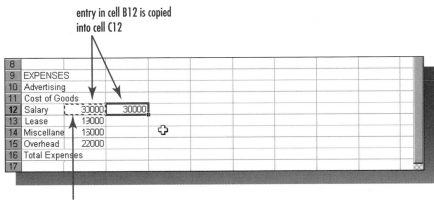

entry in cell B12 is copied into cell C12

moving border indicates the source can be pasted again

FIGURE 1-15

To complete the data for the Salary row, you could continue to paste the contents of Clipboard into the cells one after another. Instead, it is much faster to select a paste area that consists of multiple cells, called a range, and paste the contents to all cells in the selection at once.

Concept 4: Range

A selection consisting of two or more cells is a **range**. The cells in a range can be adjacent or nonadjacent. An **adjacent range** is a rectangular block of adjoining cells. In the example shown below, the shaded areas show examples of valid and invalid adjacent ranges. A **nonadjacent range** is two or more selected cells or ranges that are not adjoining. If all the valid ranges in the example were selected at the same time, they would be a non-adjacent range.

Valid Ranges   **Invalid Ranges**

You can also hold down ⇧ Shift and use the directional keys to select a range.

The paste area does not have to be adjacent to the copy area.

To complete the data for the Salary row, you want to copy the Clipboard contents to the range of cells D12 through G12. To select a range, drag the mouse from one corner of the range to the other.

- ■   Select cells D12 to G12.

- ■   Click 🖻 Paste.

Your worksheet should be similar to Figure 1-16.

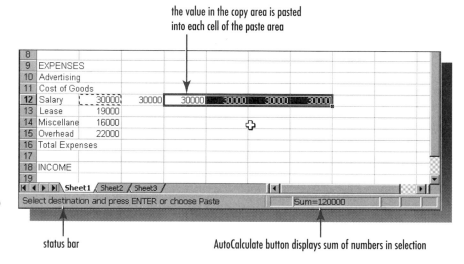

the value in the copy area is pasted into each cell of the paste area

FIGURE 1-16

status bar   AutoCalculate button displays sum of numbers in selection

You can display the average or count of numbers in a selection by choosing from the AutoCalculate button's Shortcut menu.

The paste area range selection will clear as soon as you select another cell.

Ctrl + R is the keyboard shortcut to fill to the right, and Ctrl + D to fill down.

If a range is not selected, the contents of the cell to the left or above are copied into the active cell.

Next you will copy the January lease expense to cells C13 through G13. Another way to copy is to use the Fill command on the Edit menu. This command requires that the destination range be adjacent to the source and that the entire range is selected before the command is used. You then specify the direction to fill from the Fill Command submenu. You will fill to the right.

- ■   Select cells B13 through G13.

- ■   Choose Edit/Fill/Right.

The selected range of cells to the right of the active cell is filled with the same value as in the active cell. The Fill command does not copy the source to the Clipboard; therefore, you cannot paste the source multiple times.

Finally, the numbers for the miscellaneous and overhead expenses (cells B14 and B15) need to be copied to February through June (C14 through G15). A shortcut for the Fill command is to drag the **fill handle**, the black box in the lower right corner of the selection.

■ Select the source range B14 through B15.

■ Point to the fill handle, and when the mouse pointer is a ✛, drag the mouse to extend the selection to cells B14 through G15.

■ Release the mouse button.

fill handle

Your worksheet should be similar to Figure 1-17.

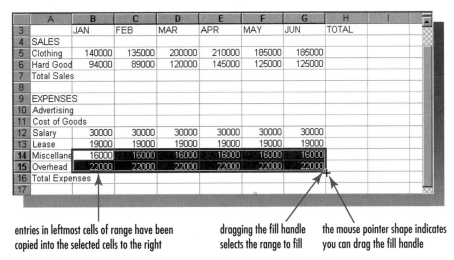

FIGURE 1-17

entries in leftmost cells of range have been copied into the selected cells to the right

dragging the fill handle selects the range to fill

the mouse pointer shape indicates you can drag the fill handle

Review of Copying Methods

To review, you have learned two methods to copy an entry:

1. Use the Copy and Paste commands: Edit/Copy ([Ctrl] + C) or 🗐 and Edit/Paste ([Ctrl] + V) or 🗐.

2. Use the Edit/Fill command: Right, Left, Up, or Down or drag the fill handle.

When you use the Copy command, the contents are copied to the Clipboard and can be copied to any location in the worksheet, another workbook, or another application. When you use Edit/Fill or drag the fill handle, the destination must be in the same row or column as the source, and the source is not copied to the Clipboard.

Entering Formulas

The remaining entries that need to be made in the worksheet are formula entries.

Concept 5: Formulas

A formula is an entry that performs a calculation. The result of the calculation is displayed in the cell containing the formula. A formula always begins with an equal sign (=), which defines it as a numeric entry. Formulas use the following arithmetic operators to specify the type of numeric operation to perform:

+	for addition
–	for subtraction
/	for division
*	for multiplication
^	for exponentiation

In a formula that contains more than one operator, Excel performs the calculation in a specific order of precedence. First exponentiations are performed, then multiplications and divisions, and finally additions and subtractions. This order can be overridden by enclosing the operation you want performed first in parentheses. Excel evaluates operations in parentheses working from the innermost set of parentheses out.

For example, in the formula =5*4–3, Excel first multiplies 5 times 4 to get 20, and then subtracts 3, for a total of 17. If you enter the formula as =5*(4–3), Excel first subtracts 3 from 4 because the operation is enclosed in parentheses. Then Excel multiplies the result, 1, by 5, for a final result of 5. If two or more operators have the same order of precedence, calculations are performed in order from left to right.

The values on which a numeric formula performs a calculation are called **operands**. Numbers or cell references can be operands in a formula. Usually cell references are used, and when the numeric entries in the referenced cell(s) change, the result of the formula is automatically recalculated. You can also use single-word row and column headings in place of cell references and formulas.

The first formula you will enter will calculate the total clothing sales for January through June by summing the numbers in cells B5 through G5. You will use cell references in the formula as the operands and the + arithmetic operator to specify addition. A formula is entered in the cell where you want the calculated value to be displayed. To enter the formula in cell H5 to sum the numbers in these cells,

Cell references can be typed in either uppercase or lowercase letters. Spaces between parts of the formula are optional.

If you enter a formula incorrectly, Excel displays an error in the cell or a message box proposing a correction.

- ■ Move to H5.

- ■ Type =.

- ■ Type **B5+C5+D5+E5+F5+G5**.

- ■ Press ⏎Enter.

- ■ Move to H5.

Your worksheet should be similar to Figure 1-18.

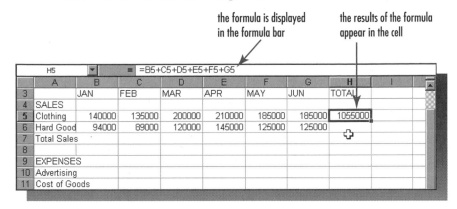

the formula is displayed
in the formula bar

the results of the formula
appear in the cell

FIGURE 1-18

You will learn more about formula entries in the next lab, when you will complete the worksheet by entering the formulas to calculate the cost of goods, total sales, total expenses, and income in the worksheet.

Recalculating the Worksheet

After considering the sales estimates for the six months, you decide that the estimated clothing sales for March are too high, and you want to reduce this number from 200000 to 175000.

■ Change the entry in cell D5 to 175000.

The total in cell H5 has been automatically recalculated, and the number displayed is now 1030000.

when the value changed in cell D5, the total formula
was recalculated and a new total value is displayed

	A	B	C	D	E	F	G	H
3		JAN	FEB	MAR	APR	MAY	JUN	TOTAL
4	SALES							
5	Clothing	140000	135000	175000	210000	185000	185000	1030000

Concept 6: Automatic Recalculation

The **automatic recalculation** of a formula whenever a number in a referenced cell in the formula changes is one of the most powerful features of electronic worksheets. Only those formulas directly affected by a change in the data are recalculated. This is called **minimal recalculation**. Without this feature, in large worksheets it could take several minutes to recalculate all formulas each time a number was changed in the worksheet. The minimal recalculation feature decreases the recalculation time by only recalculating dependent formulas.

Changing Cell Alignment

Now that many of the worksheet values are entered, you want to improve the appearance of the worksheet by changing the format of the headings.

Concept 7: Format

Formats control how information is displayed in a cell and include such features as font (different type styles and sizes), color, patterns, borders, and number formats such as commas and dollar signs. Applying different formats greatly improves both the appearance and readability of the data in a worksheet.

You decide the column headings would look better if they were right-aligned in their cell spaces. Then they would appear over the numbers in the column. You also would like to indent the row headings under the section headings. Alignment is a basic format setting that is used in most worksheets.

Concept 8: Alignment

Alignment settings allow you to change the horizontal and vertical placement and the orientation of an entry in a cell. Horizontal placement allows you to left-, center-, or right-align text and number entries in the cell space. Entries can also be indented within the cell space, centered across a selection, or justified. You can also fill a cell horizontally with a repeated entry. Vertical placement allows you to specify whether the cell contents are displayed at the top, centered, or at the bottom of the vertical cell space or justified vertically. Orientation changes the angle of text in a cell by varying the degrees of rotation. Examples of the basic alignment settings are shown below.

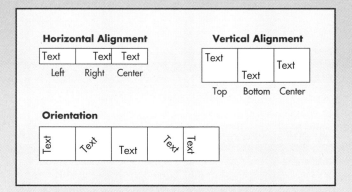

The default horizontal alignment is left for a text entry and right for a number entry. Vertical alignment is bottom for both types of entries.

First you will change the column heading in cell B3 to right-aligned using the Format menu.

■ Move to B3.

■ Choose F*o*rmat/C*e*lls.

■ Open the Alignment tab.

The shortcut key is Ctrl + 1. Format Cells is also an option on the Shortcut menu.

The dialog box on your screen should be similar to Figure 1-19.

default Horizontal alignment

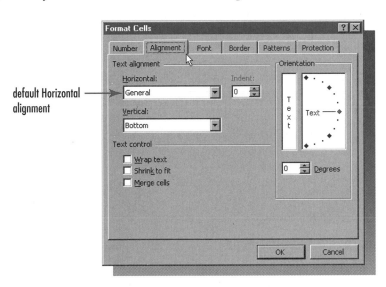

FIGURE 1-19

The Alignment tab shows the default horizontal alignment setting is General. This setting left-aligns text entries and right-aligns number entries. To change the horizontal alignment of the entry to right-aligned, from the Horizontal drop-down list,

■ Select Right.

■ Click ▢OK▢.

Your worksheet should be similar to Figure 1-20.

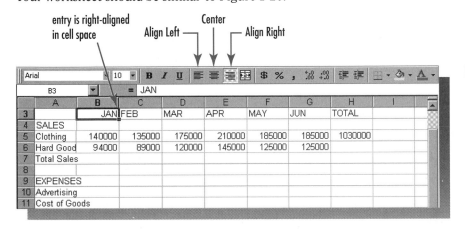

FIGURE 1-20

entry is right-aligned in cell space

Align Left

Center

Align Right

The three alignment buttons in the Formatting toolbar—▤ Align Left, ▥ Center, and ▤ Align Right—can also be used to align cell entries.

You can quickly align a range of cells by selecting the range and then using the command or button. A quick way to select a range of filled cells is to hold down ⇧ Shift and double-click on the edge of the active cell in the direction in which you want the range expanded. For example, to select the range to the right of the active cell, you would double-click the right border. To right-align the remaining month entries,

If you do not hold down ⇧ Shift while double-clicking on a border, the cell selector moves to the last-used cell in the direction indicated.

- Move to cell C3 and use the method discussed above to select cells C3 through H3.

- Click ▤ Align Right.

The entries in the selected range are right-aligned in their cell spaces.

Next you would like to indent the row headings in cells A5 through A7 and A10 through A16 under the section headings. You want to indent the headings in both ranges at the same time. To select a nonadjacent range, you select the first cell or range of cells, and then hold down Ctrl and select the other cells. To select the cells and indent them,

One indent is equal to the width of one character.

The menu equivalent is **F**ormat/**C**ells/ Horizontal/Left (Indent)/1.

- Select A5 through A7.

- Hold down Ctrl.

- Select A10 through A16.

- Click ⬚ Increase Indent.

Now, even more of the row headings are shortened because the entries are indented.

Documenting a Workbook

In the next lab you will complete the worksheet by entering the formulas to calculate the advertising, cost of goods, total sales, total expenses, and income. You will also learn how to improve the appearance of the worksheet and to adjust column widths to fully display the cell entries.

Pressing Ctrl + ; will automatically enter the current date in the active cell.

- Enter your first initial and last name in cell A1.

- Enter the current date in cell A2 in the format mm/dd/yy (for example, 10/10/98).

Your screen should be similar to Figure 1-21.

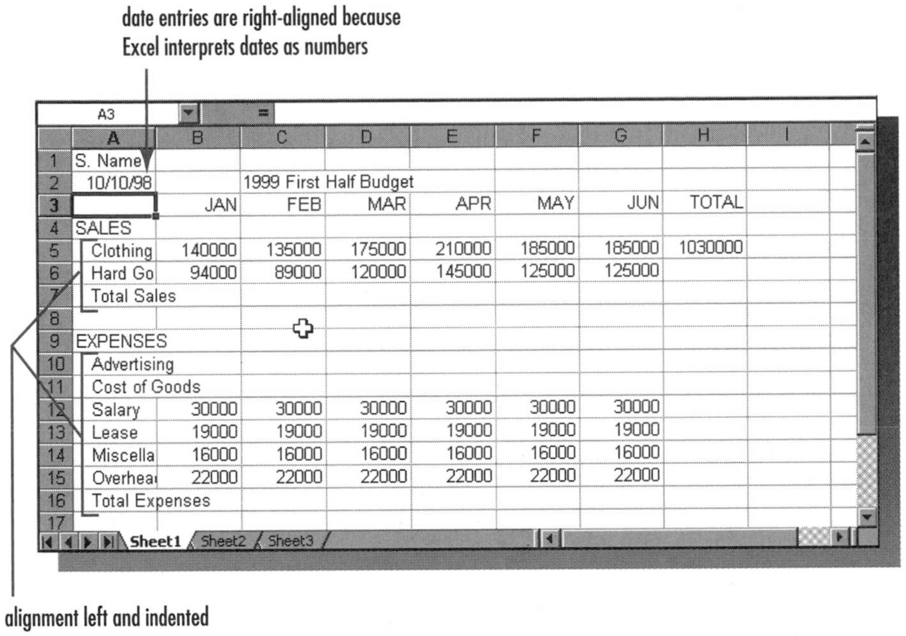

date entries are right-aligned because
Excel interprets dates as numbers

FIGURE 1-21

	A	B	C	D	E	F	G	H	I
	A3		=						
1	S. Name								
2	10/10/98		1999 First Half Budget						
3		JAN	FEB	MAR	APR	MAY	JUN	TOTAL	
4	SALES								
5	Clothing	140000	135000	175000	210000	185000	185000	1030000	
6	Hard Go	94000	89000	120000	145000	125000	125000		
7	Total Sales								
8									
9	EXPENSES								
10	Advertising								
11	Cost of Goods								
12	Salary	30000	30000	30000	30000	30000	30000		
13	Lease	19000	19000	19000	19000	19000	19000		
14	Miscella	16000	16000	16000	16000	16000	16000		
15	Overhea	22000	22000	22000	22000	22000	22000		
16	Total Expenses								
17									

Sheet1 / Sheet2 / Sheet3 /

alignment left and indented

Concept 9: Dates

Excel automatically recognizes certain types of data input, such as dates and times, and formats the entry as appropriate. It stores all dates as serial numbers with each day numbered from the beginning of the century; the date serial number 1 corresponds to the date January 1, 1900, and the integer 65380 is December 31, 2078. The integers are assigned consecutively beginning with 1 and ending with 65,380. They are called **date numbers**. Conversion of the date to a serial number allows dates to be used in calculations.

If you had preceded the date entry with =, Excel would have interpreted it as a formula and a calculation of division would have been performed on the numbers.

Now you are ready to save the changes you have made to the workbook file to your data disk. Before doing this, you want to document the workbook. Each workbook includes summary information that is associated with the file.

■   Choose **F**ile/Proper**t**ies.

■   Select each tab in the Properties dialog box and look at the recorded information.

■   Open the Summary tab.

The dialog box on your screen should be similar to Figure 1-22.

FIGURE 1-22

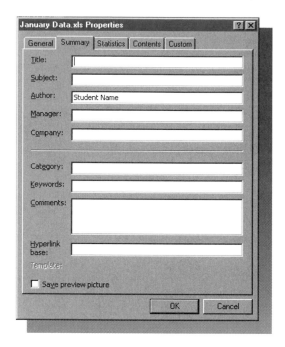

The Summary tab is used to specify information you want associated with the file such as a title, subject, author, keywords, and comments about the workbook file. This information helps you locate the workbook file you want to use as well as indicates the objectives and use of the workbook.

> The Author text box may be blank or show your school or some other name. Clear the existing contents first if necessary.

> You could also add more detailed information about the workbook in the Comments text box.

■ Enter the following information in the appropriate text boxes:

Title: **The Sports Company 1999 Budget**

Subject: **First Half**

Author: **[your name]**

■ Click [OK].

Saving a Workbook

You are now ready to save the active workbook in a file on your data disk.

> The 🖫 button is the shortcut for **F**ile/ **S**ave.

While working on a document, your changes are stored in memory. Not until you **save** the document as a file on a disk are you safe from losing your work due to a power failure or other mishap. Two commands found on the File menu of all Windows programs can be used to save a file: Save and Save As. The Save command saves a document using the same path and file name by replacing the contents of the existing disk file with the changes you have made. The Save As command allows you to select the path and provide a different file name. This command lets you save both an original version of a document and a revised document as two separate files. When you save a file for the first time, either command can be used. Although most programs create automatic backup files if your work is accidentally interrupted, it is still a good idea to save your work frequently.

You will use the Save As command and save the changes you have made to the January Data file using a different file name.

■ Choose <u>F</u>ile/Save <u>A</u>s.

The dialog box on your screen should be similar to Figure 1-23.

FIGURE 1-23

specifies location where
file will be saved

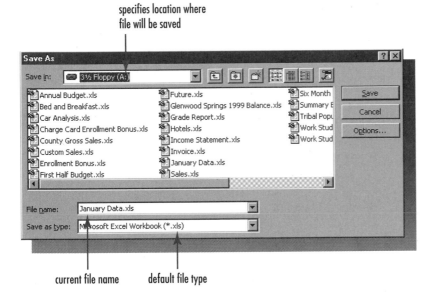

current file name   default file type

The Save As dialog box is used to specify the location to save the file to and the file name. The Save In list box displays the location of the current file as the location where the new file will be saved.

The file name of the file you opened, January Data, is displayed in the File Name text box. An Excel file name follows the same file name rules as other Windows 95 products. It is automatically saved with the file name extension .xls, which identifies it as a workbook file. You will save the file using a new file name.

■ If the Save In location is not correct, select the appropriate location from the drop-down list.

■ Replace the existing file name in the file name text box with **Six Month Budget**.

■ Click [<u>S</u>ave].

The new file name is displayed in the worksheet window title bar. The worksheet data that was on your screen and in the computer's memory is now saved on your data disk in a new file called Six Month Budget.

Always save your active workbook before closing a file or leaving the Excel program. As a safeguard against losing your work if you forget to save the workbook changes, Excel will remind you to save before closing the file or exiting the program.

Previewing and Printing a Workbook

If you have printer capability, you can print a copy of the worksheet.

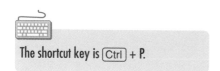

The shortcut key is (Ctrl) + P.

- ■ If necessary, turn the printer on and check to see that it is on-line. If your printer uses continuous form-feed paper, adjust the paper so that the perforation is just above the printer scale (behind the ribbon).

- ■ Choose **F**ile/**P**rint.

The dialog box on your screen should be similar to Figure 1-24.

FIGURE 1-24

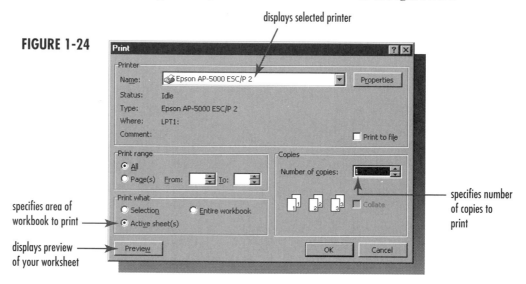

The Print dialog box is used to specify your print settings. The default print settings will print one copy of the entire worksheet. These settings are satisfactory for now. The name of the printer displayed in the Printer information area of the dialog box should be your printer.

- ■ If you need to select a different printer, open the Name drop-down list in the Printer section and select the appropriate printer.

Before printing, you may want to preview how the worksheet will appear on the printed page. To do this,

File/Print Pre**v**iew or the [🔍] button will also preview the worksheet.

- ■ Click [Preview].

Your screen should be similar to Figure 1-25.

prints the worksheet as displayed
using settings in Print dialog box

FIGURE 1-25

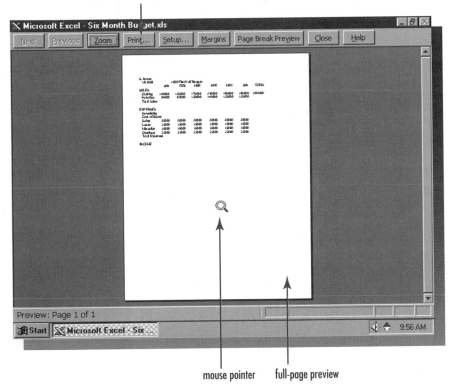

mouse pointer   full-page preview

The Print Preview dialog box window displays the worksheet as it will appear on the printed page. This is called the full-page view, but it is difficult to read. While previewing a worksheet, you can enlarge the display to a magnified view.

■ If necessary, move the mouse pointer onto the preview page.

The mouse pointer appears as a ◯ , indicating that you can switch between a full-page view and a magnified view.

■ Click the worksheet title.

The worksheet is displayed in the actual size it will appear when printed. Notice that the row and column lines are not displayed and will not print.

To display the worksheet again in the full-page view, and then print the sheet,

■ Click the worksheet.

■ Click Print... .

Your printer should be printing out the worksheet, and your printed output should look like the figure shown in the Case Study at the beginning of the lab.

The area you click on is the area that will be displayed in the Preview window.

If you do not need to change the default print settings, you can click 🖨 to print the worksheet.

SPREADSHEET

Exiting Excel

If you want to quit or exit the Excel program at this time,

- Click ☒.

The menu equivalent is <u>F</u>ile/E<u>x</u>it.

You have exited from the Excel program, and the Windows 95 desktop is displayed.

LAB REVIEW

■ ■ ■ ■ ■ ■ ■ ■ ■ ■

Key Terms

active cell   (SS10)
active sheet   (SS10)
adjacent range   (SS27)
alignment   (SS32)
automatic recalculation   (SS31)
cell   (SS10)
cell selector   (SS10)
column   (SS9)
column letter   (SS10)
constant   (SS16)
copy area   (SS26)
date number   (SS35)
destination   (SS27)
fill handle   (SS29)
format   (SS32)
Formatting toolbar   (SS9)
formula   (SS16)
formula bar   (SS9)
heading   (SS16)
minimal recalculation   (SS31)
Name box   (SS9)
nonadjacent range   (SS27)

number   (SS16)
Office Assistant   (SS11)
operand   (SS30)
paste area   (SS27)
range   (SS27)
reference   (SS10)
row   (SS9)
row number   (SS10)
save   (SS36)
sheet tab   (SS10)
source   (SS26)
spreadsheet   (SS9)
Standard toolbar   (SS9)
tab scroll button   (SS10)
text   (SS16)
variable   (SS16)
workbook   (SS9)
workbook window   (SS9)
worksheet   (SS9)
workspace   (SS9)

Command Summary

Command	Shortcut	Toolbar	Action
File/**O**pen <file name>	Ctrl + O	📂	Opens an existing workbook file
File/**C**lose			Closes open workbook file
File/**S**ave <file name>	Ctrl + S	💾	Saves current file on disk using same file name
File/Save **A**s <file name>			Saves current file on disk using a new file name
File/Proper**ti**es			Displays information about a file
File/Print Pre**v**iew		🔍	Displays worksheet as it will appear when printed
File/**P**rint	Ctrl + P	🖨	Prints a worksheet
File/E**x**it		✕	Exits Excel
Edit/**C**opy	Ctrl + C	📋	Copies selected data to Clipboard
Edit/**P**aste	Ctrl + V	📋	Pastes selections stored in Clipboard
Edit/**F**ill			Fills selected cells with contents of source cell
Edit/Cle**a**r/**C**ontents	Delete		Clears cell contents
View/**T**oolbars			Displays/hides selected toolbars
F**o**rmat/C**e**lls/Alignment/Horizontal/ Left (Indent)		▤	Left-aligns entry in cell space
F**o**rmat/C**e**lls/Alignment/Horizontal/Center		▤	Center-aligns entry in cell space
F**o**rmat/C**e**lls/Alignment/Horizontal/Right		▤	Right-aligns entry in cell space
F**o**rmat/C**e**lls/Horizontal/Left (Indent)/1		▦	Left-aligns and indents cell entry one space

Matching

1. source   _____ a. right-aligns cell entry
2. *   _____ b. moves cell selector to upper left corner of worksheet
3. ▤   _____ c. the cell you copy from
4. Ctrl + Home   _____ d. two or more worksheet cells
5. .xls   _____ e. a cell reference
6. F2   _____ f. displays current cell entry
7. =C19+A21   _____ g. an arithmetic operator
8. range   _____ h. accesses Edit mode
9. D11   _____ i. a formula summing two cells
10. formula bar   _____ j. Excel workbook file name extension

Fill-In Questions

1. In the following worksheet, several items are identified by letters. Enter the correct term for each item in the spaces that follow.

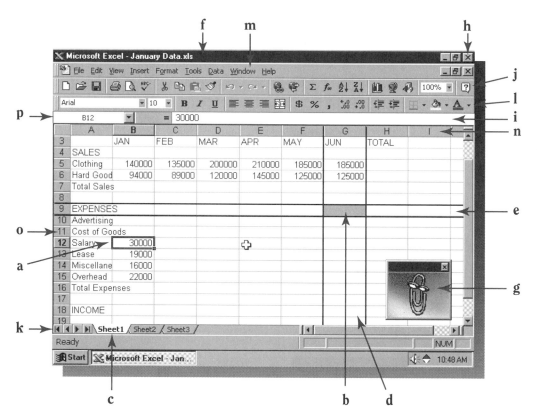

a. _____   g. _____   m. _____

b. _____   h. _____   n. _____

c. _____   i. _____   o. _____

d. _____   j. _____   p. _____

e. _____   k. _____

f. _____   l. _____

2. Complete the following statements by filling in the blanks with the correct terms.

a. The _____ occupies the center of the Excel window and can display multiple windows.

b. The worksheet displays a rectangular grid of _____ and _____.

c. A(n) _____ consists of two or more worksheet cells.

d. The intersection of a row and column creates a(n)_____.

e. _____ are text entries that are used to create the structure of the worksheet.

f. By default, text entries are _____ -aligned and number entries are _____ -aligned.

g. A(n) _____ consists of the column letter and row number used to identify a cell.

h. A(n) _____ is an entry that performs a calculation.

i. _____ is the recalculation of only those formulas in the worksheet that are directly affected by a change of data.

j. _____ control how information is displayed in a cell.

Discussion Questions

1. Discuss why it is important to design a worksheet before you begin entering actual data into it.

2. What types of entries are used in worksheets? Discuss the uses of each type of entry.

3. Discuss how formulas are created. Why are they the power behind worksheets?

4. Discuss the formatting features presented in the lab. Why are they important to the look of the worksheet?

Hands-On Practice Exercises

■ ■ ■ ■ ■ ■ ■ ■ ▪ ▪ ▫

For all exercises, go to cell A1 before you save the workbook. That way, the next time you open the workbook, the cell selector will be at the top of the worksheet.

Step by Step

Rating System	
☆	Easy
☆☆	Moderate
☆☆☆	Difficult

1. Open the workbook file Bed and Breakfast on your data disk. Scott and Toni have researched several bed and breakfast inns for a family trip to New England. This worksheet lists the inns they are considering and occupancy rates for single and double rooms with private or shared baths. Follow the directions below to modify the worksheet.

a. Change the first word in the title to uppercase.

b. Correct the names of the inns so that only the first letter of each word is in uppercase. Similarly, correct the names of the cities and make sure they are all left-aligned.

c. Center cells E3 through H3 and cell E4, and make sure all worksheet numbers are right-aligned. Indent the names of the bed and breakfast inns in column A.

d. Copy the state abbreviation "Conn" in cell D5 to cells D6 through D8. Copy the word "Bath" from cell E4 to the three adjacent cells (F4 through H4) to the right. What else was copied with the text?

e. Enter the state name "Maine" in cell D14. What happened after you typed the first three letters? Use the Office Assistant to obtain information on this feature by asking about repeated entries. Then, from the Help topic "Enter data in worksheet cells," read the information on the topic, "Quickly fill in repeated entries in a column."

Your corrected worksheet will look like the worksheet below.

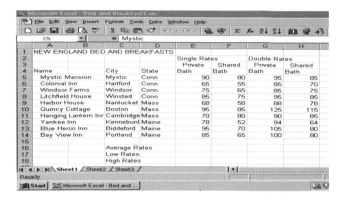

f. Enter your name and the current date on separate rows below the worksheet.

g. Move to cell A1. Use the Properties dialog box to document the workbook. Save and replace the workbook file Bed and Breakfast. Preview and print the worksheet.

You will complete this exercise as Practice Exercise 1 in Lab 2.

2. You are the owner of The Cookie Jar, a shop that sells gourmet cookies by the pound. You are interested in tracking first quarter sales for each type of cookie.

a. Create the worksheet as shown below.

	A	B	C	D	E	F	G
1	The Cookie Jar						
2							
3	Type			Jan	Feb	Mar	Total
4	Chocolate Chip			1800	1825	1835	
5	Chocolate Chip w/ Nuts			1430	1425	1390	
6	White Chocolate Macadamia			1220	1250	1295	
7	Butterscotch			750	775	800	
8	Peanut Butter			1000	1050	975	
9	Oatmeal Raisin			450	375	415	
10	Gingerbread			530	535	500	
11	Total						
12							

b. Right-align the month and total headings in row 3. Indent the types of cookies in column A.

c. Calculate a total for chocolate chip cookies only.

d. Enter your name and the current date on separate rows below the worksheet.

e. Move to A1. Use the Properties dialog box to document the workbook. Save the workbook as Cookie Jar. Preview and print the worksheet.

You will complete this exercise as Practice Exercise 2 in Lab 2.

3. Laura is changing her eating habits to include foods that obtain no more than 30 percent of their calories from fat. She has listed several of her favorite "diet" snack foods and decides to calculate the percent of fat for each one. Complete the following steps to help Laura with her task.

a. Create the worksheet as shown below.

	A	B	C	D	E	F	G
1	Food			Fat Grams	Calories	% Fat	
2	Bagel			1	240		
3	Lite Cream Cheese			5	60		
4	Peanut Butter (25% Less Fat)			13	190		
5	Saltine Crackers			1.5	60		
6	Lite Pop Corn			2	40		
7	Cholesterol Free Potato Chips			6	130		
8	Lite Frozen Fudge Pops			1.2	35		
9	Pretzels			1	110		
10							

Next you want to enter a formula to calculate the percent of fat. Each gram of fat contains nine calories. To calculate the percent of fat, multiply fat grams by nine and divide that product by the number of calories.

b. In cell F2, enter the formula =D2*9/E2 to calculate the percent of fat for bagels. Then calculate the percent of fat for lite cream cheese. Are bagels and lite cream cheese a good snack for Laura?

c. Right-align the headings in columns E and F. Indent the foods in column A.

d. Enter your name and the current date on separate rows below the worksheet.

e. Move to A1. Use the Properties dialog box to document the workbook. Save the workbook as Fat Grams. Preview and print the worksheet.

You will continue this exercise as Practice Exercise 3 in Lab 2.

4. Open the workbook file Invoice on your data disk. You are an employee of The Office Center, a discount office super store. You recently sold computer equipment to a new computer training facility. Follow the directions below to complete the transaction with the customer.

a. Replace The Office Center address with your address information, and enter the current date in the appropriate cell.

b. Make changes you feel are necessary to improve the appearance of the invoice.

c. Enter a formula to calculate a total for the Pentium computers only.

d. Enter your name below the worksheet.

Your modified worksheet will look similar to the worksheet below.

	A	B	C	D	E	F	G	H	I
1	The Office Center						Invoice #	11001	
2	Street Address						Date:	[Current Date]	
3	City, State, and Zip Code								
4									
5	Customer:	Lionel Computer Training							
6		123 Main St.							
7		Greenwich, CT 06830							
8									
9	Qty	Description				Price	Total		
10	15	Pentium-75 MHz Computers				1975	29625		
11	15	Ergonomic Mice				34.95			
12	15	Mouse Pads				4.75			
13	3	Laser Printers				850			
14	5	Power Strips				30			
15	15	Desk Chairs				95.99			
16	6	Tables				300			
17						Subtotal:			
18						State Tax:			
19						Total:			

e. Move to cell A1. Use the Properties dialog box to document the workbook. Save and replace the workbook file Invoice. Preview and print the worksheet.

You will continue this exercise as Practice Exercise 4 in Lab 2.

On Your Own

5. Open the file Income Statement on your data disk. Custom Manufacturing Company is drawing up a budgeted income statement for the next year. Sales amounts reflect past trends. Cost of goods sold is traditionally 60 percent of sales, variable costs are 15 percent of sales, and fixed costs are budgeted at $1,500 a month for the first half of the year. Other calculations are performed as follows:

Gross Profit = Sales − Cost of Goods Sold
Contribution Margin = Gross Profit − Variable Costs
Income = Contribution Margin − Fixed Costs
Income Tax Expense = 40% of Income Before Taxes
Net Income = Income Before Taxes − Income Tax Expense

Use the above information to calculate net income for the month of January only. Appropriately align the month and total headings in row 5. Enter your name and the current date on separate rows below the worksheet. Document the worksheet and save it as Income Statement. Preview and print the worksheet. Your modified worksheet will look similar to the worksheet below.

	A	B	C	D	E	F	G	H
1	Custom Manufacturing Company							
2	Budgeted Income Statement							
3	For the Year Ending December 31, 1997							
4								
5			Jan	Feb	Mar	Apr	May	
6	Sales		80000	65000	80000	100000	120000	125
7	Cost of Goods Sold		48000					
8	Gross Profit		32000					
9	Variable Costs		12000					
10	Contribution Margin		20000					
11	Fixed Costs		1500					
12	Income Before Taxes		18500					
13	Income Tax Expense		7400					
14	Net Income		11100					
15								

You will continue this exercise as Practice Exercise 5 in Lab 2.

6. Obtain an IRS Form 1040EZ. Use Excel to create a worksheet for an IRS Form 1040EZ. Enter formulas to perform the necessary calculations. Change the values you entered to see how the refund or amount you owe is affected by increases and decreases to total wages and other amounts you adjust. Move to A1. Use the Properties dialog box to document the workbook. Save the workbook file as IRS Form 1040EZ, and preview and print the worksheet.

SPREADSHEET

Creating a Worksheet: Part 1

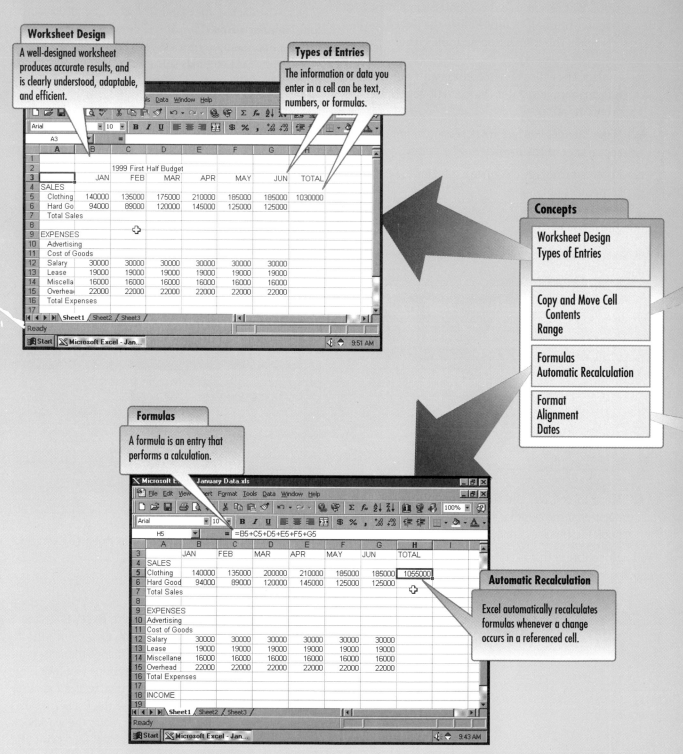

Worksheet Design

A well-designed worksheet produces accurate results, and is clearly understood, adaptable, and efficient.

Types of Entries

The information or data you enter in a cell can be text, numbers, or formulas.

Concepts

Worksheet Design
Types of Entries

Copy and Move Cell
  Contents
Range

Formulas
Automatic Recalculation

Format
Alignment
Dates

Formulas

A formula is an entry that performs a calculation.

Automatic Recalculation

Excel automatically recalculates formulas whenever a change occurs in a referenced cell.

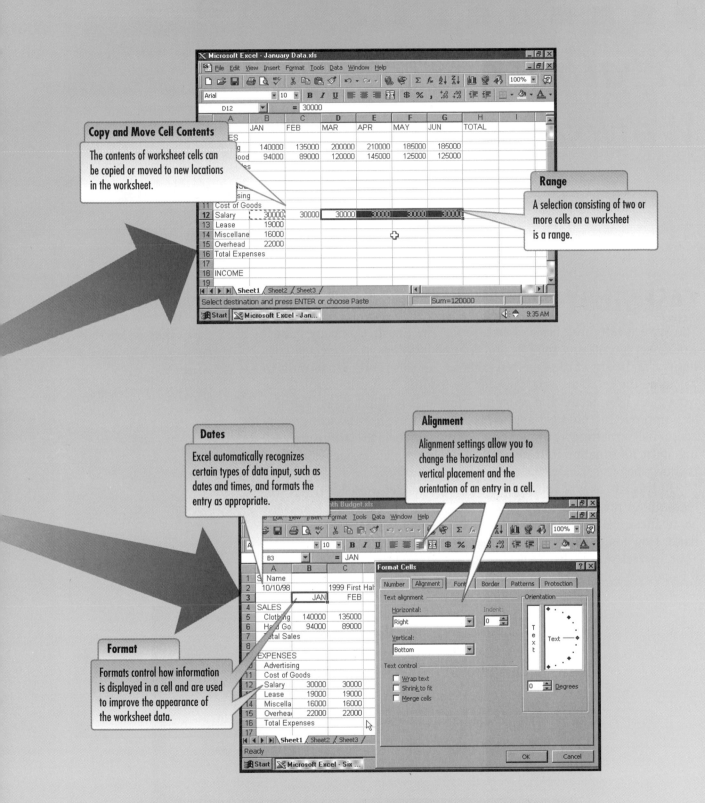

Copy and Move Cell Contents

The contents of worksheet cells can be copied or moved to new locations in the worksheet.

Range

A selection consisting of two or more cells on a worksheet is a range.

Dates

Excel automatically recognizes certain types of data input, such as dates and times, and formats the entry as appropriate.

Alignment

Alignment settings allow you to change the horizontal and vertical placement and the orientation of an entry in a cell.

Format

Formats control how information is displayed in a cell and are used to improve the appearance of the worksheet data.

ss47

Creating a Worksheet: Part 2

COMPETENCIES

After completing this lab, you will know how to:

1. Enter formulas using Point mode.
2. Copy formulas.
3. Enter functions.
4. Use the Paste Function feature.
5. Use absolute references.
6. Add cell comments.
7. Adjust column widths.
8. Use Undo.
9. Zoom the worksheet.
10. Format numbers.
11. Apply styles.
12. Insert and delete rows and columns.
13. Move and center cell contents.
14. Change fonts and font styles.
15. Add predefined headers and footers.
16. Change page orientation.

CASE STUDY

You have created the basic structure for The Sports Company budget worksheet by entering the row and column headings, the expected sales figures, and many of the expected expenses. You also entered a formula to calculate the total clothing sales for six months. You will complete the worksheet by entering the remaining formulas and functions. You will also improve the physical appearance of the worksheet by using many additional formatting features. These features also help to clarify the meaning of the information in the worksheet. The complete budget worksheet is shown below.

In this lab, as you continue to build the budget worksheet, you will learn about many features in Excel that make life easier. As you learn about these features, think what it would be like to do the same task by hand. How long would it take? Would it be as accurate or as attractive? Your appreciation of the application grows as you learn more about what it can do for you.

1999 First Half Budget

	JAN	FEB	MAR	APR	MAY	JUN	TOTAL	AVG	
SALES									
Clothing	$ 140,000	$ 135,000	$ 175,000	$ 210,000	$ 185,000	$ 185,000	$ 1,030,000	$ 171,667	59.61%
Hard Goods	$ 94,000	$ 89,000	$ 120,000	$ 145,000	$ 125,000	$ 125,000	$ 698,000	$ 116,333	40.39%
Total Sales	$ 234,000	$ 224,000	$ 295,000	$ 355,000	$ 310,000	$ 310,000	$ 1,728,000	$ 288,000	
EXPENSES									
Advertising	$ 9,360	$ 8,960	$ 11,800	$ 14,200	$ 12,400	$ 12,400	69,120	$ 11,520	
Cost of Goods	$ 135,720	$ 129,920	$ 171,100	$ 205,900	$ 179,800	$ 179,800	$ 1,002,240	$ 167,040	
Salary	$ 30,000	$ 30,000	$ 30,000	$ 30,000	$ 30,000	$ 30,000	180,000	$ 30,000	
Lease	$ 19,000	$ 19,000	$ 19,000	$ 19,000	$ 19,000	$ 19,000	114,000	$ 19,000	
Miscellaneous	$ 16,000	$ 16,000	$ 16,000	$ 16,000	$ 16,000	$ 16,000	96,000	$ 16,000	
Overhead	$ 22,000	$ 22,000	$ 22,000	$ 22,000	$ 22,000	$ 22,000	132,000	$ 22,000	
Total Expenses	$ 232,080	$ 225,880	$ 269,900	$ 307,100	$ 279,200	$ 279,200	$ 1,593,360	$ 265,560	
INCOME	$ 1,920	$ (1,880)	$ 25,100	$ 47,900	$ 30,800	$ 30,800	134,640	$ 22,440	
							Profit Margin	7.79%	

Concept Overview

The following concepts will be introduced in this lab:

1. Relative Reference	A relative reference is a cell or range reference in a formula whose location is interpreted by Excel in relation to the position of the cell that contains the formula.
2. Functions	Functions are prewritten formulas that perform certain types of calculations automatically.
3. Absolute Reference	An absolute reference is a cell or range reference in a formula whose location does not change when the formula is copied.
4. Column Width	The size or width of a column controls how much information can be displayed in a cell.
5. Number Formats	Number formats affect how numbers look onscreen and when printed.
6. Styles	A style consists of a combination of formats that have been named and that can be quickly applied to a selection.
7. Insert and Delete Cells, Rows, and Columns	Individual cells or entire rows or columns can be inserted and deleted from a worksheet.
8. Fonts	Fonts consist of typefaces, point size, and styles that can be applied to characters to improve their appearance.
9. Headers and Footers	Lines of text displayed below the top margin or above the bottom margin of each page are called headers and footers.

Part 1

Entering Formulas Using Point Mode

You will continue to build the budget worksheet by entering the remaining formulas.

- Load Excel 97.

- Put your data disk in drive A (or the appropriate drive for your system).

- Open the workbook file First Half Budget on your data disk.

- If necessary, maximize the workbook window.

Your screen should be similar to Figure 2-1.

FIGURE 2-1

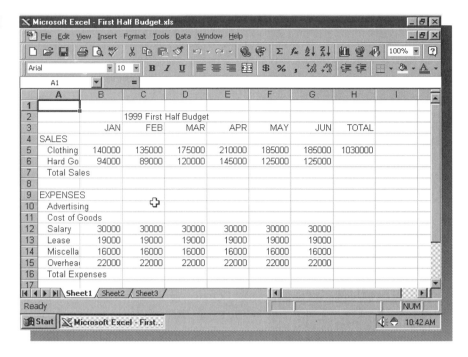

First you will enter the formula to calculate total sales. This formula will sum the numbers for clothing and hard goods sales in cells B5 and B6. Rather than typing the cell references into the formula, you will enter them by selecting the worksheet cells.

You can also use the directional keys to move to the cell.

■ Move to B7.

■ Type =.

■ Click B5.

Your worksheet should be similar to Figure 2-2.

FIGURE 2-2

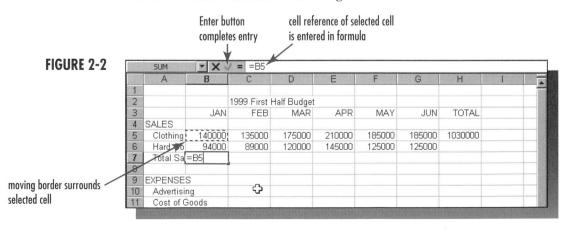

Notice that the status bar displays the current mode as Point. This tells you the program is allowing you to select cells by highlighting them. The cell reference, B5, is entered following the = sign. To continue the formula and enter the reference for the cell containing the January hard goods sales, B6,

- Type +.
- Click B6.
- Click ▭.

The formula entry in cell B7 is =B5+B6 and the calculated value is 234000.

Copying Formulas

The formulas to calculate the February through June total sales (C7 through G7) can be entered next. Just like text and numeric entries, you can copy formulas from one cell to another.

- Copy the formula in cell B7 to cells C7 through G7.
- Move to C7.

Refer to the Review of Copying Methods box on page SS29 to review how to copy.

Your worksheet should be similar to Figure 2-3.

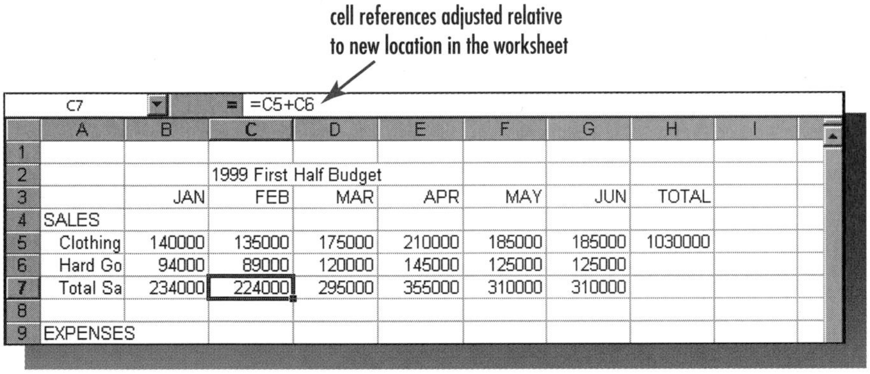

cell references adjusted relative
to new location in the worksheet

	A	B	C	D	E	F	G	H	I
	C7		=	=C5+C6					
1									
2			1999 First Half Budget						
3		JAN	FEB	MAR	APR	MAY	JUN	TOTAL	
4	SALES								
5	Clothing	140000	135000	175000	210000	185000	185000	1030000	
6	Hard Go	94000	89000	120000	145000	125000	125000		
7	Total Sa	234000	224000	295000	355000	310000	310000		
8									
9	EXPENSES								

FIGURE 2-3

The number 224000 is displayed in the cell. The formula displayed in the formula bar is =C5+C6. The formula to calculate the February total sales is not an exact duplicate of the formula used to calculate the January total sales (=B5+B6). Instead the cells referenced in the formula have been changed to reflect the new location of the formula in column C. This is because the references in the formula are relative references.

Concept 1: Relative Reference

A **relative reference** is a cell or range reference in a formula whose location is interpreted by Excel in relation to the position of the cell that contains the formula. For example in the formula to calculate total sales in cell C7, the cell reference to C5 tells Excel to use the contents of the cell two cells above the cell containing the formula. When a formula is copied, the referenced cells in the formula automatically adjust to reflect the new worksheet location. The relative relationship between the referenced cell and the new location is maintained. Because relative references automatically adjust for the new location, the relative references in a copied formula refer to different cells than the references in the original formula. The relationship between cells in both the copied and pasted formula is the same although the cell references are different.

■ Move to D7.

This formula has also changed to reflect the new column location, and appropriately calculates the total based on the March sales.

Next you will enter the formulas to calculate the advertising and cost of goods sold. These numbers are estimated by using a formula to calculate the number as a percent of total sales. As a general rule, The Sports Company calculates advertising expenses at 4 percent of sales and cost of goods expenses at 58 percent of sales. The formula to make these calculations for January takes the number in cell B7 and multiplies it by the percentage.

To make the process of entering and copying entries even easier, you can enter data into the first cell of a range and have it copied to all other cells in the range at the same time by using Ctrl + ←Enter to complete the entry. You will use this feature to enter the formulas to calculate the advertising expenses for January through June.

Even when a range is selected, you can still point to specify cells in the formula.

■ Select cells B10 through G10.

■ Type =B7*4%.

■ Press Ctrl + ←Enter.

The formula to calculate the January advertising expenses was entered in cell B10 and copied to all cells of the selected range.

■ In the same manner, select the range B11 through G11 and enter the formula =B7*58% in cell B11 to calculate the cost of goods sold for January through June.

Your worksheet should be similar to Figure 2-4.

FIGURE 2-4

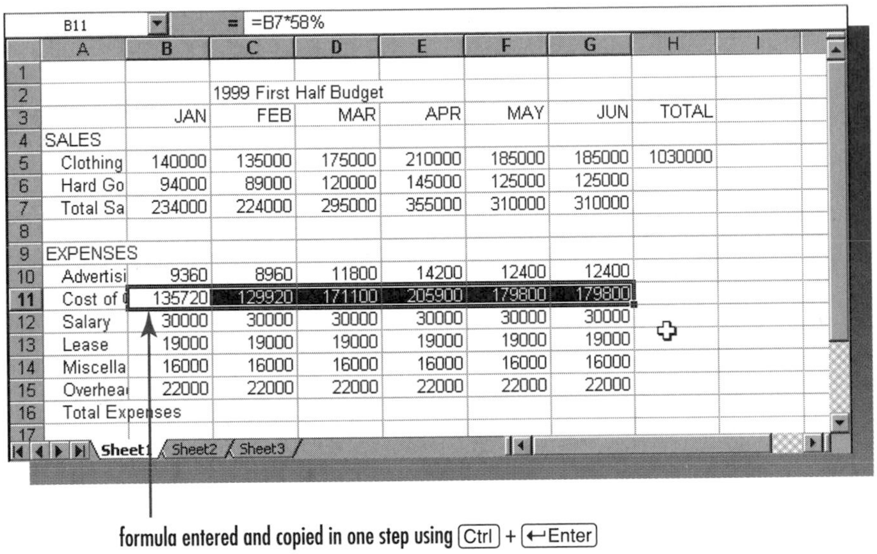

	B11	▼	= =B7*58%						
	A	B	C	D	E	F	G	H	I
1									
2			1999 First Half Budget						
3		JAN	FEB	MAR	APR	MAY	JUN	TOTAL	
4	SALES								
5	Clothing	140000	135000	175000	210000	185000	185000	1030000	
6	Hard Go	94000	89000	120000	145000	125000	125000		
7	Total Sa	234000	224000	295000	355000	310000	310000		
8									
9	EXPENSES								
10	Advertisi	9360	8960	11800	14200	12400	12400		
11	Cost of	135720	129920	171100	205900	179800	179800		
12	Salary	30000	30000	30000	30000	30000	30000		
13	Lease	19000	19000	19000	19000	19000	19000		
14	Miscella	16000	16000	16000	16000	16000	16000		
15	Overhea	22000	22000	22000	22000	22000	22000		
16	Total Expenses								
17									

Sheet1 / Sheet2 / Sheet3 /

formula entered and copied in one step using ⌐Ctrl⌐ + ⌐←Enter⌐

Entering Functions

Now that all the expenses have been entered into the worksheet, the total expenses can be calculated. The formula to calculate the total expenses for January needs to be entered in cell B16 and copied across the row through June. You could use a formula similar to the formula used to calculate the total sales (B7). The formula would be =B10+B11+B12+B13+B14+B15. However, it is faster and more accurate to use a function.

Concept 2: Functions

Functions are prewritten formulas that perform certain types of calculations automatically. The **syntax** or rules of structure for entering all functions is:

Function name (argument1, argument2,...)

The function name identifies the type of calculation to be performed. Most functions require that you enter one or more arguments following the function name. An **argument** is the data the function uses to perform the calculation. The type of data the function requires depends upon the type of calculation being performed. Most commonly the argument consists of numbers or references to cells that contain numbers. The argument is enclosed in parentheses, and multiple arguments are separated by commas. If a function starts the formula, enter an equals sign before the function name (=SUM(D5:F5)/25).

Excel includes several hundred functions* divided into 9 categories. Some common functions and the results they calculate are shown below.

Category	Function	Calculates
Financial	PMT	Calculates the payment for a loan based on constant payments and a constant interest rate.
	PV	Returns the present value of an investment: the total amount that a series of future payments is worth now.
Time & Date	TODAY	Returns the serial number that represents today's date.
	DATE	Returns the serial number of a particular date.
	NOW	Returns the serial number of the current date and time.
Math & Trig	SUM	Adds all the numbers in a range of cells.
	ABS	Returns the absolute value of a number, a number without its sign.
Statistical	AVERAGE	Returns the average (arithmetic mean) of its arguments.
	MAX	Returns the largest value in a set of values. Ignores logical values and text.
Lookup & Reference	COLUMNS	Returns the number of columns in an array or reference.
	CHOOSE	Chooses a value or action to perform from a list of values, based on an index number.
Database	DSUM	Adds the numbers in the field (column) or records in the database that match the conditions you specify.
	DAVERAGE	Averages the values in a column in a list or database that match conditions you specify.
Text	DOLLAR	Converts a number to text, using currency format.
	UPPER	Converts text to uppercase.
Logical	IF	Returns one value if a condition you specify evaluates to True and another value if it evaluates to False.
	AND	Returns True if all its arguments are True; returns False if any arguments is False.
Information	ISLOGICAL	Returns True if value is a logical value, either True or False.
	ISREF	Returns True if value is a reference.

*Use Help for detailed explanations of every function.

You will use the SUM function to calculate the total expenses for January. Because the SUM function is the most commonly used function, it has its own toolbar button.

- ■ Move to B16.

- ■ Click Σ AutoSum.

Your worksheet should be similar to Figure 2-5.

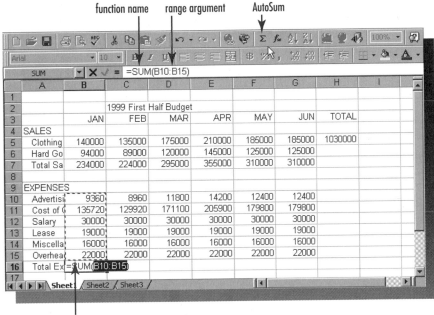

FIGURE 2-5

Pressing Alt + = is the keyboard shortcut for AutoSum.

moving border identifies proposed range to sum

Excel automatically proposes a range based upon the data above or to the left of the active cell. The name of the function followed by the range argument enclosed in parentheses is displayed in the formula bar. Excel displays a range reference as the leftmost cell and rightmost cell in the range separated by a colon (B10:B15). To accept the proposed range and enter the function,

- ■ Click ✓ Enter.

The result, 232080, calculated by the SUM function is displayed in cell B16. Next you need to calculate the total expenses for February through June.

- ■ Copy the function from cell B16 to cells C16 through G16.

- ■ Move to C16.

If you used the ←Enter key, move to B16.

The result calculated by the function, 225880, is displayed in cell C16, and the copied function is displayed in the formula bar. The range reference in the function adjusted relative to its new cell location because it is a relative reference.

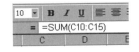

You can point to specify the cell references in the formula.

Now that the total expenses are calculated, the formula to calculate income can be entered. This number is the difference between sales and total expenses.

■   Select the range B18 through G18.

■   Enter the formula =B7–B16 in cell B18.

■   Press Ctrl + ↵Enter.

The calculated income numbers are displayed in cells B18 through G18. The income number for February shows a loss, while January and March through June show positive numbers. You are not concerned that the February income number is negative, because this is a projected budget to help the store manager make adjustments for the actual budget.

Finally, the total over the six months needs to be entered down column H.

■   Move to H6.

The AutoSum button can also calculate a grand total if your worksheet contains subtotals. Select a cell below or the right of a cell that contains a subtotal and then click AutoSum.

■   Click Σ AutoSum.

Your worksheet should be similar to Figure 2-6.

incorrect proposed range to sum

	A	B	C	D	E	F	G	H	I
				SUM	▼ X ✓ =	=SUM(H5)			
3		JAN	FEB	MAR	APR	MAY	JUN	TOTAL	
4	SALES								
5	Clothing	140000	135000	175000	210000	185000	185000	1030000	
6	Hard Go	94000	89000	120000	145000	125000	125000	=SUM(H5)	
7	Total Sa	234000	224000	295000	355000	310000	310000		
8									
9	EXPENSES								
10	Advertisi	9360	8960	11800	14200	12400	12400		
11	Cost of (	135720	129920	171100	205900	179800	179800		
12	Salary	30000	30000	30000	30000	30000	30000		
13	Lease	19000	19000	19000	19000	19000	19000		

FIGURE 2-6

range you want to sum

Notice that the moving border is around cell H5 and not the row. AutoSum first checks for values above and then to the left of the active cell. If the values above are not the range you want to sum, you can edit the function by selecting another range.

As you drag, the mouse pointer displays the number of rows (R) and the number of columns (C) selected ([1R x 6C]).

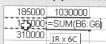

185000	1030000
125000	=SUM(B6:G6)
310000	
	1R x 6C

■   Select B6 through G6.

■   Press ↵Enter.

■   Copy the function down the column to cell H18.

■   Move to H8.

Your screen should be similar to Figure 2-7.

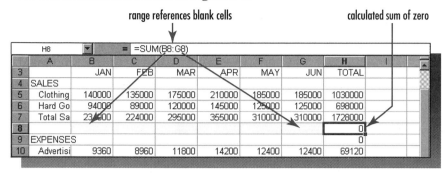

range references blank cells   calculated sum of zero

FIGURE 2-7

This cell displays a zero because the formula was copied into a cell that references empty cells. Cells H9 and H17 also display zeros for the same reason. You will clear the formulas from these cells using the fill handle.

- Select H8 through H9.

- Point to the fill handle of the selected range, and when the mouse pointer changes to , drag the mouse up until the entire selection is gray.

- Release the mouse button.

- In the same manner, delete the formula from cell H17.

Using the Paste Function Feature

Next you decide you want to add a new column showing the average values for the six months.

- Enter and right-align the heading AVG in cell I3.

- Move to I5.

Another way to enter a function is to use the Paste Function feature. This feature simplifies entering functions by prompting you to select a function from a list and then helps you to enter the arguments correctly.

- Click f_x Paste Function.

> Refer to Changing Cell Alignment on page SS32 in Lab 1 to review this feature.

> The menu equivalent is Insert/Function and the shortcut key is ⇧Shift + F3 .

The Paste Function dialog box on your screen should be similar to Figure 2-8.

displays function categories

list of function names in selected category

FIGURE 2-8

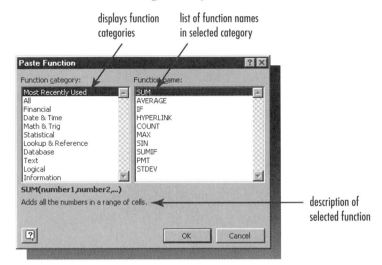

The Most Recently Used function category initially displays 10 of the most common functions.

First, you select the type of function you want to use. The Function Category list box displays the names of the function categories, and the Function Name list box displays the names of the functions in the selected category. The currently selected category is Most Recently Used. This category displays the names of the last 10 functions used.

■   Select AVERAGE from in the Function Name list box.

If AVERAGE is not displayed in the list box, select it from the Statistical category.

■   Click [OK] .

Your screen should be similar to Figure 2-9.

proposed argument range

hides dialog box while you point to select a range

displays values in selected range

FIGURE 2-9

Formula Palette dialog box

description of Average function

average result calculated

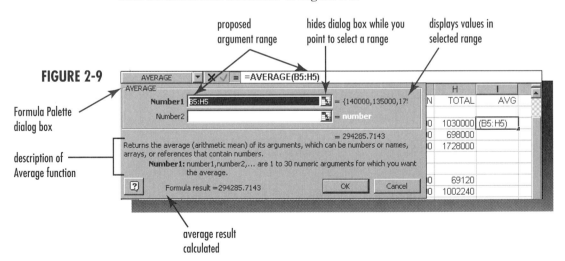

Next, the Formula Palette dialog box is displayed to help you enter the arguments required for the selected function. The upper section displays the proposed argument range in the Number 1 text box. Also notice the actual numbers in the selected range are displayed to the right of the textbox. The lower section describes the Average function and what the function requires for arguments.

Because the proposed argument range is incorrect (it includes the total value in cell H5) you need to specify the correct range (B5:G5) in the Number1 text box. The numbers or the cell references containing the numbers can be entered in the text box directly, or can be entered by selecting the cell or range from the worksheet. Selecting the range is usually faster, and it avoids the accidental entry of incorrect references. To select the range B5 through G5 from the worksheet,

■   Click

Your worksheet should be similar to Figure 2-10.

name box changes to a
drop-down function list

dialog box reduced to a single bar to
allow easy access to worksheet

restores display of
dialog box

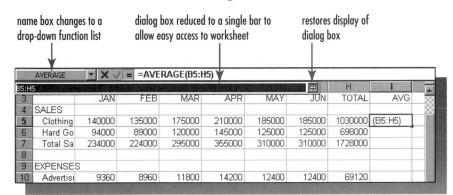

FIGURE 2-10

■   Select B5 through G5.

The new range appears in the formula bar and the cell, as well as in the dialog box bar. To redisplay the dialog box and complete the function,

■   Click 🖳 .

■   Click [OK] .

The average of the clothing sales for the six months, 171666.7, is calculated and displayed in cell I5. By default numbers are displayed with as many decimal places as cell space allows and are rounded appropriately.

■   Copy the function down column I through row 18.

You can also display the Formula Palette by clicking ⊡ Edit Formula in the Formula bar.

Keyboard users must type the range B5:G5 in the text box.

When the Formula Palette is open, the name box changes to a drop-down function list.

Your worksheet should be similar to Figure 2-11.

indicates a division error   values rounded to 10ths

FIGURE 2-11

	A	B	C	D	E	F	G	H	I
	I5		=	=AVERAGE(B5:G5)					
	A	B	C	D	E	F	G	H	I
3		JAN	FEB	MAR	APR	MAY	JUN	TOTAL	AVG
4	SALES								
5	Clothing	140000	135000	175000	210000	185000	185000	1030000	171666.7
6	Hard Go	94000	89000	120000	145000	125000	125000	698000	116333.3
7	Total Sa	234000	224000	295000	355000	310000	310000	1728000	288000
8									#DIV/0!
9	EXPENSES								#DIV/0!
10	Advertisi	9360	8960	11800	14200	12400	12400	69120	11520

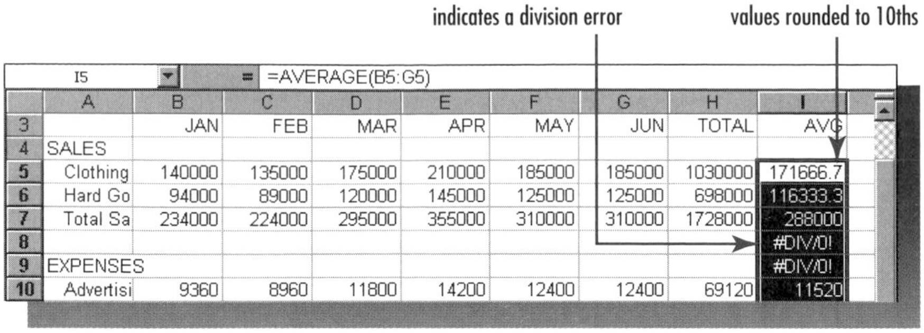

The average value has been correctly calculated for each row. Notice three cells display #DIV/0!. This indicates a division error occurred because the formula divides by zero.

■   Clear the function from the three cells that display #DIV/0!.

Using Absolute References

Next you decide to enter a formula to calculate what proportion the total clothing sales and total hardware sales for six months are of the total sales. You will display the proportion in the column to the right of the Average column. The formula to calculate the proportion for clothing is Total Clothing Sales/Total Sales.

■   Move to J5

■   Enter the formula =H5/H7 in cell J5.

The value 0.596065 is displayed in cell J5. This shows that the clothing sales are approximately 60 percent of total sales.

Next, to calculate the proportion that hardware sales are of total sales, you will copy the formula from J5 to J6. Another quick way to copy cell contents is to drag the cell border while holding down Ctrl. This method is most useful when the distance between cells is short and they are both visible in the window. It cannot be used if you are copying to a larger range than the source range.

The mouse pointer appears as ↖+ to show that it will copy the cell contents.

■   Point to the border of cell J5 and when the mouse pointer shape is ↖, hold down Ctrl, and drag the mouse pointer to cell J6.

Your worksheet should be similar to Figure 2-12.

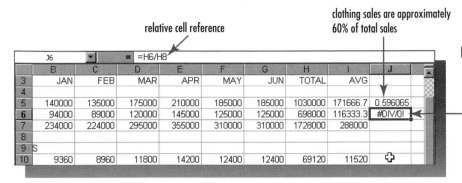

relative cell reference

clothing sales are approximately
60% of total sales

FIGURE 2-12

division error occurs because formula adjusted
relative to its new location when copied and
reference in cell H8 is blank

A #DIV/0! error occurred because the reference to cell H7 changed to cell H8, a
blank cell, when the formula was copied. The formula in J5 needs to be entered
so that the row of the referenced cell, row 7, does not change to row 8 when it is
copied. To do this you need to make the cell reference absolute.

Concept 3: Absolute Reference

An **absolute reference** is a cell or range reference in a formula whose location does not change
when the formula is copied.

To stop the relative adjustment of cell references, enter a $ (dollar sign) character before the
column letter and row number. This changes the cell reference to absolute. When a formula containing an absolute cell reference is copied to another row and column location in the worksheet, the
cell reference does not change. It is an exact duplicate of the cell reference in the original formula.

A cell reference can also be a **mixed reference**. In this type of reference, either the column
letter or the row number is preceded with the $. This makes only the row or column absolute. When
a formula containing a mixed cell reference is pasted to another location in the worksheet, only the
part of the cell reference that is not absolute changes relative to its new location in the worksheet.

The table below shows examples of relative and absolute references and the results when a
reference in cell C10 to cell B28 is copied to cell E13.

Cell Contents of C10	Copied to Cell E13	Type of Reference
$B$28	$B$28	Absolute reference
B$28	D$28	Mixed reference
$B28	$B31	Mixed reference
B28	D31	Relative reference

You can change a cell reference to absolute or mixed by typing in the dollar
sign directly or by using the ABS (Absolute) key, F4. To use the ABS key, the
program must be in the Edit mode.

■ Move to cell J5 and turn on the Edit mode.

Press F2 or double-click cell J5.

SPREADSHEET

Your worksheet should be similar to Figure 2-13.

the Range Finder feature uses matching colors to
identify cells or range references in formulas

FIGURE 2-13

	B	C	D	E	F	G	H	I	J
	AVERAGE	▼	✗ ✓	=	=H5/H7				
	JAN	FEB	MAR	APR	MAY	JUN	TOTAL	AVG	
3									
4									
5	140000	135000	175000	210000	185000	185000	1030000	171666.7	=H5/H7
6	94000	89000	120000	145000	125000	125000	698000	116333.3	#DIV/0!
7	234000	224000	295000	355000	310000	310000	1728000	288000	
8									
9	S								
10	9360	8960	11800	14200	12400	12400	69120	11520	✛

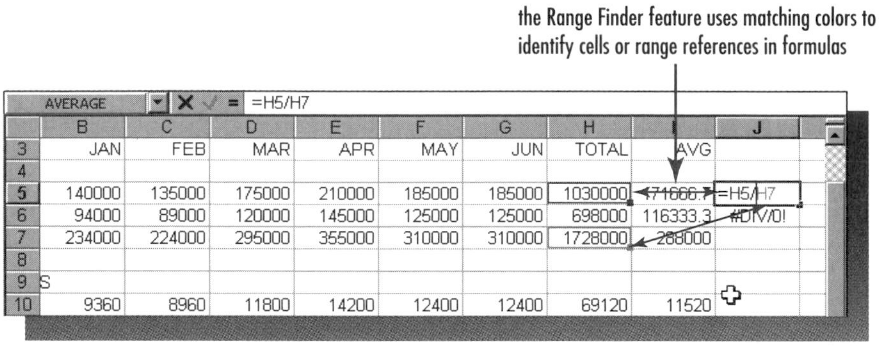

Notice that the cell references in the formula are color coded to match the borders Excel displays around the referenced worksheet cells. This is Excel's Range Finder feature. It is designed to provide visual cues to the relationships between the cells that provide values to the formulas or the cells that depend on the formulas.

You need to change the H7 cell reference to absolute. When using the ABS key, first position the insertion point on or immediately to the right of the cell reference that you want to change.

- If necessary, move the insertion point to the cell reference H7.

- Press F4.

The cell reference now displays $ characters before the column letter and row number, making this cell reference absolute. If you continue to press F4, the cell reference will cycle through all possible combinations of cell reference types. Leaving the cell reference absolute, as it is now, will stop the relative adjustment of the cell reference when you copy it again.

```
=H5/$H$7
  #DIV/0!
```

- Click ✓ Enter.

- Copy the revised formula to cell J6.

- Move to J6.

> A mixed reference of H$7 would also have solved the problem.

Your worksheet should be similar to Figure 2-14.

absolute reference stopped the
adjustment of the cell reference
when the formula was copied

hard goods sales are
approximately
40% of total sales

FIGURE 2-14

	B	C	D	E	F	G	H	I	J
	J6	▼		=	=H6/$H$7				
	JAN	FEB	MAR	APR	MAY	JUN	TOTAL	AVG	
3									
4									
5	140000	135000	175000	210000	185000	185000	1030000	171666.7	0.596065
6	94000	89000	120000	145000	125000	125000	698000	116333.3	0.403935
7	234000	224000	295000	355000	310000	310000	1728000	288000	
8									✛
9	S								
10	9360	8960	11800	14200	12400	12400	69120	11520	

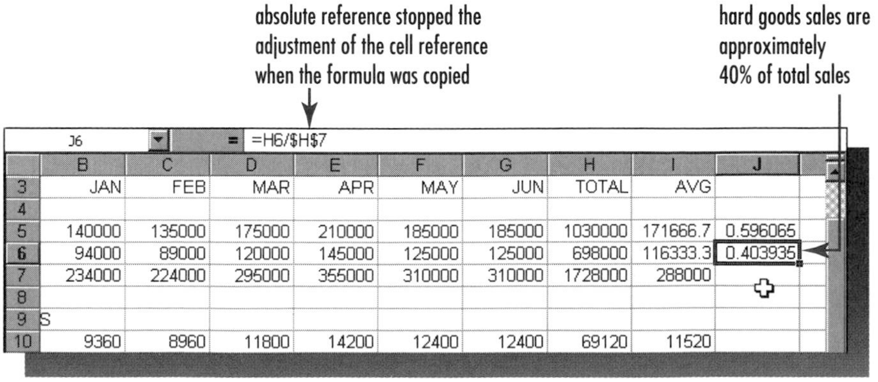

Adding Cell Comments

To clarify the meaning of the two proportion values, you decide to add cell comments. Cell comments are notes that are attached to a cell and that automatically appear whenever the mouse pointer rests on the cell. To add a comment to clarify the hard goods proportion value,

■ Choose **I**nsert/Co**m**ment.

Your worksheet should be similar to Figure 2-15.

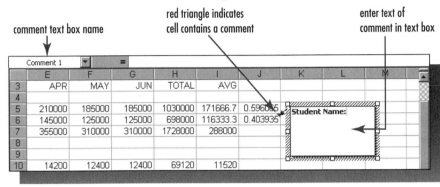

comment text box name

red triangle indicates
cell contains a comment

enter text of
comment in text box

FIGURE 2-15

Notice the cell displays a red triangle in the upper right corner. This indicates the cell contains a comment. In the comment text box you enter the text you want to appear in the comment.

■ Select the name and type your name.

■ Press ⏎Enter.

■ Type **Total hard goods sales as a percent of total sales**.

■ To close the comment, click anywhere outside the comment box.

■ To display the comment, point to cell J6.

Your worksheet should be similar to Figure 2-16.

> The comment text box displays the user name assigned to the program by default.

> The text wraps within the comment text box as you type.

> The cell does not need to be active to display the cell comment.

the comment is displayed
when you point to the cell

FIGURE 2-16

	E	F	G	H	I	J	K	L	M
4	APR	MAY	JUN	TOTAL	AVG				
5									
6	210000	185000	185000	1030000	171666.7	0.596065			
7	145000	125000	125000	698000	116333.3	0.403935			
8	355000	310000	310000	1728000	288000				
9									
10									
11	$ 14,200	$ 12,400	$ 12,400	$ 69,120	$ 11,520				

Student Name:
Total hard goods sales
as a percent of total
sales.

> You can copy the text from the comment text box of cell J6 and edit it in the comment text box for cell J5.

> To delete a comment, use Edit/Clear/Comment.

> As long as the cells to the left are blank, when you right-align an entry, it will overlap into the cell to the left.

> Reminder: Use [Ctrl] + [Home] to quickly move to cell A1.

- Add the comment, "Total clothing sales as a percent of total sales," to cell J5.

- Close the comment text box and display the comment.

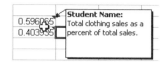

The last formula you need to add to the worksheet is to calculate the total profit margin for the first six months. You will enter the formula in cell H20 and a descriptive text entry in cell G20.

- In cell G20 enter and right-align the entry, Profit Margin.

- In cell H20 enter the formula =H18/H7.

The profit margin for the first half of the year is approximately 8 percent (0.077917).

- Move to A1.

Note: If you are stopping at the end of Part 1, enter your name in cell A1, save the workbook file as 1999 First Half Budget, print the worksheet, and exit Excel. When you begin Part 2, open the file 1999 First Half Budget.

Part 2

Adjusting Column Widths

Now that the worksheet data is complete, you want to improve its appearance by adjusting column widths, using underlining, and setting different number format styles.

After entering the numbers for January in column B, any long headings in column A were cut off or interrupted. To allow the long text entries in column A to be fully displayed, you can increase the column's width.

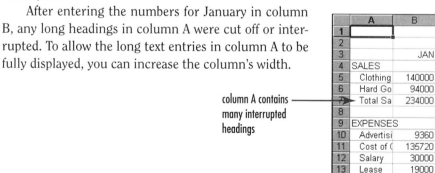

column A contains many interrupted headings

Concept 4: Column Width

The size or width of a column controls how much information can be displayed in a cell. A text entry that is larger than the column width will be fully displayed only if the cells to the right are blank. If the cells to the right contain data, the text is interrupted. On the other hand, when numbers are entered in a cell, the column width is automatically increased to fully display the entry.

The default column width setting in Excel is 8.43. The number represents the average number of digits that can be displayed in a cell using the standard font. The column width can be any number from 1 to 255.

When the worksheet is printed, it appears as it does currently on the screen. Therefore, you want to increase the column width to display the largest entry. Likewise, you can decrease the column width when the entries in a column are small.

The column width can be quickly adjusted by dragging the column divider line located to the right of the column letter. Dragging it to the left decreases the column width, while dragging it to the right increases the width. As you drag, a temporary column reference line shows where the new column will appear, and the mouse pointer displays the width of the column.

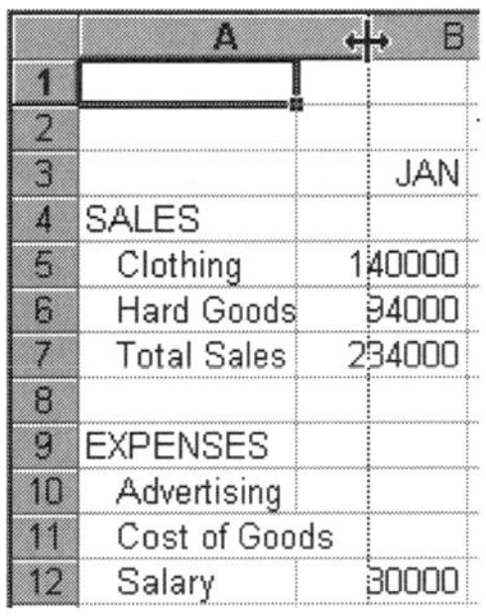

- Point to the column divider line to the right of the column letter A and drag the mouse pointer to the right.

- When the mouse pointer displays 15.00, release the mouse button.

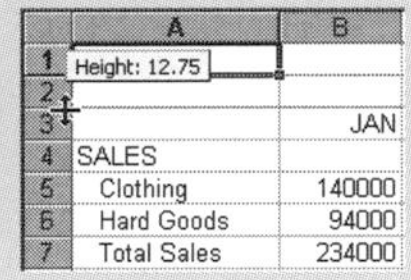

Your worksheet should be similar to Figure 2-17.

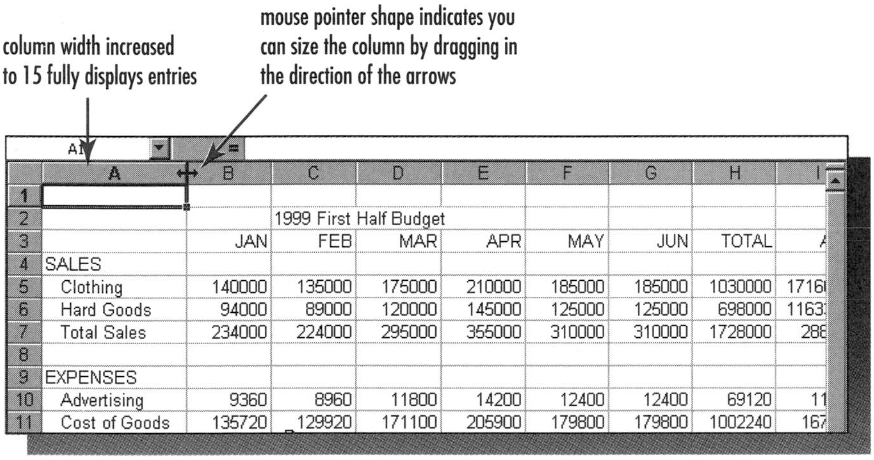

The menu equivalent is Format/Column/Width.

The mouse pointer changes to ↔ when you can size a column.

You can also adjust the height of a row by dragging the row divider line.

column width increased to 15 fully displays entries

mouse pointer shape indicates you can size the column by dragging in the direction of the arrows

FIGURE 2-17

Next you want to see how the worksheet would look if you decreased the column widths of all the other columns in the worksheet. You can decrease the width of each column individually, but it would be faster to change the width of all the columns at once. First you need to select the columns you want to change.

- Click on the column letter B.

- Drag the mouse to the right until columns B through J are selected.

Clicking the column letter selects the entire column to the last worksheet row. Next you want to reduce the column width of all selected columns to 5.

- Drag the right border of any column in the selected range to the left until the mouse pointer displays 5.00.

- Release the mouse button.

- Move to cell A1.

Your screen should be similar to Figure 2-18.

> When you drag beyond the visible window, the window will scroll in the same direction.

FIGURE 2-18

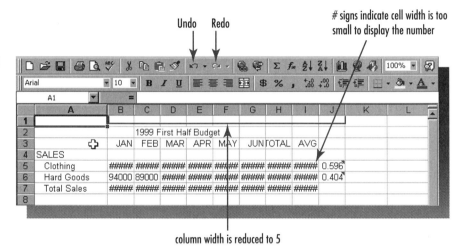

Undo   Redo

\# signs indicate cell width is too small to display the number

column width is reduced to 5

All the cells in the selected columns have changed to five character spaces. Notice that a series of number signs (#####) appears in most of the worksheet cells. Whenever the width of a cell is too small to display the entire number, number signs are displayed.

Using Undo

As you can see, this new column width is much too small. To cancel the most recent operation and restore the worksheet to how it was prior to your change,

- Click [↶ ▾] Undo.

> The menu equivalent is **E**dit/**U**ndo Column Width, and the shortcut key is [Ctrl] + Z.

The effects of the column width setting are reversed and the columns are restored to the prior column width setting. The previously selected range is highlighted again.

The Undo feature is primarily used to undo errors and is an important safeguard against mistakes that may take a lot of time to fix. Clicking Undo reverses the effects of the most recent command performed or deletes the last entry you typed. If the action cannot be undone, the ⟲ button appears dimmed.

To Undo several actions at once, open the Undo drop-down list and select the actions you want to reverse. All actions above the selected action are also reversed.

■ Move to cell A1 to clear the selection.

Zooming the Worksheet

Before adjusting the column widths any more, you want to improve the appearance of the numbers in columns B through J. This range, however, is not entirely visible in the window. You can change how much information is displayed in the window to make it easier to navigate, view, and select the worksheet data by adjusting the zoom percentage. The 100% ▾ Zoom button at the right end of the Standard toolbar shows the current zoom percentage is 100 percent. This is the default display percent setting, and it displays data onscreen as it will appear on the printed page. You can reduce or enlarge the amount of information displayed onscreen by changing the magnification from between 10 to 400 percent. You want to decrease the zoom percent to display more information in the window.

■ Open the 100% ▾ Zoom drop-down menu.

■ Select 75%.

Your screen should be similar to Figure 2-19.

Immediately after you undo an action, the command changes to Redo and the ⟳ Redo button is available to allow you to restore the action(s) you just undid.

The Zoom feature is common to all Office 97 programs.

The menu equivalent is **V**iew/**Z**oom.

The Selection option adjusts the percentage to fit the selected range in the current window size.

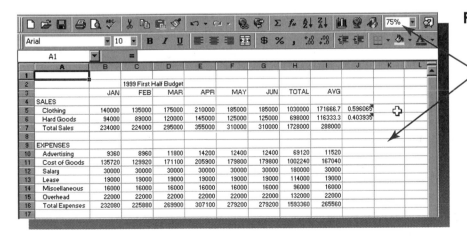

FIGURE 2-19

reducing the zoom percentage displays more information in the window

Formatting Numbers

Now you can more easily select the range to change. You want to improve the appearance of the numbers in the worksheet by changing their format.

Concept 5: Number Formats

Number formats affect how numbers look onscreen and when printed. They do not affect the way Excel stores or uses the values in calculations. The default format setting that controls how numbers are displayed in the worksheet is General. The General format setting automatically sets the number format to a Date, Time, Comma, Currency, Percent, or Scientific number format setting depending on the symbols you used when entering the data.

The table below shows samples of how Excel automatically formats a number based on how it appears when you enter it.

Entry	Format
10,000	Comma
$102.20	Currency with two decimal places
90%	Percent with zero decimal places
10/30/98	Date
9:10	Time

If no symbol is used, Excel leaves the number unformatted. Unformatted numbers are displayed without a thousands separator such as a comma, with negative values preceded by a – (minus sign), and with as many decimal place settings as cell space allows.

First you will change the number format of cells B5 through I18 to display dollar signs, commas, and decimal places.

A quick way to select a range is to click on the first cell of the range and then hold down ⇧Shift while clicking on the last cell of the range. This method is particularly useful when the range is large or if it is not entirely visible in the window.

- Use this method to select the range B5 through I18.

- Choose F̲ormat/C̲ells.

- If necessary, open the Number tab.

- Select Currency.

The keyboard shortcut is Ctrl + 1. Format Cells is also an option on the Shortcut menu.

The dialog box on your screen should be similar to Figure 2-20.

selected format category

example of how a number appears in the selected format

FIGURE 2-20

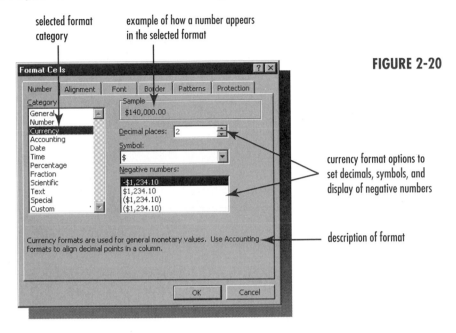

currency format options to set decimals, symbols, and display of negative numbers

description of format

The Currency category includes options that allow you to specify the number of decimal places, how negative numbers will appear, and whether a currency symbol such as a dollar sign will be displayed.

- If a dollar sign is not displayed in the Symbol drop-down list box, turn it on by selecting $English (United States) from the drop-down list.

- Click .

The number entries in the selected range appear with a currency symbol, comma, and two decimal places. The column widths for most columns increased automatically to fully display the formatted values.

A second format category that displays numbers as currency is Accounting.

- Click **$** .

	A	B	C
			=C7*0.04
1			
2			1999 First Ha
3		JAN	FEB
4	SALES		
5	Clothing	$140,000.00	$135,000.00
6	Hard Goods	$94,000.00	$89,000.00
7	Total Sales	$234,000.00	$224,000.00

Your screen should be similar to Figure 2-21.

FIGURE 2-21

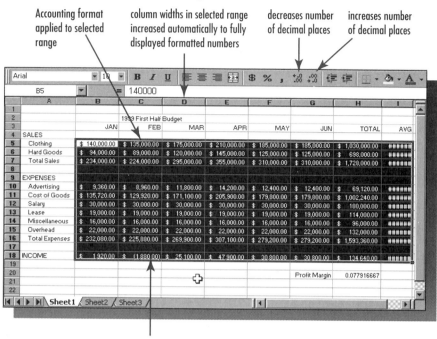

Accounting format applied to selected range

column widths in selected range increased automatically to fully displayed formatted numbers

decreases number of decimal places

increases number of decimal places

negative numbers displayed in parentheses

The numbers now appear in Accounting format. The primary difference between the Accounting and the Currency formats is that the Accounting format aligns numbers at the decimal place and places the dollar sign in a column at the left edge of the cell space. In addition, it does not allow you to select different ways of displaying negative numbers, but displays them in black in parentheses. You feel the Accounting format will make it easier to read the numbers in a column.

As you look at the numbers, you decide it is not necessary to display the decimal places since most of the values are whole numbers. To do this,

> The menu equivalent is F**o**rmat/C**e**lls/ Accounting.

> The ⌷⌷ button increases the number of decimal places.

■ Click ⌷⌷ Decrease decimal (2 times).

Now that the numbers are displayed with zero decimal places, the column widths are larger than they need to be. Because Excel does not automatically reduce column widths, you need to make this change yourself. You will do this using the AutoFit feature. This feature automatically sets the column widths to the minimum necessary to display the contents of the selected cells.

■ Choose F**o**rmat/**C**olumn/**A**utoFit Selection.

Your screen should be similar to Figure 2-22.

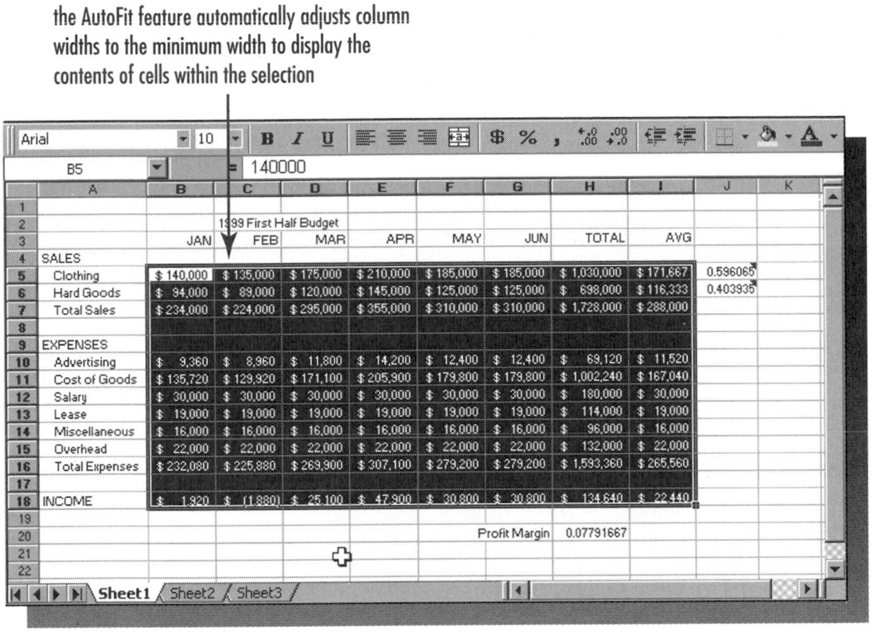

the AutoFit feature automatically adjusts column
widths to the minimum width to display the
contents of cells within the selection

FIGURE 2-22

The width of columns B through I automatically decreased to the minimum
column width needed to fully display the numbers. The width of column A remained the same because it was not included in the selection.

Applying Styles

Next you want to format the two proportion values in cells J5 and J6 and the
profit margin to display as a percent. You could apply the Percent format using
the Format/Cells menu command as you just did. Another way, however, is to
select a predefined format style.

Concept 6: Styles

A **style** consists of a combination of formats that have been named and that
can be quickly applied to a selection. Normal is the default style. It sets the
number format to General and controls other format
settings that are applied to all entries.

Examples of the six predefined styles are shown
on the right. Notice the two Currency styles. They will
display dollar signs, commas, and two or zero decimal
places, just as if you had selected these formats from
the Format Cells dialog box.

Style	Examples
Normal	89522
Comma	89,522.00
Comma[0]	89,522
Currency	$89,522.00
Currency[0]	$ 89,522
Percent	89.52200%

■ Select J5 and J6.

■ Choose F**o**rmat/**S**tyle.

The dialog box on your screen should be similar to Figure 2-23.

FIGURE 2-23

current format style

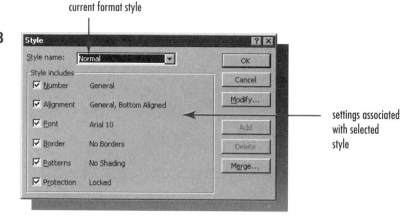

settings associated with selected style

The Style Name list box displays the current style, Normal. The check boxes in the Style Includes area of the dialog box show the options that are included in this style and a description or sample. You want to use the Percent style.

■ Open the Style Name drop-down list box.

■ Select Percent.

■ Click [OK].

Your worksheet should be similar to Figure 2-24.

changes format to percent

Percent style applied to cells

FIGURE 2-24

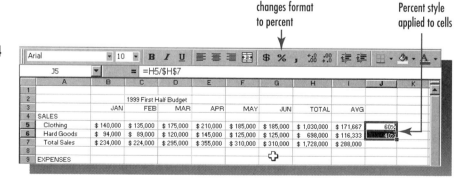

Setting the cell format to Percent takes the value in the cell and multiplies it by 100. The decimal value is converted to a percent by moving the decimal point two places to the right and rounding the value to the nearest whole.

■ To make the percentage more accurate, increase the decimal place setting to 2.

Next you need to change the profit margin number to display as a percent with two decimal places. To quickly change the value to percent, you can also use the % button on the formatting toolbar.

■   Move to H20.

■   Click % Percent.

■   Format the profit margin percent to display two decimal places.

■   Press Ctrl + Home.

Inserting Rows

The appearance of the worksheet is greatly improved already. However, it looks crowded and could be further improved by inserting a blank row below the worksheet title as row 3.

Concept 7: Insert and Delete Cells, Rows, and Columns

Individual cells or entire rows or columns can be inserted and deleted from a worksheet. A cell is inserted by moving the contents of the active cell down or to the right. When inserting a row, the new row is added at the cell selector position, moving the current row and all others down. When a column is added, the current column and all other columns move to the right. The formats associated with surrounding cells are applied to the newly inserted cell, row, or column.

You can also delete individual cells as well as entire columns and rows. When you delete the cell, column, or row, the surrounding cells, columns, and rows shift to fill the space. Deleting cells is different from clearing cells. When you clear a cell, the cell contents, formats, or comments are erased, leaving a blank cell on the worksheet. Be very careful when you delete, however, because any information in the cell, column, or row will be erased.

When you insert or delete cells, rows, or columns, all cell references in formulas and functions are automatically adjusted to their new locations. This keeps your formulas up to date. However, a worksheet formula containing a reference to a deleted cell displays a #REF! error message.

To insert a blank row into the worksheet, begin by moving the cell selector to the row where the new blank row will be inserted.

■   Move to A3.

■   Choose Insert/Rows.

To delete a cell, row, or column, select it and choose Edit/Delete/Entire Row or Entire Column.

To insert a column, choose Insert/Columns.

Insert and Delete are also on the Shortcut menu.

Your worksheet should be similar to Figure 2-25.

FIGURE 2-25

blank row inserted into worksheet

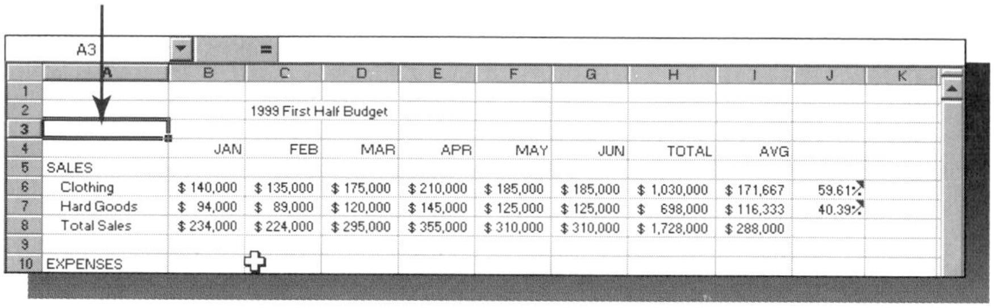

A blank row has been inserted into the worksheet at the cell selector location by moving everything below row 3 down one row.

Moving Cell Contents

Next you want the worksheet title centered in the range A2 through I2 so it appears centered over the worksheet data. To center-align across a selection, the text you want aligned must be in the leftmost cell of the range. To move the worksheet title in cell C2 to cell A2, you could cut and paste the contents, or you can drag the cell border to move the cell contents. This is similar to copying by dragging. Dragging is quickest and most useful when the distance between cells is short and they are visible within the window, whereas Cut and Paste are best for long-distance moves.

As you drag, an outline of the cell appears and the mouse pointer displays the cell reference to show its new location in the worksheet.

If you move cells containing formulas, the formulas are not adjusted relative to their new worksheet locations.

■   Move to C2.

■   Point to the border of the cell and when the mouse pointer shape is ⬚, drag the mouse pointer to cell A2 and release the mouse button.

The contents of cell C2 are copied into cell A2 and cleared from the original cell.

Centering Across a Selection

Now you are ready to center the worksheet title. The text will be centered across cells A2 through I2.

■   Select A2 through I2.

The menu equivalent is Format/Cells/Alignment/Horizontal/Center Across Selection.

■   Click ⊞ Merge and Center.

Your worksheet should be similar to Figure 2-26.

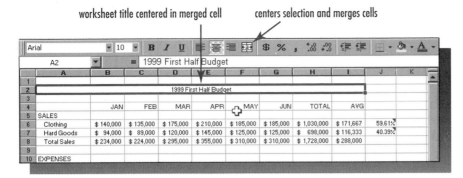

worksheet title centered in merged cell   centers selection and merges cells

FIGURE 2-26

Combining all cells in the selected range into one has created a **merged cell**. The cell reference for the merged cell is the upper left cell in the range. The contents of the leftmost cell of the range are centered within the merged cell space.

Changing Fonts and Font Styles

Finally, you want to improve the worksheet appearance by enhancing the appearance of the title. To do this you can change the font settings.

> The Font settings are common to all Office 97 programs.

Concept 8: Fonts

Fonts consist of typefaces, size, and style. The **typeface** is the appearance and shape of characters. Two common typefaces are Times New Roman and Courier. Size refers to the size of the printed characters and is commonly measured in points, abbreviated pt. A point is about 1/72 inch in height. A common point size for text is 12 pt. This means the printed character is about 12/72 inch in height. Arial 10 pt is the default font for a worksheet. Additionally, you can change the font style, such as bold, italics, and underlines, associated with a cell entry. The box below shows several examples of the same text in various typefaces, sizes, and styles.

Typeface	Font Size (12 pt/18 pt)	Font Style (Bold)
Arial	This is 12 pt. This is 18 pt.	**Bold 18 pt**
Courier New	This is 12 pt. This is 18 pt.	**Bold 18 pt**
Times New Roman	This is 12 pt. This is 18 pt.	**Bold 18 pt**

The fonts on your computer system will be either printer or true-type fonts. True-type fonts appear onscreen as they will appear when printed. They are installed when Windows is installed. Printer fonts are supported by your printer and are displayed as close as possible to how they will appear onscreen, but may not match exactly when printed.

The ⬚ Font and ⬚ Font Size drop-down list boxes on the Formatting toolbar show the typeface and point size associated with the current cell. First you will change the typeface.

■   Open the ⬚ Font drop-down list box.

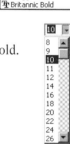

The Font drop-down menu displays the available typefaces in alphabetical order. If a font name is preceded with a ⬚, this means it is a font associated with your printer. Those preceded with **T̅r̅** are true-type fonts.

■   Select **T̅r̅** Times New Roman.

The title appears in the selected typeface. Next you will increase the font size to 14 and change the font style to bold.

■   Open the ⬚ Font Size drop-down list box.

■   Select 14.

■   Click **B** Bold.

Your worksheet should be similar to Figure 2-27.

Font button displays font of selected cell   Font Size button displays point size of selected cell   Bold button is depressed, indicating bold has been applied to the selected cell   cell contents appear in selected font, size, and style

FIGURE 2-27

row height automatically increases to accommodate larger font size

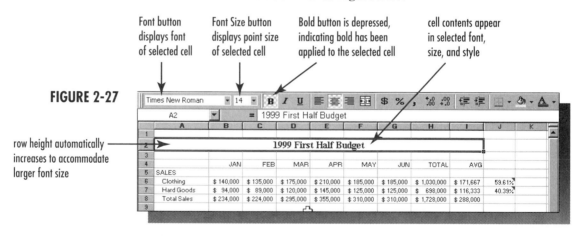

The title is in the typeface, size, and style you specified. Notice that the height of the row has increased to accommodate the larger character size of the heading in that row.

You also want to add bold, italics, and underlines to several other worksheet entries.

■   Format the row headings in cells A8 and A17 to bold.

Next you would like to change the row headings in cells A5, A10, and A19 to bold and italic.

■   Move to A5.

■   Click **B** Bold, **I** Italic.

You could repeat the same sequence for cells A10 and A19, but a quicker method is to copy the format from one cell to another using 🖌 Format Painter on the Standard toolbar. To copy the format of the active cell to the other cells,

- Double-click 🖌 Format Painter.

- Click A10.

- Click A19.

- Click 🖌 Format Painter.

The formatting was quickly added to each cell as it was selected, and the feature is off.

Finally, you want to bold and underline the column headings.

- Select B4 through I4.

- Click **B** Bold, **U** Underline.

- Move to A4.

The last formatting change you would like to make to the worksheet is to adjust the width of column A to fully display the row headings again. You will use the AutoFit shortcut to make this change.

- Double-click the right column boundary of column A.

Your screen should be similar to Figure 2-28.

A single click on 🖌 allows you to copy formats to a single cell.

The keyboard shortcut for underline is Ctrl + U.

The mouse pointer displays as a +.

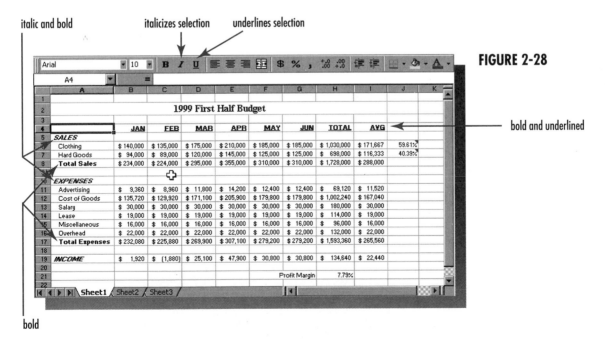

FIGURE 2-28

The six-month budget is now complete.

- Return the zoom percentage to 100%.

> Use **F**ile/Prope**r**ties/Summary to update the documentation.

- Update the workbook documentation to include your name.

- Save the changes you have made to the workbook file as 1999 First Half Budget.

Adding Predefined Headers and Footers

You would like to include your name and the date in a header.

Concept 9: Headers and Footers

A **header** is a line or several lines of text that appears at the top of each page just below the top margin. A **footer** is a line or several lines of text that appears at the bottom of each page just above the bottom margin. The text can be formatted like any other text. In addition, you can control the placement of the header and footer text by specifying where it should appear: left-aligned, centered, or right-aligned in the header or footer space. Information that is commonly placed in a header or footer is the date and page number.

To add a header,

- Preview the worksheet.

> Click ⌕ Print Preview to preview the worksheet.

- Click Setup... .

- Open the Header/Footer tab.

The dialog box on your screen should be similar to Figure 2-29.

FIGURE 2-29

> The **F**ile/Page Set**u**p command can also be used to modify page layout settings.

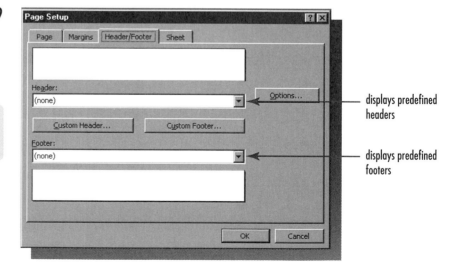

displays predefined headers

displays predefined footers

The Header drop-down list box contains a list of predefined headers that you select to appear in the header.

■ Open the Header drop-down list box and select the Prepared By **[your name] [date]**, Page 1 option.

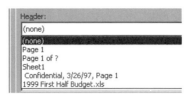

Header:
(none)
(none)
Page 1
Page 1 of ?
Sheet1
Confidential, 3/26/97, Page 1
1999 First Half Budget.xls

The selected header is displayed in the header area of the dialog box.

■ Click  OK .

> Footers are entered in the same way as headers.

Your screen should be similar to Figure 2-30.

changes page layout settings   predefined header added to worksheet   worksheet too large to print on one page

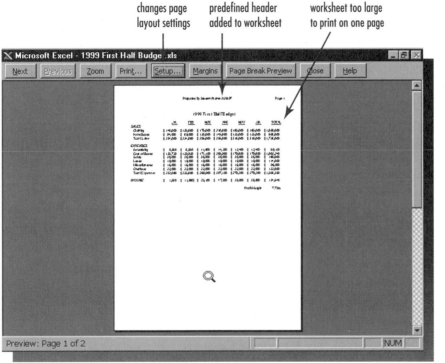

FIGURE 2-30

Changing Page Orientation

Notice that the entire sheet does not fit across the width of the page. To see the second page,

■ Click Next .

The sheet requires two pages to print using the default settings. To print the entire sheet on a single page, you can change the orientation (layout of the printed worksheet on the paper) so that the worksheet prints across the length of the paper. This type of layout is called **landscape** style. You also feel the worksheet may be easier to read if the row and column lines were printed. To change the orientation of the worksheet on the page from **portrait** (prints across the width of the page) to landscape and to print the gridlines,

Not all printers can print landscape style. If your printer does not have this capability, skip the instructions on changing the orientation.

- Click Previous .

- Click Setup... .

- From the Page tab select Landscape.

- From the Sheet tab select Gridlines.

- Click OK .

Your screen should be similar to Figure 2-31.

changing the orientation to landscape
displays the entire worksheet

gridlines are displayed

FIGURE 2-31

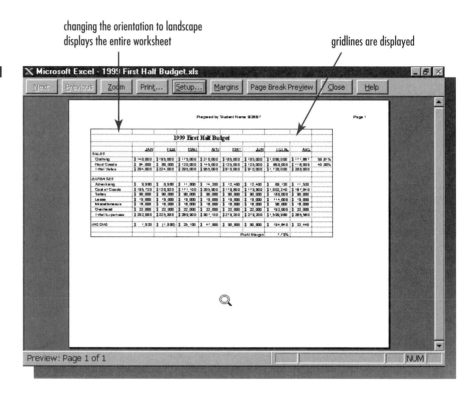

The Preview screen is recreated showing how the sheet will appear in landscape orientation and with gridlines. To print the workbook,

- Click Print... .

- If necessary, select the appropriate printer for your system.

- Click OK .

- When you are ready, exit Excel, saving the workbook file using the same file name.

LAB REVIEW

■ ■ ■ ■ ■ ■ ■ ■ ■ ■

Key Terms

absolute reference (SS61)
argument (SS54)
font (SS75)
footer (SS78)
function (SS54)

header (SS78)
landscape (SS79)
merged cell (SS75)
mixed reference (SS61)
portrait (SS80)

relative reference (SS52)
style (SS71)
syntax (SS54)
typeface (SS75)

Command Summary

Command	Shortcut	Toolbar	Action
File/Page Set**u**p/**H**eader/Footer			Adds header and/or footer
File/Page Set**u**p/**L**andscape			Prints worksheet across length of paper
Edit/**U**ndo	Ctrl + Z	↶ ▾	Undoes last editing or formatting change
Edit/Cle**a**r/**C**omment			Removes comment from cell
Edit/**D**elete/Entire **R**ow			Deletes selected rows
Edit/**D**elete/Entire **C**olumn			Deletes selected columns
View/**Z**oom		100% ▾	Changes magnification of window
Insert/**R**ows			Inserts a blank row
Insert/**C**olumns			Inserts a blank column
Insert/**F**unction	⇧Shift + F3	*fx*	Inserts a function
Insert/Co**m**ment			Inserts a comment to a cell
Fo**r**mat/C**e**lls/Number/Currency			Applies Currency format to selection
Fo**r**mat/C**e**lls/Number/Accounting			Applies Accounting format to selection
Fo**r**mat/C**e**lls/Alignment/Center Across Selection		▦	Centers cell contents across selected cells
Fo**r**mat/C**e**lls/Font			Changes font and attributes of cell contents
Fo**r**mat/**C**olumn/**W**idth			Changes width of columns
Fo**r**mat/**C**olumn/**A**utofit Selection			Changes column width to match widest cell entry
Fo**r**mat/**S**tyle			Applies selected style to selection

Matching

1. General _____
2. F4 _____
3. point _____
4. $B$4 _____
5. footer _____
6. style _____
7. SUM _____
8. landscape _____
9. ###### _____
10. _____

a. function to add a series of numbers

b. prints across length of paper

c. an absolute cell reference

d. indicates insufficient cell width to display numbers

e. method of entering a cell range or reference in a formula

f. a line of text that appears at the bottom of each page

g. centers across selection

h. a named group of format settings

i. in Edit mode, the ABS key

j. default cell format

Fill-In Questions

1. Complete the following statements by filling in the blanks with the correct terms.

a. _____ are predefined formulas that perform certain types of calculations automatically.

b. To display more characters in a cell, you would increase the _____.

c. When a formula is copied, and a cell reference does not adjust to the new location, the reference is _____.

d. To print a worksheet across the length of the page, you would change the orientation to _____.

e. A(n) _____ is a named group of formats.

f. When column widths are adjusted based on their contents, the _____ command is used.

g. _____ appear when a cell width is too small to display the entire number in that cell.

h. A(n) _____ character is used to make a reference absolute.

i. A(n) _____ is the data the function uses to perform the calculation.

j. _____ consist of typefaces and size.

Discussion Questions

1. How is the formula F6+F7+F8 changed when it is copied from cell F10 to cell B16? How would the formula change if all the cell references were made absolute? How would the formula change if all the cell references were mixed references with the row number fixed?

2. Discuss the differences between relative, mixed, and absolute cell references.

3. What are the advantages of using a function instead of a formula to calculate a value?

4. Discuss the differences between the way numbers are displayed when the following formats are used: Currency, Accounting, Percent, and Date.

Hands-On Practice Exercises

Step by Step

Rating System		
☆	Easy	
☆☆	Moderate	
☆☆☆	Difficult	

☆

1. To complete this problem, you must have completed Practice Exercise 1 in Lab 1. Open the workbook file Bed and Breakfast on your data disk. In this exercise you will continue to modify the worksheet comparing prices of bed and breakfast inns in New England.

a. Delete column B. Size column A to fully display the names of the inns. Change the width of columns B, and C to accommodate the widest entries. Center the title across columns A to G. Increase the title font and bold it.

b. Format the numbers in columns D through G to display dollar signs and two decimals.

c. Insert a row at row 2 and row 6.

d. Bold the contents of cells A1 through G5, and underline the row 5 headings.

e. Center the heading Single Rates across columns D and E, and center Double Rates across columns F and G. Increase the font size of those two headings by two points.

f. In cell D18, enter the formula =AVERAGE(D7:D16) to calculate the average rate for a single room with a private bath. Copy the formula to the three adjacent cells to the right. Use the Office Assistant to look up the MIN and MAX functions, and calculate the low and high rates for the four occupancy categories.

g. Italicize the row headings Average Rates, Low Rates, and High Rates.

h. Clear your name and the date from the worksheet.

i. Save and replace the workbook file Bed and Breakfast. Preview the worksheet. Add a predefined header that displays your name and the date, then print the worksheet with gridlines.

2. To complete this problem, you must have completed Practice Exercise 2 in Lab 1. Open the workbook file Cookie Jar on your data disk. In this exercise you will continue to modify the quarterly sales worksheet for the gourmet cookie shop, The Cookie Jar.

a. Delete columns B and C and widen column A appropriately.

b. Format the sales numbers to display commas without dollar signs and with two decimals.

c. Delete the formula that you used to calculate a total for chocolate chip cookies. Replace it with a SUM function, and copy the function down the column. Calculate totals for the three months, and sum the Total column. List three different ways you can total a column. Which do you think is the most efficient?

d. Make the necessary changes to column widths.

e. Center the worksheet title across the columns. Bold the title. Select a different font and increase the size to 14 pt.

f. Bold and underline the column headings. Insert a blank row between the column headings and the chocolate chip cookie information.

g. Italicize the names of the cookies. Bold, italicize, and right-align the row heading Total.

h. Clear your name and the date from the worksheet.

i. Preview the worksheet. Add a predefined header that displays your name and the date. Print the worksheet. Save and replace the workbook file Cookie Jar.

You will complete this exercise as Practice Exercise 5 in Lab 3.

3. To complete this problem, you must have completed Practice Exercise 3 in Lab 1. Open the workbook file Fat Grams on your data disk. In this exercise you will continue to modify the fat analysis worksheet.

a. Eliminate columns B and C, and change the width of column A to accommodate the widest entry.

b. Bold and underline the column headings and make any necessary adjustments to column width.

c. Enter a title centered above the worksheet. Insert a blank row below the title.

d. Insert a blank row between the column headings and the bagel information.

e. By law, all prepared foods must contain nutrition facts, including calories and fat grams per serving. Go to the kitchen and look up the nutrition facts on some of your favorite snacks. Insert a few rows below the Pretzels row and use this information to add your snacks to the list. Copy the lite cream cheese fat formula down the column. What foods should Laura eliminate? What foods, if any, should you eliminate?

f. Display one decimal place for all numbers in the Fat Grams column. Format the % Fat column to display a percent sign and two decimals.

g. Add the following cell comments:

Cell D5: **Warning: "Lite" cream cheese is VERY high in fat!**

Cell D6: **Stay away from the peanut butter!**

h. Delete the date and your name from the worksheet.

i. Save and replace the workbook file Fat Grams. Preview the worksheet. Add a predefined header that displays your name and the date then print the worksheet with gridlines.

You will complete this exercise as Practice Exercise 1 in Lab 3.

4. To complete this problem, you must have completed Practice Exercise 4 in Lab 1. Open the workbook file Invoice on your data disk. In this exercise you will continue to modify the invoice worksheet of computer equipment you sold to a new computer training facility.

a. Use the formatting techniques you learned to improve the appearance of the invoice.

b. Copy the total for the Pentium computers down the column and calculate a subtotal.

c. Calculate the tax based on the tax rate in your state, and then calculate the total amount due.

d. Format numbers using settings of your choice.

e. As you are ringing up the total for a customer, he decides he needs some diskettes. Insert a row between Tables and the Subtotal. Enter the following information:

Qty	Description	Price
1	Formatted 2HD Diskettes100 Pk	49.95

f. Calculate a total for the diskettes and edit the subtotal formula.

g. Clear the date and your name from the worksheet. Make any last-minute formatting changes you wish.

h. Save and replace the workbook file Invoice. Preview the worksheet. Add a predefined header that displays your name and the date, then print the worksheet.

You will complete this exercise as Practice Exercise 2 in Lab 5.

On Your Own

5. To complete this problem, you must have completed Practice Exercise 5 in Lab 1. Open the workbook file Income Statement on your data disk. In this exercise you will continue to modify the budget income worksheet for the Custom Manufacturing Company.

Copy the January formulas and the fixed cost entries to the months February through June. Calculate totals in column I.

Format the Sales and Net Income numbers to display dollar signs, commas, and two decimals. Change all other numbers to display commas and two decimals.

Make changes you feel are necessary to improve the appearance of the invoice, such as font size, type and style changes, and centering the worksheet title.

You are interested in seeing how each month's net income compares to the total net income for the six months. Below the Net Income row, calculate the percent of total net income for each month. Format the new calculated values appropriately and add a row heading.

Delete your name and date from the worksheet. Add a predefined header that displays your name and the date, then print the worksheet on one page. Save and replace the workbook file.

You will continue this exercise as Practice Exercise 2 in Lab 3.

6. While attending college at night, Ilsa has a full-time day job. To better keep track of her weekly hours, she uses the time sheet shown below. Now that she has a computer, Ilsa will maintain her time sheet information using Excel. Follow the example below to create a time sheet.

	A	B	C	D	E
1	Time Sheet Of:	[Student's Name]			
2	Week Of:	[Starting Date]			
3		**Total**	**Regular**	**Overtime**	**Adjusted**
4	**Day**	**Hours**	**Hours**	**Hours**	**Total Hours**
5	Monday	10	8		
6	Tuesday	11	8		
7	Wednesday	8	8		
8	Thursday	9	8		
9	Friday	7	7		
10			Weekly Total:		
11					
12					

Enter the formulas to calculate Overtime Hours and Adjusted Total Hours. Overtime Hours is the difference between Regular Hours and Total Hours multiplied by 1.5. The Adjusted Total Hours is the sum of Regular and Overtime Hours. Sum the Adjusted Total Hours to calculate a Weekly Total. (The Weekly Total should be equal to 48.) Enter last Monday's date as the Starting Date in B2. Use the formatting techniques you learned to improve the appearance of the time sheet.

Document and save the workbook file as Time Sheets. Add a predefined header that displays your name and the date, then print the worksheet changing the page setup as needed.

You will complete this exercise as Practice Exercise 6 in Lab 3.

Creating a Worksheet: Part 2

Relative Reference

A relative reference is a cell or range reference in a formula whose location is interpreted by Excel in relation to the position of the cell that contains the formula.

Absolute Reference

An absolute reference is a cell or range reference in a formula whose location does not change when the formula is copied.

Concepts

Relative Reference
Absolute Reference

Functions

Column Width
Insert and Delete
   Cells, Rows, and Columns

Number Formats
Fonts
Styles

Headers and Footers

Insert and Delete Cells, Rows, and Columns

Individual cells or entire rows or columns can be inserted and deleted from a worksheet.

Column Width

The size or width of a column controls how much information can be displayed in a cell.

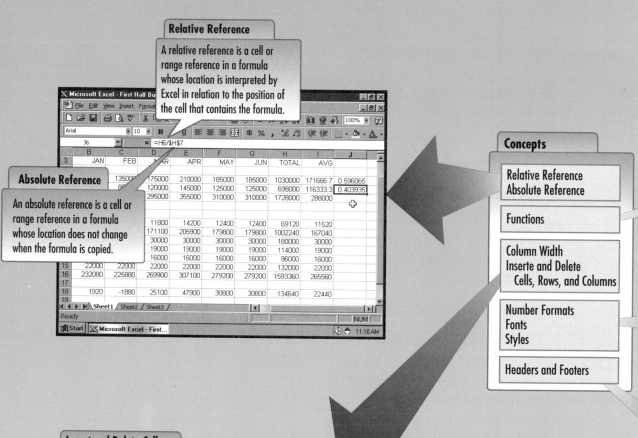

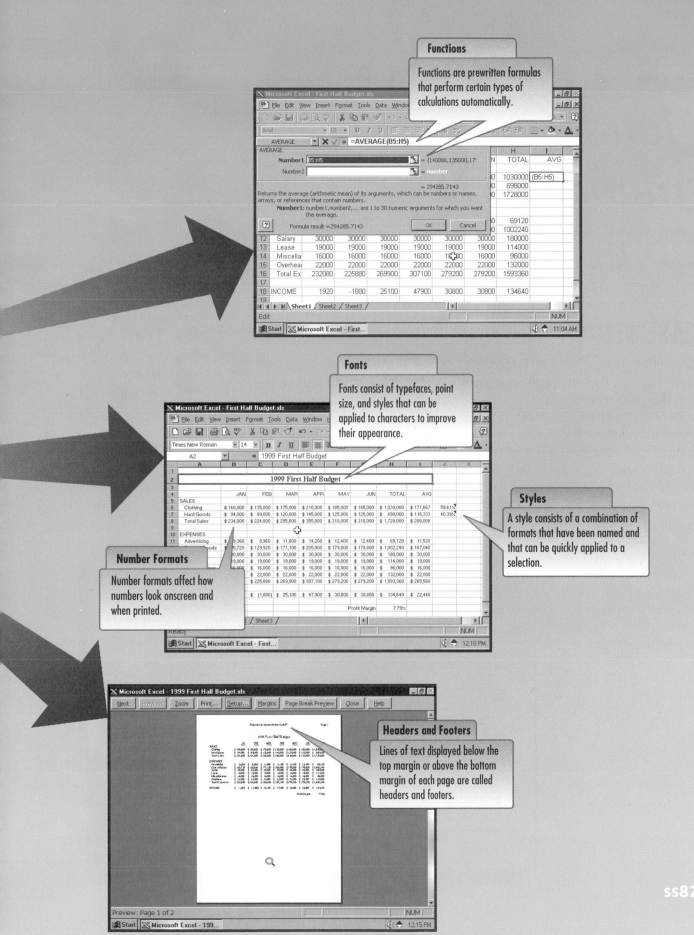

Functions

Functions are prewritten formulas that perform certain types of calculations automatically.

Fonts

Fonts consist of typefaces, point size, and styles that can be applied to characters to improve their appearance.

Styles

A style consists of a combination of formats that have been named and that can be quickly applied to a selection.

Number Formats

Number formats affect how numbers look onscreen and when printed.

Headers and Footers

Lines of text displayed below the top margin or above the bottom margin of each page are called headers and footers.

ss87

Managing and Analyzing a Complex Workbook

CASE STUDY

After looking at the first-half budget for 1999, the store manager expressed some concern that the profit margin is so low and wants you to look at how this value can be adjusted to be closer to the industry standard of 10 percent for the first six-month time period. You have also been asked to create a worksheet for the data for the second half of the year, in which the profit margin should reflect the industry standard of 13.5 percent.

Additionally, you are to create another worksheet (shown here) for the annual budget that displays the profit margin for each month and for the year. The annual profit margin should be between 12 and 13 percent. Finally, the manager wants you to create a summary worksheet showing only the total values for the year and the projected values for the year 2000.

As you develop the budget workbook and it grows in size and complexity, you will learn about many of the Excel features that help you efficiently manage a large workbook. In addition, you will learn to use several of the built-in tools designed to help you analyze data and to make future projections.

Concept Overview

The following concepts will be introduced in this lab:

1. Sheet Names   Each sheet in a workbook can be assigned a descriptive name to identify the contents of the sheet.

2. AutoFill   The AutoFill feature makes entering long or complicated headings easier by logically repeating and extending the series.

3. Referencing Sheets   A formula reference to cells in different worksheets in a workbook allows you to use data from other worksheets and to calculate new values based on this data.

4. Split Windows   A sheet window can be split into sections called panes to make it easier to view different parts of the sheet at the same time.

5. Freeze Panes   Freezing panes prevents the data in the pane from scrolling as you move to different areas in the worksheet.

6. What-If Analysis   What-if analysis is a technique used to evaluate the effects of changing selected factors in a worksheet.

7. Solver   Solver is an Excel tool that answers what-if problems by determining the value of a cell by changing values in one or more cells in the worksheet.

8. Spelling Checker   A spelling checker feature locates misspelled words, duplicate words, and capitalization irregularities and proposes the correct spelling.

9. Link Workbooks   A link creates a connection between files that updates the linked data automatically in one file whenever the data changes in the other file.

10. Goal Seek   Goal Seek is an Excel tool that is used to find the value needed in one cell to attain a result you want in another cell.

Part 1

Copying a Sheet

First you want to add the budget data to the workbook for the second half of 1999. You want this data in a separate sheet in the same workbook file.

■   Load Excel 97 for Windows 95.

■   Place your data disk in drive A (or the appropriate drive for your computer system).

■   Open the file Six Month 1999 Budget.

Your screen should be similar to Figure 3-1.

FIGURE 3-1

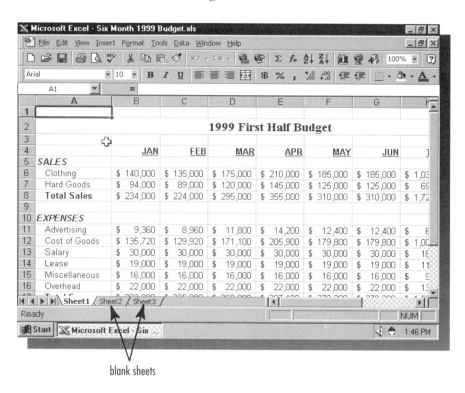

blank sheets

By default new Excel workbook files include three blank sheets. You used the first sheet to hold the first half budget data. To move to the next blank sheet,

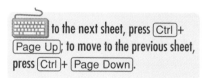
to the next sheet, press [Ctrl]+ [Page Up]; to move to the previous sheet, press [Ctrl]+ [Page Down].

■   Click Sheet2 tab.

Your worksheet should be similar to Figure 3-2.

blank second sheet in workbook

FIGURE 3-2

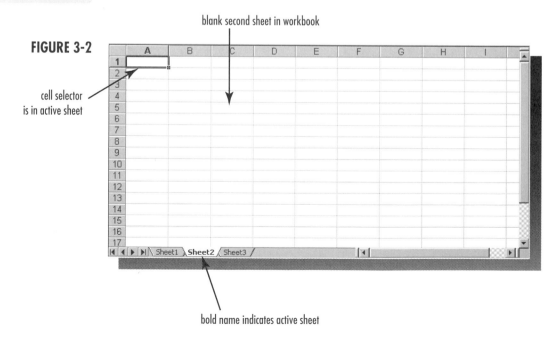

cell selector is in active sheet

bold name indicates active sheet

The blank worksheet, Sheet 2, is the active sheet because it contains the cell selector and is the sheet that will be affected by any actions. The name of the active sheet is always bold in the sheet tab. Sheet1, containing the budget for the first six months, is behind Sheet2.

To make it easier to enter the budget for the next six months, you want to copy the contents of the first half budget in Sheet1 into another sheet in the workbook. Then you will change the month headings, the title, and the number data. Although the workbook already includes two extra blank sheets, if you pasted the data into an existing sheet, the column width settings would not be copied and you would need to reset the widths. Instead, to duplicate an existing sheet with all its formats, you need to create a new sheet.

To copy the active sheet into a new sheet, you hold down Ctrl while dragging the sheet tab to where you want the new sheet inserted. The mouse pointer changes to a ▨ as you drag the mouse from one tab to another. The + indicates that the sheet is being copied. A black triangle ▼ also appears, indicating where the sheet will be inserted.

> To move a sheet, drag the sheet tab without holding down Ctrl. The mouse pointer appears as ▨ when the sheet is being moved.

- ■ Click on the Sheet1 tab.

- ■ Hold down Ctrl.

- ■ Drag the Sheet1 tab to the Sheet2 tab. (The ▼ appears between the Sheet1 and Sheet2 tabs.)

> The menu equivalent is **E**dit/**M**ove or Copy Sheet.

- ■ Release the mouse button and then Ctrl.

Your worksheet should be similar to Figure 3-3.

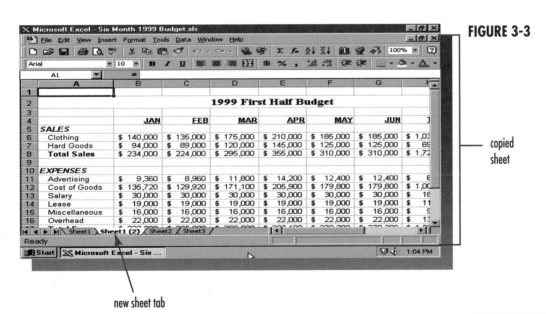

FIGURE 3-3

copied sheet

new sheet tab

Excel names the copy of the sheet Sheet1 (2) and inserts it before Sheet2. The new sheet is the active sheet and contains a duplicate of the first half budget in Sheet1.

> To create a new blank sheet, use **I**nsert/ **W**orksheet.

Naming Sheets

As more sheets are added to a workbook, remembering what information is in each sheet becomes more difficult. To help clarify the contents of the sheets, you can rename the sheets.

> **Concept 1: Sheet Names**
>
> Each sheet in a workbook can be assigned a descriptive name to help identify the contents of the sheet. The following guidelines should be followed when naming a sheet. A sheet name:
>
> - Can be up to 31 characters
> - Can be entered in uppercase or lowercase letters or a combination (it will appear as entered)
> - Can contain any combination of letters, numbers, and spaces
> - Cannot contain the characters : ? * / \
> - Cannot be enclosed in square brackets ([ ])

Double-clicking the sheet tab activates the tab and highlights the existing sheet name. The existing name is cleared as soon as you begin to type the new name. You will change the name of Sheet1 to First Half and Sheet1 (2) to Second Half.

The menu equivalent is F**o**rmat/S**h**eet/**R**ename.

- ■ Double-click the Sheet1 tab.

- ■ Type **First Half**.

- ■ Press [←Enter].

- ■ Change the name of the Sheet1 (2) tab to "**Second Half**".

Using AutoFill

Now you can change the worksheet title and data in the second half sheet to the budget data for the second half of 1999.

- ■ Change the title to **1999 Second Half Budget**.

- ■ Change the month heading in cell B4 to JUL.

Now you need to change the remaining month headings to AUG through DEC. You will use the AutoFill feature to enter the remaining month headings.

Concept 2: AutoFill

The AutoFill feature makes entering a series of headings easier by logically repeating and extending the series. AutoFill recognizes trends and automatically extends data and alphanumeric headings as far as you specify. For example, the entry Qtr 1 would be extended to Qtr 2, Qtr 3, and so on, as far as you specify. Other examples of time series are increments of days, weeks, or months. A linear series increases or decreases values by a constant value, and a growth series multiplies values by a constant factor.

Dragging the fill handle activates the AutoFill feature if Excel recognizes the entry in the cell as an entry that can be incremented. When AutoFill extends the entries, it uses the same style as the original entry. For example, if you enter the heading for July as JUL (abbreviated with all letters uppercase), all the extended entries in the series will be abbreviated and uppercase. Dragging down or right increments in increasing order, and up or left increments in decreasing order.

A starting value of a series may contain more than one item that can be incremented, such as JAN-98, in which both the month and year can increment. If you only want one value to increment, hold down the right mouse button as you drag, and then click the appropriate command on the AutoFill shortcut menu to specify which value to increment.

The entry in cell B4, JUL, is the starting value of a series of months.

■ To automatically complete the month entries, drag the fill handle to extend the range from cell B4 through cell G4.

Your screen should be similar to Figure 3-4.

If a series is created when you drag the fill handle that you do not want incremented, select the original values again and hold down Ctrl as you drag the fill handle. The entries will be copied, not incremented.

The mouse pointer displays the entry that will appear in each cell.

month headings automatically incremented

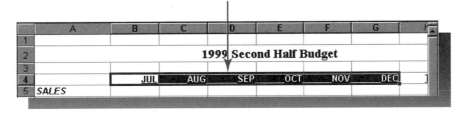

FIGURE 3-4

- Finally, to update the budget for July through December clothing and hard goods sales, enter the new numbers as shown in the table below.

Clothing		Hard Goods	
Cell	Number	Cell	Number
B6	**200000**	B7	**135000**
C6	**180000**	C7	**120000**
D6	**172000**	D7	**114000**
E6	**175000**	E7	**118000**
F6	**160000**	F7	**110000**
G6	**390000**	G7	**280000**

The worksheet has been recalculated and now contains the data for the second half.

- To see more worksheet data in the window, set the zoom to 75%.

Your screen should be similar to Figure 3-5.

FIGURE 3-5

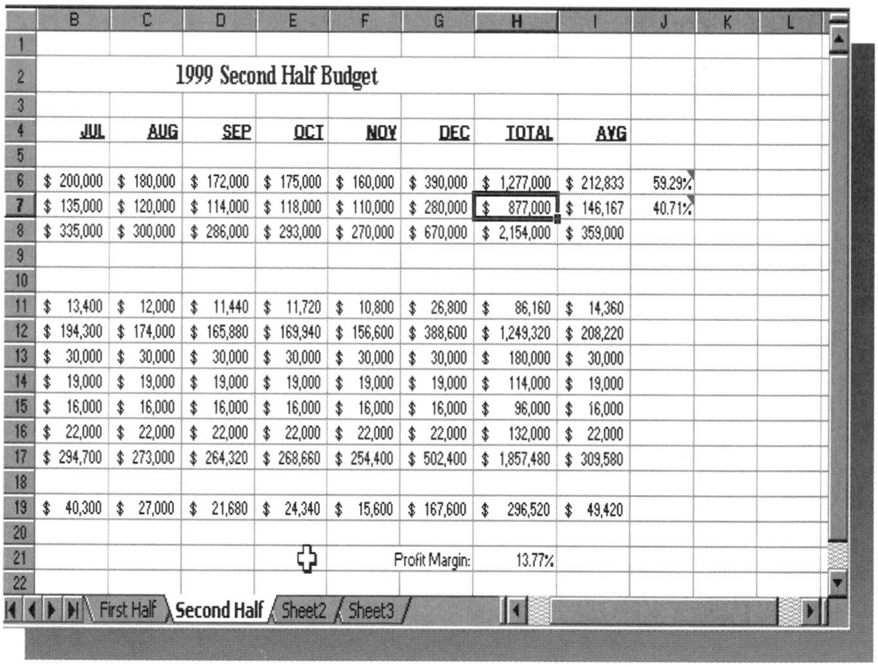

	B	C	D	E	F	G	H	I	J	K	L
1											
2			1999 Second Half Budget								
3											
4	JUL	AUG	SEP	OCT	NOV	DEC	TOTAL	AVG			
5											
6	$ 200,000	$ 180,000	$ 172,000	$ 175,000	$ 160,000	$ 390,000	$ 1,277,000	$ 212,833	59.29%		
7	$ 135,000	$ 120,000	$ 114,000	$ 118,000	$ 110,000	$ 280,000	$ 877,000	$ 146,167	40.71%		
8	$ 335,000	$ 300,000	$ 286,000	$ 293,000	$ 270,000	$ 670,000	$ 2,154,000	$ 359,000			
9											
10											
11	$ 13,400	$ 12,000	$ 11,440	$ 11,720	$ 10,800	$ 26,800	$ 86,160	$ 14,360			
12	$ 194,300	$ 174,000	$ 165,880	$ 169,940	$ 156,600	$ 388,600	$ 1,249,320	$ 208,220			
13	$ 30,000	$ 30,000	$ 30,000	$ 30,000	$ 30,000	$ 30,000	$ 180,000	$ 30,000			
14	$ 19,000	$ 19,000	$ 19,000	$ 19,000	$ 19,000	$ 19,000	$ 114,000	$ 19,000			
15	$ 16,000	$ 16,000	$ 16,000	$ 16,000	$ 16,000	$ 16,000	$ 96,000	$ 16,000			
16	$ 22,000	$ 22,000	$ 22,000	$ 22,000	$ 22,000	$ 22,000	$ 132,000	$ 22,000			
17	$ 294,700	$ 273,000	$ 264,320	$ 268,660	$ 254,400	$ 502,400	$ 1,857,480	$ 309,580			
18											
19	$ 40,300	$ 27,000	$ 21,680	$ 24,340	$ 15,600	$ 167,600	$ 296,520	$ 49,420			
20											
21						Profit Margin:	13.77%				
22											

As you can see, the profit margin of 13.77 percent for this half is above the industry standard of 13.5 percent for that period.

Referencing Multiple Sheets

You also want to display a year-to-date income total in cell H22. The formula to make this calculation will sum the total income numbers from First Half cell E19 and Second Half cell E19. To reference data in another sheet in the same workbook, you enter a formula that references cells in other worksheets.

Concept 3: Referencing Sheets

A formula reference to cells in different worksheets of the same workbook allows you to use data from multiple sheets and to calculate new values based on this data. The formula contains a sheet reference as well as a cell reference. The sheet reference consists of the name of the sheet enclosed in quotes. It is separated from the cell reference by an exclamation point. For example, ="Sheet2"!B17 would display the entry in cell B17 of Sheet2 in the active cell of the current sheet. A formula can be created using references on multiple sheets; for example, =Sheet1!A1+Sheet2!B2.

The link can also be created by entering a 3-D reference in a formula. A **3-D reference** is a reference to the same cell or range on multiple sheets in the same workbook. A 3-D reference consists of the names of the beginning and ending sheets enclosed in quotes and separated by a colon. This is followed by an exclamation point and the cell or range reference. The cell or range reference is the same on each sheet in the specified sheet range. For example the formula =SUM("Sheet1:Sheet4"!H6:K6) sums the values in cell H6 of sheets 1 through 4. The formula =SUM ("Sheet1:Sheet4"!H6:K6) sums the values in the range H6 through K6 of sheets 1 through 4. Any sheets stored between the starting and ending names of the reference are included. If a sheet is inserted or deleted, the range is automatically updated. 3-D references make it easy to analyze data in the same cell or range of cells on multiple worksheets.

Just like a formula that references cells within a sheet, a formula that references cells in multiple sheets is automatically recalculated when data in a referenced cell changes.

You will enter a 3-D reference formula in cell H22 and a descriptive text entry in cell G22.

- In cell G22 enter and right-align the entry, **Year-To-Date**.

- Move to H22.

- Click Σ AutoSum.

The SUM function argument will consist of a 3-D reference to cell H19 in the First and Second Half sheets. Although a 3-D reference can be entered by typing it using the proper syntax, it is much easier to enter it by pointing to the cells on the sheets. To enter a 3-D reference, select the cell or range in the beginning sheet and then hold down ⇧Shift and click on the sheet tab of the last sheet in the range. This will include the indicated cell range on all sheets between and including the first and last sheet specified.

- Click H19.

- Hold down ⇧Shift and click the First Half tab.

- Release ⇧Shift.

- Press ⏎Enter.

- Move to H22.

To reference a cell or range in another sheet, begin the formula or function, hold down ⇧Shift, switch to the other sheet, and select the cell(s).

Keyboard users must enter the 3-D reference by typing it.

Your screen should be similar to Figure 3-6.

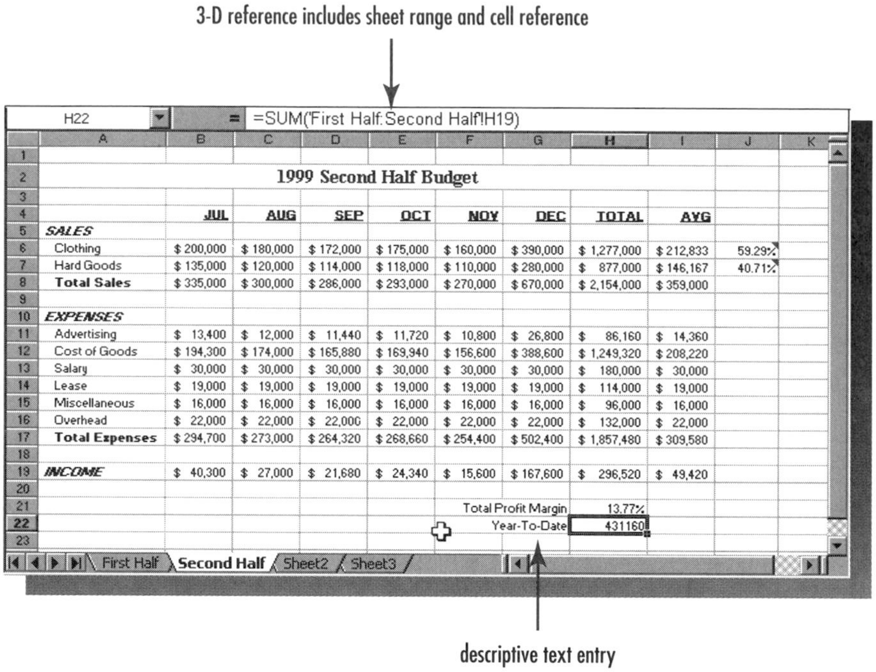

3-D reference includes sheet range and cell reference

FIGURE 3-6

descriptive text entry

The calculated number 431,160 appears in cell H22, and the function containing a 3-D reference appears in the formula bar. The number does not display in Accounting format because it is outside the range you selected when setting the cell format.

- Change the format of cell H22 to Accounting with zero decimal places.

- Return the zoom to 100%.

- Move to cell A1 of both sheets.

- Update the workbook summary properties.

- Save the workbook file as 1999 Budget.

- Close the workbook file.

Splitting Windows

You presented the completed first and second half worksheets of the estimated operating budget for 1999 to the regional manager. The manager wants you to create another worksheet showing the entire annual budget and to include a row to calculate the monthly profit margin. Several of the changes requested by the manager have already been made and saved on your data disk in the workbook file Annual Budget.

■   To see the revised and expanded budget, open the workbook file Annual Budget.xls.

Your screen should be similar to Figure 3-7.

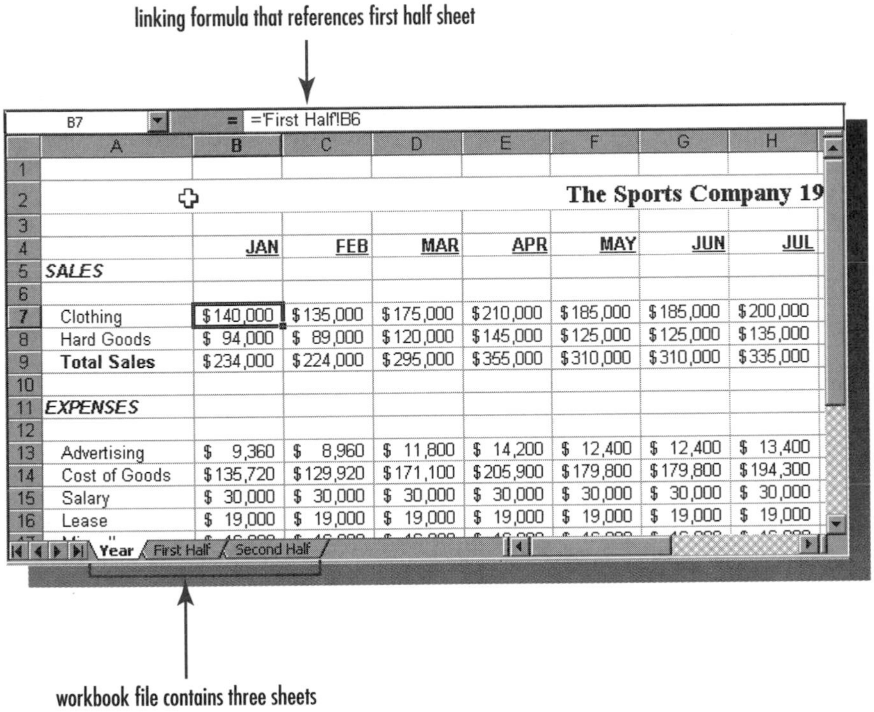

linking formula that references first half sheet

FIGURE 3-7

workbook file contains three sheets

The workbook file now contains three sheets: Year, First Half, and Second Half. The Year sheet contains the numbers for 12 months. Most of the monthly values in the Year sheet, such as cell B7, contain linking formulas that reference the appropriate cells in the First Half or Second Half sheets. Others, such as the total formulas and the formula to calculate the income, do not reference cells outside the Year worksheet.

Note: Although there are quicker ways to move to cells in the worksheet, use the arrow keys when directed. Your screen will then show the same rows and columns as the figures in the text.

To view the rest of the worksheet below row 16 and to the right of column H, using the directional keys,

■   Move to B23.

■   Move to O23.

If row 23 is already visible in your window, move to B28 and then to O28.

Your screen should be similar to Figure 3-8.

when row and column headings are not visible, it is difficult to know what the data represents

	H	I	J	K	L	M	N	O	P
8	$135,000	$120,000	$115,000	$118,000	$110,000	$280,000	$1,576,000	$131,333	
9	$335,000	$300,000	$287,000	$293,000	$270,000	$670,000	$3,883,000	$323,583	
10									
11		⊹							
12									
13	$ 13,400	$ 12,000	$ 11,480	$ 11,720	$ 10,800	$ 26,800	$ 155,320	$ 12,943	
14	$194,300	$174,000	$166,460	$169,940	$156,600	$388,600	$2,252,140	$187,678	
15	$ 30,000	$ 30,000	$ 30,000	$ 30,000	$ 30,000	$ 30,000	$ 360,000	$ 30,000	
16	$ 19,000	$ 19,000	$ 19,000	$ 19,000	$ 19,000	$ 19,000	$ 228,000	$ 19,000	
17	$ 16,000	$ 16,000	$ 16,000	$ 16,000	$ 16,000	$ 16,000	$ 192,000	$ 16,000	
18	$ 22,000	$ 22,000	$ 22,000	$ 22,000	$ 22,000	$ 22,000	$ 264,000	$ 22,000	
19	$294,700	$273,000	$264,940	$268,660	$254,400	$502,400	$3,451,460	$287,622	
20									
21	$ 40,300	$ 27,000	$ 22,060	$ 24,340	$ 15,600	$167,600	$ 431,540	$ 35,962	
22									
23									
24									

Year / First Half / Second Half /

FIGURE 3-8

The row (23) where you need to enter the formula to calculate the profit margin is now visible, as are the Total and Average columns and the numbers for the remaining months. However, it is difficult to know what the numbers represent because the row and column headings are not visible. For example, the number in cell J17 is $16,000. Is this number a lease expense, an advertising expense, or a miscellaneous expense? Which month do the numbers in column J refer to? Without seeing the row and column headings, it is difficult for you to know.

Whenever you scroll a large worksheet, you will find that information you may need to view in one area scrolls out of view as you move to another area. Although you could reduce the zoom percent to view more of the worksheet in the window, you still could not see the entire worksheet because it is too large. To view different areas of the same sheet at the same time, you can split the window into panes.

Concept 4: Split Windows

A sheet window can be split into sections called **panes** to make it easier to view different parts of the sheet at the same time. The panes can consist of any number of columns or rows along the top or left edge of the window. You can divide the sheet into two panes either horizontally or vertically, or four panes if you split the window both vertically and horizontally.

Each pane can be scrolled independently to display different areas of the sheet. When split vertically, the panes scroll together when you scroll vertically, but scroll independently when you scroll horizontally. Horizontal panes scroll together when you scroll horizontally, but independently when you scroll vertically.

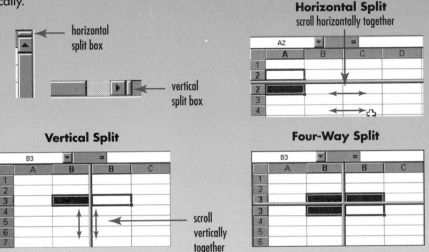

Dragging the split box at the top of the vertical scroll bar downward creates a horizontal split, and dragging the split box at the right end of the horizontal scroll bar leftward creates a vertical split. The **W**indow/**S**plit command can be used to quickly create a four-way split at the active cell.

Panes are most useful for viewing a worksheet that consists of different areas or sections. Creating panes allows you to display the different sections of the worksheet in separate panes and then to quickly switch between panes to access the data in the different sections without having to repeatedly scroll to the areas.

To display the column headings in the window at the same time as you are viewing data in cell J17, you will divide the window into two horizontal panes. Pointing to the vertical split box and dragging the split bar to the left creates a vertical pane.

- ■ Point to the split box in the vertical scroll bar.

- ■ Drag down and position the bar at row 10.

> The mouse pointer changes to ⬍ when you can drag to create a split.

Your screen should be similar to Figure 3-9.

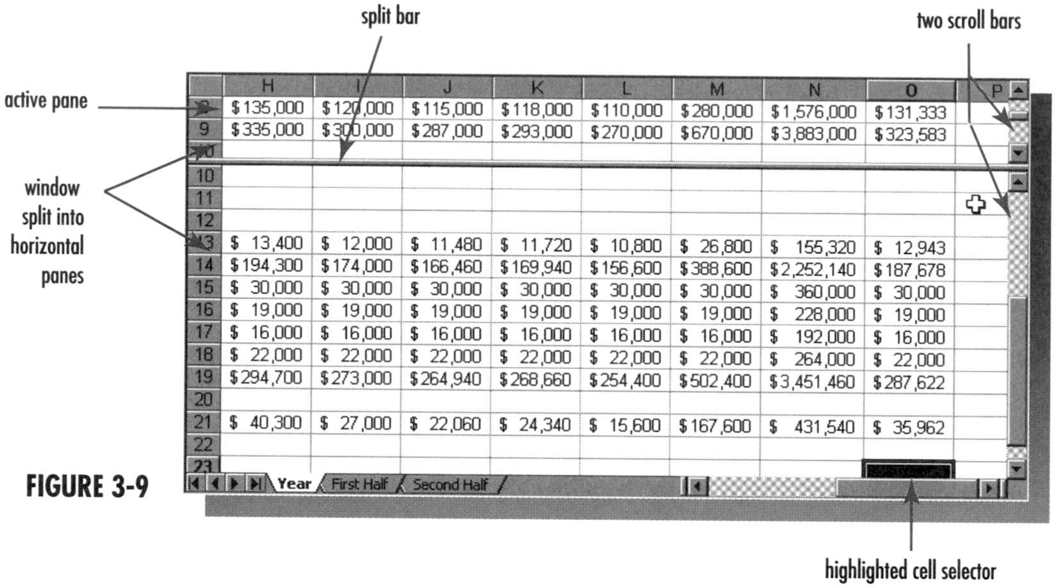

FIGURE 3-9

There are now two horizontal panes with two separate scroll bars. The highlighted cell selector is visible in the lower pane. The top pane also has a cell selector in cell O23, but it is not visible because that area of the worksheet is not displayed in the upper pane. When the same area of a worksheet is visible in multiple panes, the cell selector in the panes that are not active is highlighted whereas the cell selector in the **active pane** is clear. The active pane will be affected by your movement vertically. The cell selector moves in both panes, but only the active pane scrolls.

You will scroll the top pane vertically to display the month headings and then scroll horizontally to display the row headings.

- Click J10 in the upper pane to display the active cell selector in the pane.
- Press ⬆ (6 times).
- Press [Home].

Your worksheet should be similar to Figure 3-10.

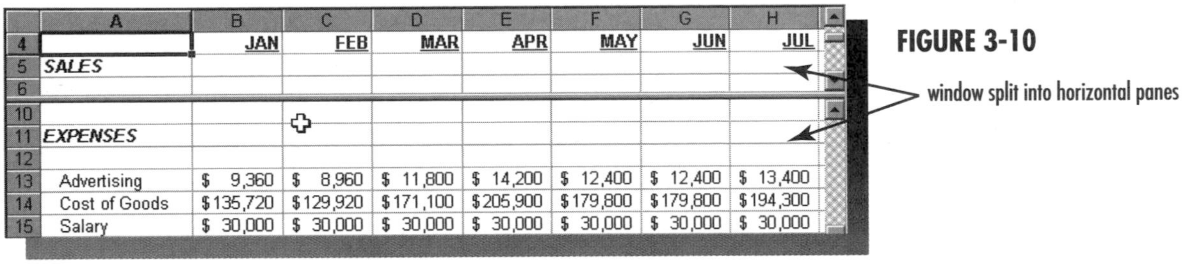

	A	B	C	D	E	F	G	H
4		JAN	FEB	MAR	APR	MAY	JUN	JUL
5	*SALES*							
6								
10								
11	*EXPENSES*							
12								
13	Advertising	$ 9,360	$ 8,960	$ 11,800	$ 14,200	$ 12,400	$ 12,400	$ 13,400
14	Cost of Goods	$135,720	$129,920	$171,100	$205,900	$179,800	$179,800	$194,300
15	Salary	$ 30,000	$ 30,000	$ 30,000	$ 30,000	$ 30,000	$ 30,000	$ 30,000

FIGURE 3-10

window split into horizontal panes

The lower pane did not scroll when you moved vertically through the upper pane to display the month headings. However, both panes scrolled together when you moved horizontally. The cell selector in the lower pane is in the same cell location as in the upper pane (A4), although it is not visible.

Creating panes is helpful when you want to display and access distant areas of a worksheet quickly. After scrolling the data in the panes to display the appropriate worksheet area, you can then quickly switch between panes to make changes to the data that is visible in the pane. This saves you the time of scrolling to the area each time you want to view or make changes to it. To clear the horizontal split from the window,

■ Double-click anywhere on the split bar.

The menu equivalent is **W**indow/Remove **S**plit.

Freezing Panes

Next you need to enter the formula to calculate the profit margin in row 23. To make it easier to enter the formula, you will first split the window into frozen panes.

Concept 5: Freeze Panes

Freezing panes prevents the data in the pane from scrolling as you move to different areas in a worksheet. You can freeze the information in the top and left panes of a window only.

The Freeze command on the Window menu is used to freeze panes. To create two horizontal panes with the upper pane frozen, move the cell selector in the leftmost column in the window to the row below where you want the split to appear before choosing the command.

To create two vertical panes with the left pane frozen, move the cell selector in the top row of the window and select the column to the right of where you want the split to appear.

To create four panes, click the cell below and to the right of where you want the split.

This feature is most useful when your worksheet is organized using row and column headings. It allows you to keep the titles on the top and left edge of your worksheet in view as you scroll horizontally and vertically through the worksheet data.

Top Pane Frozen

	A	B	C
9	Total Sales	$234,000	$224,000
10			
19	Total Expenses	$232,080	$225,880
20			
21	*INCOME*	$ 1,920	$ (1,880)
22			

Left Pane Frozen

	A	M	N
9	Total Sales	$670,000	$3,883,000
10			
11	*EXPENSES*		
12			
13	Advertising	$ 26,800	$ 155,320
14	Cost of Goods	$388,600	$2,252,140

Top and Left Panes Frozen

	A	M	N
3			
4		DEC	TOTAL
11	*EXPENSES*		
12			
13	Advertising	$ 26,800	$ 155,320
14	Cost of Goods	$388,600	$2,252,140

You want to keep the month headings in row 4 and the row headings in column A visible in the window at all times while entering the formula to calculate the profit margin in row 23. To do this, you will create four panes and freeze the headings in the upper and left panes. When creating frozen panes, first position the sheet in the window to display the information you want to appear in the top and left panes. This is because data in the frozen panes cannot be scrolled like data in regular panes. The worksheet is already positioned appropriately in the window.

■   Move to B5

■   Choose **W**indow/**F**reeze Panes

Your worksheet should be similar to Figure 3-11.

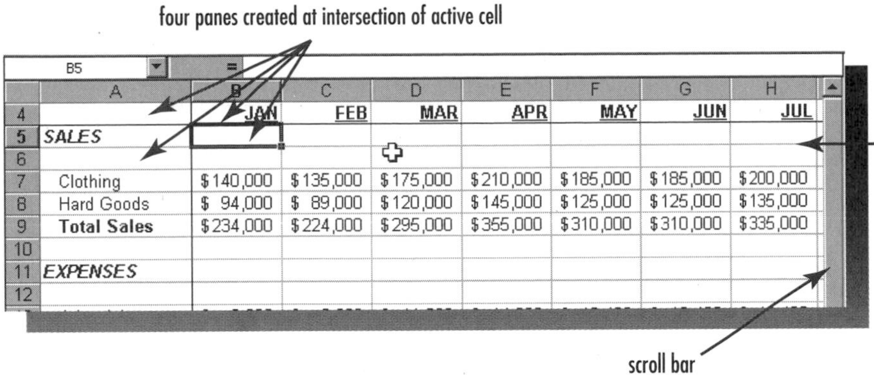

four panes created at intersection of active cell

FIGURE 3-11

unfrozen pane

scroll bar

Only one scroll bar is displayed because the only pane that can be scrolled is the larger lower right pane.

Now, to verify that the rows and columns in the top and left panes are frozen,

- Press ↑ (3 times).

- Press ←.

- Press ↓ (3 times).

- Press →.

The cell selector moved through the top and left panes, but the data in the panes did not scroll because the panes are frozen. Also, there is only one cell selector that moves from one pane to another over the pane divider, making it unnecessary to click on the pane to make it active before moving the cell selector in it.

Now, while the panes are frozen, you will enter the formula to calculate the profit margin in cell B23. The formula to calculate the monthly profit margin divides the monthly income by the monthly total sales.

- Move to B23.

- Enter the formula =**B21/B9 in cell B23**.

- Change the display of this number to a percent with two decimal places.

The profit margin for January is .82%. Next you need to copy the formula across the row through the Total column. Because the column headings are frozen in the upper pane, it will be easy to see which column is the Total column while you are specifying the paste range.

- Copy the formula in cell B23 across the row through the Total column (N23).

> Look at the Name box to check the location of the cell selector as you move within the frozen panes.

> Use ☒ to set the format to percent and ☒ to increase the decimal places.

SPREADSHEET

Your screen should be similar to Figure 3-12.

FIGURE 3-12

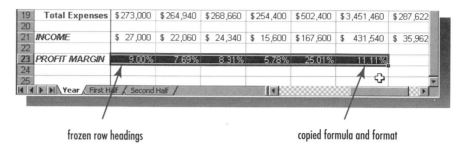

19	Total Expenses	$273,000	$264,940	$268,660	$254,400	$502,400	$3,451,460	$287,622
20								
21	*INCOME*	$ 27,000	$ 22,060	$ 24,340	$ 15,600	$167,600	$ 431,540	$ 35,962
22								
23	*PROFIT MARGIN*	9.00%	7.69%	8.31%	5.78%	25.01%	11.11%	
24								
25								

Year / First Half / Second Half /

frozen row headings   copied formula and format

The total profit margin for the year displayed in cell N23 is 11.11%. As you can see, freezing panes makes it much easier to navigate in and use a large worksheet.

Using What-If Analysis

The manager wants the store to show an annual profit margin of between 12 and 13 percent. Using the figures as budgeted for the year, the total profit margin of 11.11 percent is below this objective. In addition, the manager wants the first half profit margin to meet the industry standard of 100% for that period. After some consideration, you decide to reduce monthly salary expenses by scheduling fewer employees to work during the slow period of January to June to increase the first half profit margin. This change will also increase the profit margin for the year.

You want to see the effect on the first half profit margin as you substitute different salary expense values for the six months. The process of evaluating what effect reducing the salary expenses will have on the profit margin is called what-if analysis.

Concept 6: What-If Analysis

What-if analysis is a technique used to evaluate the effects of changing selected factors in a worksheet. This technique is a common accounting function that has been made much easier with the introduction of spreadsheet programs. By substituting different values in cells that are referenced by formulas, you can quickly see the effect of the changes when the formulas are recalculated.

You want to see the effect on the total profit margin of reducing salary expenses a set amount each month. First you want to see the effect of reducing the salary expenses to $28,000 per month.

■ Switch to the First Half sheet.

■ Scroll the window so that the month headings are displayed in the top row in the window.

■ Freeze the window at cell B5.

■ Enter 28000 in cell B13 and copy this value to cells C13 through G13.

■ Move to H21.

Your screen should be similar to Figure 3-13.

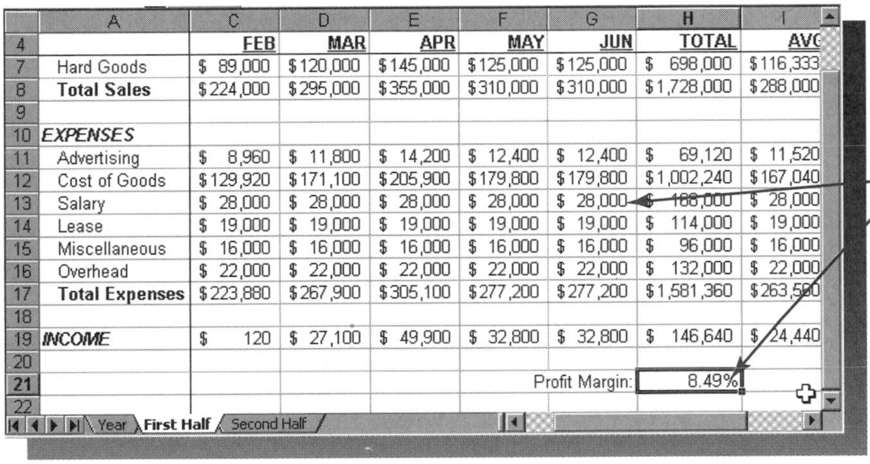

FIGURE 3-13

decreasing salary expenses increases the probit margin

Now by looking in cell H21 you can see that decreasing the salary expenses has increased the profit margin for the first half to 8.49 percent. This is still below the industry standard of 10 percent for the period.

Using Solver

As you can see, it may take several guesses before you find the salary expense number that will increase the first half profit margin to 10 percent. A quicker way to find the salary expense value is to use the Solver tool.

Solver is an Excel add-on program that must be installed. If it is not on your system, skip this section and enter the value 23604 in B13 through G13 to attain a 10 percent total profit margin.

Concept 7: Solver

Solver is an Excel tool that answers what-if problems by determining the value of a cell by changing values in one or more cells in the worksheet. Solver calculates a formula to achieve a given value by changing one of the variables that affect the formula. To do this Solver works backward from the result of a formula to find the numbers. The cells you select must be related through formulas on the worksheet. If not related, changing one will not change the other.

You will use Solver to find the salary numbers that will make the solution to the formula in cell H21 10 percent.

■ Choose **T**ools/Sol**v**er.

The dialog box on your screen should be similar to Figure 3-14.

target cell   enter value to obtain

FIGURE 3-14

enter range —
that can be
changed

hides dialog
box while you
specify range

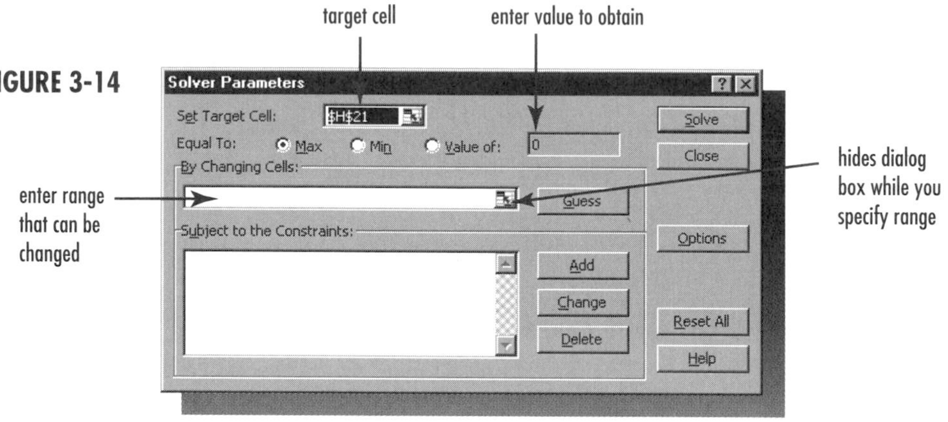

In the Solver Parameters dialog box, you need to supply three items of information. The cell reference of the cell containing the formula you want to solve is entered in the Set Target Cell text box. The cell reference of the active cell, H21, is already correctly entered in this box.

The number you want as the result of the formula is entered in the Equal To text box. You can set the number to be a maximum, minimum, or an exact number. The maximum option sets the target cell to the highest possible number, while the minimum option sets the target cell for the lowest possible number. In this case, however, you are looking for a specific number. To specify an exact number of 10 percent,

- Select **V**alue of.

- Type **.10**.

The final item needed is the cells whose contents can be changed when the formula is computed. These are the adjustable cells. This range is entered in the By Changing Cells text box. Specifying this range is the same as specifying a range when using the Paste Function feature. In this case, the cells to change are the range of cells B13 through G13. To enter the range and have Solver find the values to meet the parameters,

- Click 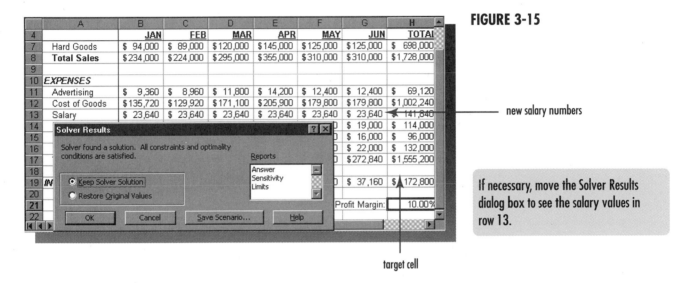.

- Select the range B13 through G13.

- Click .

- Click Solve .

The status bar briefly displays the message "Setting Up Problem" while Solver finds the solution.

Your screen should be similar to Figure 3-15.

FIGURE 3-15

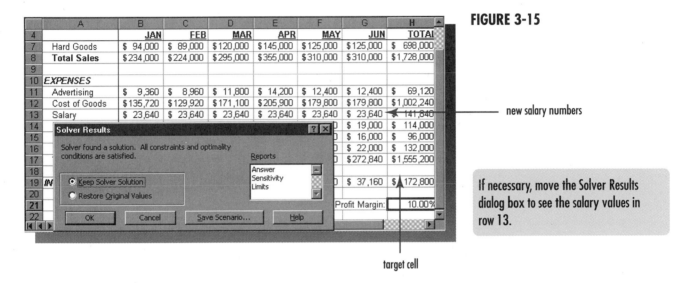

new salary numbers

If necessary, move the Solver Results dialog box to see the salary values in row 13.

target cell

The Solver Results dialog box is displayed indicating Solver found a solution. The new salary numbers are entered in the worksheet range and the worksheet is automatically recalculated. The profit margin is 10 percent if salary expenses are reduced to $23,640 per month. This was a lot quicker than making multiple guesses as to the correct value and changing it manually each time.

The Solver Results dialog box allows you to keep the Solver solution, restore original values, or create a report of the results. The default selection to keep the Solver results is acceptable. In addition, you can create several different reports of the Solver results: Answer, Sensitivity, and Limits. These reports are used to help you analyze how the new numbers affect the worksheet. To create a report of the Solver solution,

- Select Answer from the Reports list box.

- Choose OK .

The message "Forming Answer Report" is briefly displayed in the status bar as the Answer report is created. A new sheet tab named Answer Report 1 has been inserted before the First Half sheet.

■ Make the Answer Report 1 sheet active.

Your screen should be similar to Figure 3-16.

FIGURE 3-16

value solved for ——

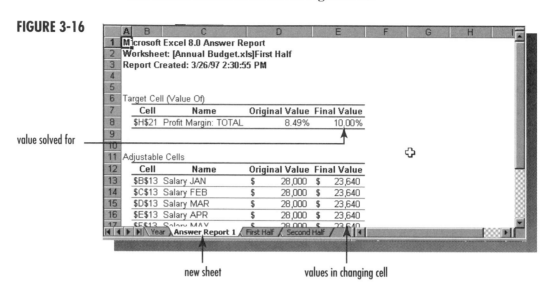

new sheet   values in changing cell

The target cell section of the report shows the original profit margin value of 8.49 percent and the final value of 10 percent. The Adjustable Cells area shows the original and final values for each cell that was changed to achieve the profit margin of 10 percent. The final value entered in each adjustable cell will be the same number even if the original values were different in each cell.

Now you want to see what effect changing the salary values in the first half had on the annual profit margin.

■ Make the Year sheet active.

The total profit margin in cell N23 is now 12.10 percent and falls within the range of the industry standard. The total profit margin for the year increased because reducing the salary expense in the first six-month sheet changed the values in the annual sheet, which in turn affected the annual profit margin.

Moving a Sheet

Next you want to move the Answer Report 1 sheet after the Second Half sheet. You can quickly rearrange sheets in a workbook by dragging the sheet tab to the new location. Just as when copying a sheet, the ▾ symbol indicates where the sheet will appear.

■ Drag the Answer Report 1 tab to the right end of the Second Half tab.

■ Unfreeze the panes in the First Half and Year sheets

Note: If you are exiting Excel at the end of Part 1, enter your name in cell A4 of the Answer Report and print the Answer Report only. Save the workbook as 1999 Annual Budget. When you begin Part 2, load Excel, open the 1999 Annual Budget workbook, and display the Year sheet.

> The **W**indow/Un**f**reeze command is used to unfreeze panes.

Part 2

Opening a Second Workbook

Next you want to create a summary of the annual budget in a separate workbook file. The summary will contain the worksheet headings and the total numbers only. The headings for the summary worksheet budget have already been entered and saved for you in a workbook file.

■ To see this workbook, open the file Summary Budget.xls.

Excel displays the Summary Budget workbook file in a second window on top of the Annual Budget workbook window. There are now two active workbook files. To view both files side by side, you will tile the windows.

■ Choose **W**indow/**A**rrange/**T**iled/ OK .

Your screen should be similar to Figure 3-17.

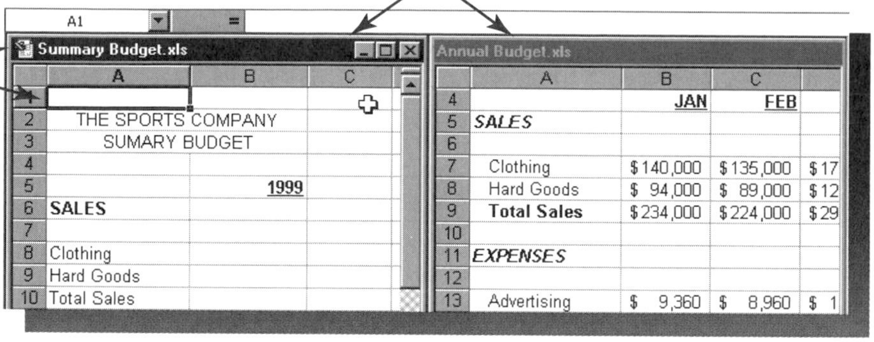

tiled windows

active window
has blue title bar
and cell selector

FIGURE 3-17

The two open workbook windows are displayed side by side in the workspace. The title bars display the file names. The window displaying the Summary Budget workbook file is the active window. The file in the active window will be affected by your changes. You can tell it is the active window because it contains the cell selector and the title bar is blue. Simply clicking on the window makes it the active window.

You can also press Ctrl+F6 to switch to the workbook window, or Ctrl+⇧Shift +F6 to switch to the previous window.

■   Click on the Annual Budget workbook window.

■   Scroll the window to display cell N23.

The cell selector is in the same location it was last in when using that window. If a range was selected, it is still active. You can also display different parts of a sheet or different sheets in a workbook in separate windows. As you will see, using multiple windows makes it easier to enter, edit, and compare data within and between workbooks.

Spell-Checking a Sheet

You notice that the word "Summary" in the title of the Summary Budget worksheet is spelled incorrectly. Just to make sure there are no other spelling errors, you will check the spelling of all text entries in this worksheet.

Concept 8: Spelling Checker

Excel includes a Spelling Checker tool that locates misspelled words, duplicate words, and capitalization irregularities and proposes the correct spelling. The Spelling Checker compares each word to a dictionary of words. If the word does not appear in the main dictionary or in a custom dictionary, it is identified as misspelled. The **main dictionary** is part of the Word program; a **custom dictionary** is one you can create to hold words you commonly use but that are not included in the main dictionary.

Excel also includes an AutoCorrect feature that corrects typing errors automatically as you type by comparing each completed word to a list of commonly mistyped words and phrases. You can also add words and phrases you commonly mistype to the list and they will be corrected automatically as you type.

If you have Microsoft Office, the same spelling dictionary and listing of AutoCorrect entries is shared with the other Office applications.

Excel begins checking all worksheet entries from the active cell forward. To check the spelling in the Summary sheet,

■ Make the Summary Budget window active.

■ Click [ABC] Spelling.

Your screen should be similar to Figure 3-18.

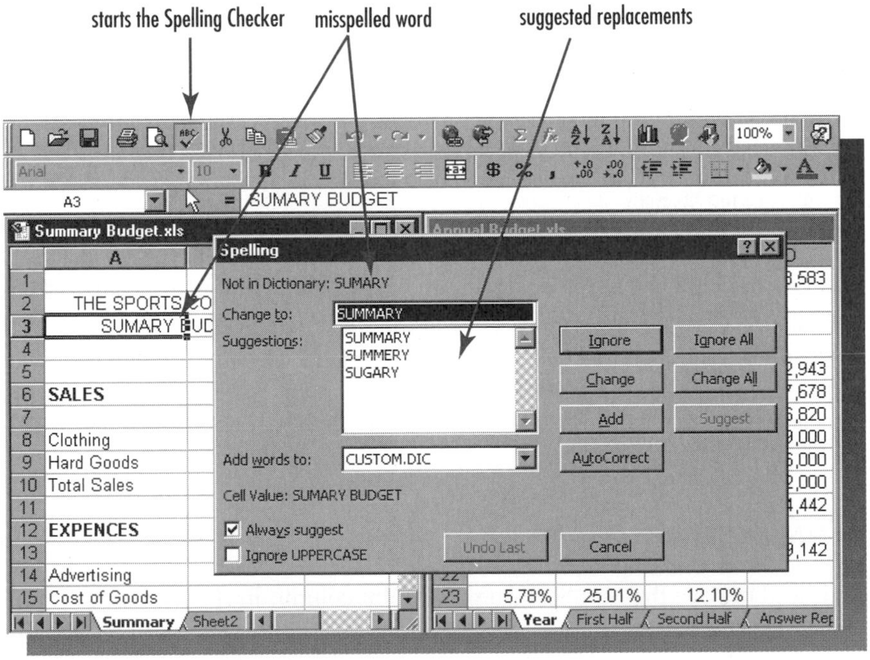

> The menu equivalent is **T**ools/**S**pelling or [F7].

starts the Spelling Checker   misspelled word   suggested replacements

FIGURE 3-18

> The Spelling Checker operates the same way in all Office 97 programs.

Immediately Excel begins checking the worksheet for words that it cannot locate in its main dictionary. The cell selector moves to the first cell containing a misspelled word, and the Spelling dialog box is displayed. The word it cannot locate in the dictionary is displayed in the first line of the dialog box. The Change To text box displays the suggested replacement. A list of other possible replacements is displayed in the Suggestions list box. If the Change To replacement is not correct, you could select from the suggestions list or type in the correct word in the Change To text box.

The option buttons shown in the table below have the following effects:

Option	Effect
Ignore	Leaves selected word unchanged
Ignore All	Leaves this and all identical words in worksheet unchanged
Change	Changes selected word to word displayed in Change To text box
Change All	Changes this and all identical words in worksheet to word displayed in Change To text box
Add	Adds selected word to a custom dictionary so Excel will not question word during subsequent spell checks

To accept the suggested replacement,

■ Click [Change].

The correction is made in the worksheet, and the program continues checking the worksheet and locates the second error, Expenses.

■ Correct the word.

The program continues checking the worksheet and does not locate any other errors. A dialog box is displayed, indicating that the entire worksheet has been checked. When it reaches the end of the sheet, if the cell selector was not at the beginning of the sheet when checking started, the program will ask if you want to continue checking at the beginning of the sheet. To end spell-checking,

■ Click [OK].

Linking Workbooks

You need to copy the numbers from the Total column in the Year sheet of the Annual Budget workbook file into the Summary sheet of the Summary Budget workbook file. However, because you are concerned that more changes may be made to the annual budget, you want to create a link between cells in the two workbook files. Linking the workbooks will ensure that the Summary Budget file will be automatically updated if changes are made in the Annual Budget workbook.

Concept 9: Link Workbooks

A link creates a connection between files that updates the linked data automatically in one file whenever the data changes in the other file. The link between the workbook files is formed by entering an **external reference formula** in one workbook that refers to a cell in another workbook. When data in a linked cell changes, the workbook that is affected by this change is automatically updated whenever it is opened.

The formula is entered in the workbook that receives the data. This workbook file is called the **dependent workbook**. The workbook that supplies the data is called the **source workbook**. The cell containing the external reference formula (the dependent cell) refers to the cell (the source cell) in the source file that contains the data to be copied.

An external reference formula uses the following format:

=[workbook]file reference!cell reference

The file reference consists of the file name of the source file followed by the name of the sheet. The cell reference of the cell or range of cells containing the number to be copied into the dependent workbook follows the file reference. The two parts of the formula are separated by an exclamation point.

You will create a link between the Summary Budget and Annual Budget workbooks by entering external reference formulas in the Summary worksheet that references the cells containing the total numbers in the Year worksheet. The Annual Budget workbook is the source workbook, and the Summary Budget workbook is the dependent workbook.

The first external reference formula you will enter will link the total clothing sales numbers. To create an external reference formula, you copy the contents of the source cell to the Clipboard, switch to the dependent workbook, and then use the Edit/Paste Link command to create the external reference formula in the specified cell of the dependent workbook. The source cell is cell N7 of the Year sheet in the Annual Budget workbook.

- Move to cell N7 of the Year sheet in the Annual Budget workbook.

- Click 📋 Copy.

- Move to cell B8 of the Summary worksheet.

- Choose **E**dit/Paste **S**pecial/ Paste Link .

Your screen should be similar to Figure 3-19.

FIGURE 3-19

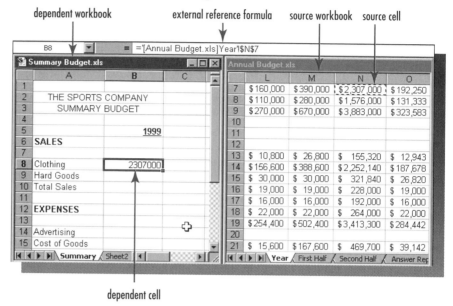

dependent workbook   external reference formula   source workbook   source cell

dependent cell

The link is created by entering an external reference formula in the selected cell of the dependent workbook. The formula is displayed in the formula bar, and the number in cell N7 of the source workbook is copied into the dependent workbook and displayed in cell B8. Notice that Excel uses absolute references in the external reference formula. Also notice that the cell format was not copied.

Next you want to create a link between the other total numbers in the source workbook. To do this quickly, you can copy the external reference formula down the column. However, you must first change the cell reference in the external reference formula to relative.

> **Double-click cell B8 to change to Edit mode.**

- Display the formula in cell B8 in Edit mode.

- Position the insertion point on the N7 cell reference in the formula.

- Press F4 (3 times).

- Press ←Enter.

The cell reference (N7) is now a relative cell reference and will adjust appropriately as the formula is copied. You also want to change the cell format to Accounting before copying, so that the format and formula can be copied at the same time.

- Format cell B8 to Accounting format with dollar signs and zero decimal places.

- Copy the external reference formula in B8 down column B through row 24.

- Clear the formula from any blank cells.

- Change the format of the profit margin in cell B24 to Percent style with two decimal places.

Your screen should be similar to Figure 3-20.

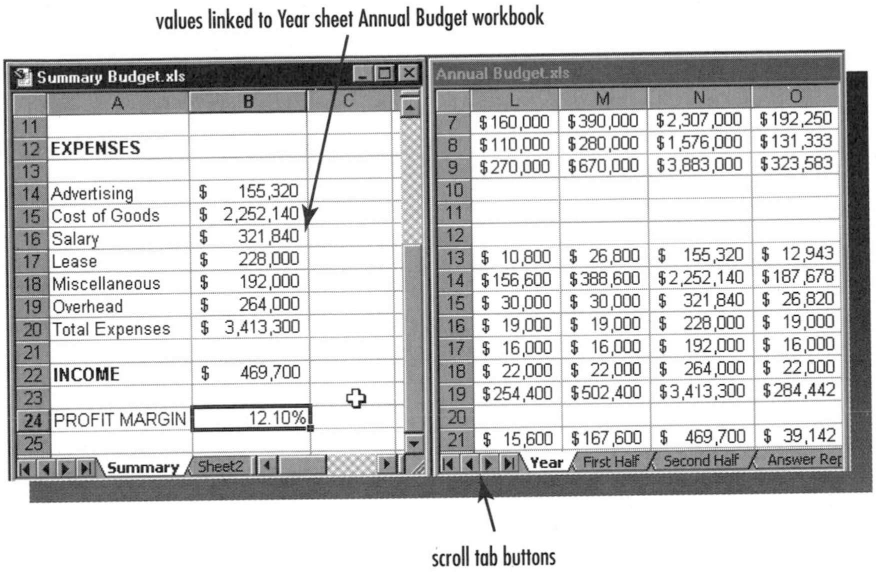

values linked to Year sheet Annual Budget workbook

FIGURE 3-20

scroll tab buttons

You showed the Summary Budget and Annual Budget workbook files to the store manager. As you expected, you need to make some changes to the data in the Annual Budget workbook. The manager advises you that the lease for the store will increase to $19,500 a month beginning in July of 1999.

■ Change the lease expenses for July through December in the Second Half worksheet to 19500.

All affected formulas are recalculated. You can easily see the effect on the annual profit margin in the Summary Budget workbook window. It has decreased to 12.02 percent. However, this value is still acceptable because it is within the industry standard.

Once an external reference formula is entered in a worksheet, whenever the number(s) in the cell referenced in the source file changes, the dependent file is automatically updated if it is open. However, if the dependent file is not open, it is not updated. To ensure that a dependent file gets updated whenever the source file is opened, an alert message is displayed asking if you want to update references to unopened documents. If you respond Yes, Excel checks the source documents and updates all references to them so that you will have the latest values from the source worksheet.

> Use the tab scroll buttons to display tabs that may not be visible.

Using Goal Seek

In addition, the manager has asked you to include a projected budget for the year 2000 in the Summary Budget worksheet. This data has already been entered for you and saved in a separate file named Future. You will open this file in another workbook window and copy the data to column C of the Summary workbook.

- Maximize the Summary Budget window.

- Open the file Future from your data disk.

- Move to B23.

Your screen should be similar to Figure 3-21.

FIGURE 3-21

	A	B	C	D	E	F	G	H
8	Hard Goods	$ 1,619,160						
9	Total Sales	$ 4,053,980						
10								
11	**EXPENSES**							
12								
13	Advertising	$ 162,159						
14	Cost of Goods	$ 2,391,848						
15	Salary	$ 332,000						
16	Lease	$ 231,000						
17	Miscellaneous	$ 195,000						
18	Overhead	$ 270,560						
19	Total Expenses	$ 3,582,567						
20								
21	**INCOME**	$ 471,413						
22								
23	**PROFIT MARGIN**	11.63%						
24								

Sheet1 / Sheet2 / Sheet3 /

You see that the profit margin for 2000 is 11.63 percent. The first change you need to make to the 2000 budget is to adjust the salary expenses so the profit margin is at least 12 percent for the year. To find this number quickly, you will use the Goal Seek tool.

Concept 10: Goal Seek

The Goal Seek tool is similar to Solver in that it is used to find the value needed in one cell to attain a result you want in another cell. The difference is that the value of only one cell can be changed. Goal Seek varies the value in the cell you specify until a formula that is dependent on that cell returns the desired result.

- Choose **T**ools/**G**oal Seek.

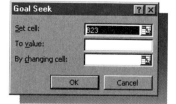

In the Goal Seek dialog box you need to specify the location of the cell containing the formula to be solved, the desired calculated value, and the cell containing the number that can be adjusted to achieve the result. You want the formula in cell B23 to calculate a result of .12 by changing the salary number in cell B15. The Set Cell text box correctly displays the current cell as the correct location of the formula to be solved.

- To complete the settings, enter **.12** in the To Value text box and cell B15 in the By Changing Cell text box.

- Click [OK].

The dialog box on your screen should be similar to Figure 3-22.

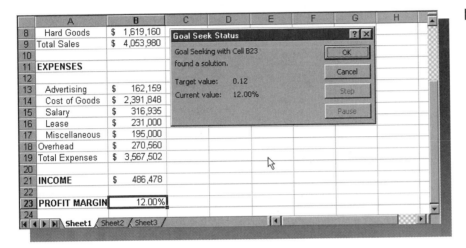

FIGURE 3-22

Goal Seek found the value of 316,935 for salary expense, making the profit margin 12 percent. To close the message box,

- Click [OK].

Next you want to copy the data in cells B4 through B23 of the Future file to cells C5 through C24 in the Summary Budget file.

- Select B4 through B23 of the Future workbook.

- Click [📋].

- Choose **W**indow/Summary Budget.

- Move to C5.

- Click [📋].

- Increase the column width of column C to 12 to fully display the numbers.

- Press Ctrl + Home.

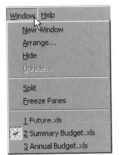

> The Window menu displays the file names of all open workbooks at the bottom of the menu.

Adding Color and Borders

Before sending the Summary Budget worksheet to the store manager, you want to enhance its appearance.

- Realign the worksheet titles in cells A2 and A3 so they are centered across columns A through C.

> You can align both titles simultaneously using the Format/Cells/Alignment command. If you use [📊] each cell must be aligned independently.

The font color, fill, and borders features work similarly in all Office 97 programs.

Next you will add color to the title text, add a box around the title, and add color shading within the title box. Color is applied to cell contents using the  Font Color button. If you click ▲ the color displayed in the button is applied to your selection. You can apply another color by opening the button's drop-down list and selecting another color from the palette of 40 color choices.

The menu equivalent is F**o**rmat/C**e**lls/Font/**C**olor.

- Select the range A2 through C3.
- Open the ▲ ▾ Font Color drop-down list.
- Select a color of your choice from the color palette.

Your worksheet should be similar to Figure 3-23.

applies color to entry

FIGURE 3-23

Next you will create a box around the title. A box is created using the Borders button. This button also applies the displayed border style to a selection. You can change the border style by selecting another from the Borders button's drop-down list of 12 border and line styles options. The range A2 through C3 should still be selected.

The menu equivalent, F**o**rmat/C**e**lls/Border, includes additional border styles.

- Open the Borders drop-down list.
- Click □ (bottom right option).

The selected range of cells is surrounded by a heavy outline border box, and the selected border style appears in the button.

Finally, you want to add shading to the cells within the box. The Fill Color button applies the displayed color to the background of a selection. Like the Font Color button, you can change the selected color by choosing another from the button's drop-down menu palette of 40 colors.

The menu equivalent is F**o**rmat/C**e**lls/Patterns.

- Open the Fill Color drop-down list box.
- Select a color of your choice from the palette.
- Move to A1.

Your worksheet should be similar to Figure 3-24.

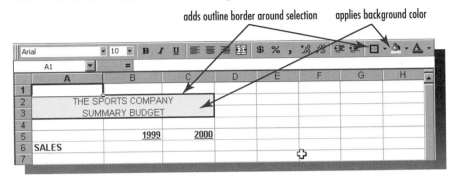

adds outline border around selection   applies background color

FIGURE 3-24

The last formatting change you want to make is to add lines to separate the numbers being summed from the total numbers in the column. To add a single line below the Hard Goods row to separate it from the Total Sales data,

- ■ Select B9 through C9.

- ■ Open the ▣ Borders drop-down menu.

- ■ Click ▦ .

- ■ Press ←.

Your worksheet should be similar to Figure 3-25.

adds bottom border to selection

FIGURE 3-25

Arial		10	B I U	...	$ % ,	...		...	A ...

	A	B	C	D	E	F	G	H
1								
2	THE SPORTS COMPANY							
3	SUMMARY BUDGET							
4								
5		1999	2000					
6	**SALES**							
7								
8	Clothing	$ 2,307,000	$2,434,820					
9	Hard Goods	$ 1,576,000	$1,619,160					
10	Total Sales	$ 3,883,000	$4,053,980					

single-line bottom border

The solid line creates a visual separation between the numbers being summed and the total sales numbers. The border line is different from an underline in that it extends along the entire edge of the cell, whereas an underline would appear only under the text within the cell.

Next you want to add the same type of line below the Overhead row to separate it from the Total Expenses row. Rather than reselect the same commands, you can use the Repeat command to redo the last command you entered. To use this feature,

The keyboard equivalent is Ctrl +Y.

- Select B19 through C19.

- Choose **E**dit/**R**epeat Borders.

The same solid border line is added below the selected range of cells.

- Finally, add a double-line style bottom border below the Income row of data in cells B22 through C22.

Aligning a Sheet on a Page

The Summary Budget workbook is complete.

- Update the workbook summary properties documentation to display your name and a title.

Click Setup... to access the Header/Footer tab.

- Preview the worksheet.

- Add a footer that displays your name, date, and page number.

The changes you made to the header and footer are reflected in the Preview screen (see Figure 3-26).

You would also like to center the worksheet horizontally on the page. To make this change,

- Click Setup... .

- Choose Margins/Hori**z**ontally.

- Click OK .

Your screen should be similar to Figure 3-26.

FIGURE 3-26

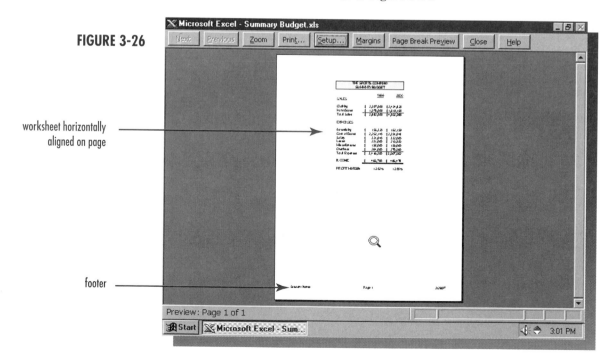

worksheet horizontally aligned on page

footer

The worksheet appears the way you want it to appear when printed.

- Print the worksheet.

- Save the Summary Budget workbook as 1999-2000 Summary Budget.

- Close the file.

- Save the Future workbook file as Future Revised.

- Close the file.

> The colored text and fill will appear shaded if you have a black and white printer.

Previewing a Workbook

The Annual Budget workbook window is displayed. To preview all sheets in the workbook,

- Choose **F**ile/**P**rint/**E**ntire Workbook/ Previe**w** .

The first page of the Year worksheet is displayed in the Preview window.

- Use the Next button to view the other sheets in the workbook.

- Change the orientation of the Second Half sheet to Landscape.

Now you like the way the First Half and Second Half budgets are displayed, but you would like to change the Year sheet to display a custom header and fit on one page.

- Display the first page of the Year sheet and change the orientation to Landscape.

Creating Custom Headers and Footers

You would like to add a custom header to this sheet.

- Choose Setup... /Header/Footer.

- Choose Custom Header.

The Header dialog box on your screen should be similar to Figure 3-27.

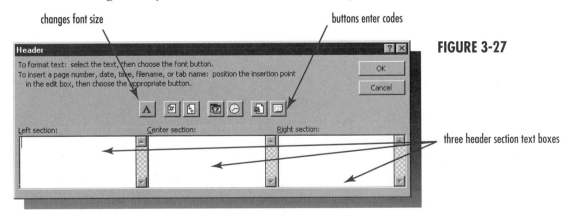

FIGURE 3-27

The Left Section text box will display the header text you entered aligned with the left margin, the Center Section will center the text, and the Right Section will right-align the text. The insertion point is currently positioned in the Left Section text box. You want to enter your name, class, and the date in this box.

■   Type **Created by [your name]**.

■   Press ←Enter.

■   Enter the name of your class and the section or time.

■   Press ←Enter.

Next you will enter the date. However, instead of typing today's date, you will enter a code that will automatically insert the current date whenever the worksheet is printed. The buttons above the section boxes are used to enter the codes for common header and footer information.

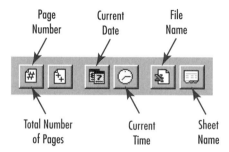

■   Click 🗓 Date.

■   Click ___OK___ .

The header as you entered it appears in the sample header area of the dialog box.

■   Click ___OK___ .

You would also like the worksheet printed on one page. To do this,

■   Click Setup... .

■   Open the Page tab.

■   Choose **F**it to.

■   Click ___OK___ .

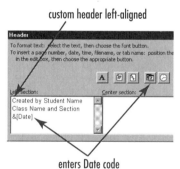

custom header left-aligned

enters Date code

> By default Excel fits the worksheet to one page wide and one page tall.

Your screen should be similar to Figure 3-28.

custom header   text fit to one page

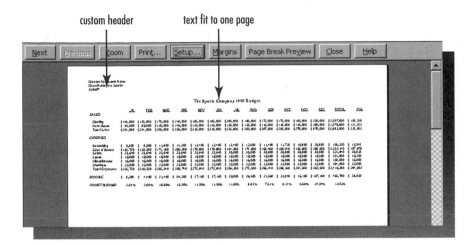

FIGURE 3-28

To print the Year worksheet only, you need to close the preview of the entire workbook and then print the Year sheet. To do this,

■ Click Close.

Because the Year sheet is displayed, you can use the 🖨 button to print the active sheet.

■ Click 🖨 Print.

■ Save the file as 1999 Annual Budget, then close the workbook and exit Excel.

> If you need to specify a different printer, use the Print command on the File menu to print the worksheet.

LAB REVIEW

Key Terms

3-D reference (SS95)
active pane (SS100)
custom dictionary (SS111)
dependent workbook (SS113)
external reference formula (SS113)
freeze (SS102)
main dictionary (SS111)
pane (SS99)
source workbook (SS113)
what-if analysis (SS104)

Command Summary

Command	Shortcut	Toolbar	Action
File/**P**rint/**E**ntire Workbook			Prints all sheets in workbook
Edit/**R**epeat	Ctrl + Y		Repeats last-used command
Edit/Paste **S**pecial/Paste **L**ink			Creates a link to source document
Edit/**M**ove or Copy Sheet			Moves or copies selected sheet
Insert/**W**orksheet			Creates an additional worksheet in active workbook
F**o**rmat/C**e**lls/Font/**C**olor			Adds color to text
F**o**rmat/C**e**lls/Border/**O**utline			Adds border around selection
F**o**rmat/C**e**lls/Border/**B**ottom			Adds border to bottom edge of selection
F**o**rmat/C**e**lls/Patterns			Adds shading to selection
F**o**rmat/S**h**eet/**R**ename			Renames sheet
Tools/**S**pelling	F7		Spell-checks worksheet
Tools/**G**oal Seek			Adjusts value in specified cell until a formula dependent on that cell reaches specified result
Tools/Sol**v**er			Calculates a formula to achieve a given value by changing one of variables that affects formula
Window/**A**rrange/**T**iled			Arranges open windows side by side
Window/Un**f**reeze			Unfreezes window panes
Window/**F**reeze Panes			Freezes top and/or leftmost panes
Window/**S**plit			Divides window into four panes at active cell
Window/Remove **S**plit			Removes split bar from active worksheet

Matching

1. =[ANNUAL.XLS] YEAR!$B$12   _____   **a.** prevents scrolling of information in upper and left panes of a window

2. pane   _____   **b.** spell-checks worksheet

3. freeze   _____   **c.** finds a specific value for a cell by adjusting value of only one other cell

4.   _____   **d.** the sections of a divided window

5.   _____   **e.** an external reference formula

6. dependent workbook   _____   **f.** worksheet that supplies data in a linking formula

7. current workbook   _____   **g.** worksheet that receives data in a linking formula

8.   _____   **h.** a workbook that is open and available for use

9. Goal Seek   _____   **i.** adds text color

10. source workbook   _____   **j.** applies bottom border

Fill-In Questions

1. Complete the following statements by filling in the blanks with the correct terms.

  a. Excel checks spelling by comparing text entries to words in a(n) _____.

  b. When a column or row is _____, it is visible in the window all the time.

  c. A worksheet window can be divided into four _____.

  d. _____ is a what-if tool that changes values in a specified range to attain a result in another cell.

  e. The _____ calculates a formula to achieve a given value by changing one of the variables that affect the formula.

  f. To view two windows side by side, the Window/_____ command is used.

  g. The link between workbook files is formed by entering a(n) _____ in one file that refers to a cell in another file.

  h. The workbook file that receives the data from a link is called the _____ workbook.

  i. A(n) _____ is a line of text that appears at the top of each printed page.

  j. Use _____ to find the value in a single cell to achieve the result you want in another cell.

Discussion Questions

1. Discuss the differences between splitting a window and freezing a window. When would it be appropriate to split a window? When would it be appropriate to freeze a window?

2. Discuss what happens to formulas that are linked to another workbook when the original workbook is updated. When would it be appropriate to link data between workbooks?

3. Discuss how the features on the Format menu can be used to enhance a worksheet. What should you consider when adding style changes to a worksheet?

4. Discuss how what-if analysis is used in a worksheet. How can Goal Seek and Solver help with the analysis of data in a worksheet?

Hands-On Practice Exercises

Step by Step   **Rating System**   Easy
                                         ☆☆ Moderate
                                         ☆☆☆ Difficult

☆

1. To complete this problem, you must have completed Practice Exercise 3 in Lab 2. Open the file Fat Grams from your data disk. In this exercise you will continue to modify the worksheet.

  a. Remove the underlines from the column headings. Draw a bottom border across that row.

  b. Enclose the worksheet title in a box. Add text color to the title and a background color. Add a background color to the % Fat column of data.

  c. Name the sheet tab.

  d. Preview the worksheet. Add a custom footer that displays the file name and the sheet name. Center the worksheet horizontally. Print the worksheet. Save and replace the workbook Fat Grams.

2. To complete this problem, you must have completed Practice Exercise 5 in Lab 2. In this exercise you will continue to modify the income statement for Custom Manufacturing. The sales representatives have recently completed an intensive sales seminar. The results seem positive, and the sales manager is confident that a net income of $85,000 is an attainable goal for the first six months.

  a. Open the workbook file Income Statement on your data disk. Appropriately name the sheet tab. Freeze the worksheet panes below the column headings and to the right of the row headings.

b. Use Solver to determine what monthly sales will be required to reach the new net income goal. Keep the Solver solution.

c. Preview the worksheet and add a header that displays the sheet name centered. Print the worksheet centered horizontally on the page and use landscape orientation. Update the documentation to reflect the new sales goal. Save and replace the workbook file.

Next you will link Income Statement to the file Custom Sales on your data disk. This file contains the actual sales for the first six-month period.

d. Open the Custom Sales file and sum the columns and rows. Format the values to display commas and two decimal places. Center the title over the columns. Draw a single bottom border under the column headings and under the Region 4 values. Draw a double-line border under the Total row. Make any other formatting changes you wish.

e. Tile the windows. Make the Income Statement file active. Enter an external reference formula to copy the January total sales number from the Custom Sales file into the corresponding cell of the Income Statement file. Adjust the formula so it can be copied across the row. Maximize the Income Statement file window. Copy the formula. What is the total net income?

f. Unfreeze the panes. Add a note to the Sales heading in column A that informs the users that the sales numbers are linked to the total sales numbers in the Custom Sales workbook.

g. Save and replace the workbook file Income Statement. Print the worksheet using the previously defined settings. Close the file.

h. Preview the Custom Sales worksheet. Add a header that includes your name and the date. Print the worksheet centered horizontally using landscape orientation. Save and replace the workbook file Custom Sales. Close the file.

3. Kevin O'Neal is a student at Metro Community College. He has just completed his final semester and will graduate with an associate's degree in Information Systems Technology. In this exercise you will calculate semester and cumulative totals and GPA for each semester.

a. Open the file Grade Report on your data disk. Rename the first four sheet tabs Fall 97, Spring 98, Fall 98, and Spring 99.

b. You can edit several sheets at once by selecting the sheets you want to change and modifying the first sheet in the group. In this portion of the exercise, you will draw an outline border around the first four rows of information on the Fall 97 through Spring 99 sheets.

• Make the Fall 97 sheet active.

• Hold down ⇧Shift as you click the Spring 99 sheet. All four sheets should be selected.

• Select cells A1 through G4 of the Fall 97 sheet.

• Draw an outline border around those cells.

• Change the color of the text and the background.

• Click A1 to clear the highlight.

• Right-click the Fall 97 sheet tab and choose the command Ungroup Sheets. Look at each sheet to see that the formatting was copied.

c. Following the above procedure, draw a bottom border across cells A7 to H7 of the four sheets. While the sheets are still selected, bold the column headings in rows 6 and 7 and bold the Semester Total and Cumulative Total headings in rows 14 and 15. Remember to ungroup the sheets when you are done.

d. In the Fall 97 sheet, multiply the Grade by the Credits Earned to calculate Total Points for Intro to Business. Copy that formula down the column. Sum the Credits Attempted, Credits Earned, and Total Points columns and display the results in the Semester Total row.

e. In cell H14, divide the Semester Total's Total Points by the Semester Total's Credits Earned to calculate the GPA for the semester. Use what-if analysis to see what Kevin's GPA would be if he had earned a 3 instead of a 2 in Western Civ. Change the grade back to a 2.

f. Go to the Spring 98 sheet. Select the Spring 98 through Spring 99 sheets and follow the above procedure to calculate Total Points, Semester Total, and GPA on three sheets at once. When you are finished, click the Fall 97 sheet. Clicking a sheet that is not selected is another way of ungrouping the sheets. Look at each sheet to see that the calculations were performed.

g. Go to cell E15 in the Fall 97 sheet. Enter the reference formula =E14 to copy the Semester Total Credits Attempted number to the Cumulative Total row. Copy the formula to cells F15 and G15 to calculate Credits Earned and Total Points.

h. Go to the Spring 98 sheet and calculate a Cumulative Total for Credits Attempted by summing the Spring 98 Semester Total and the Fall 97 Cumulative Total. (Hint: You can use pointing to enter the Cumulative Totals formula.)

i. Copy that formula to the adjacent cells to calculate Cumulative Totals for Credits Earned and Total Points. Repeat this procedure on the Fall 98 and Spring 99 sheets.

j. Go to the Fall 97 sheet. Select all four sheets. In cell H15, calculate the GPA for the Cumulative Total. Format the Semester Total GPA and the Cumulative Total GPA to display two decimals. Look at each sheet to see the GPA for each semester. (Hint: Kevin's GPA at the end of the Spring 99 semester is 3.15.) Display the Sheet tab Shortcut menu and ungroup the Sheets.

k. Go to the Fall 97 sheet and preview the workbook. Enter your name in the left footer position and the current date in the right footer position.

l. Document the workbook. Save and replace the workbook file Grade Report. Print all of the sheets.

You will continue this exercise as Practice Exercise 7 in this lab.

4. Marion manages a computer lab at a community college. She has four work-study students to assist her. The students are allowed to earn no more than $900 per semester at $4.75 an hour. Marion has created a worksheet that calculates the amount of money the students have left at the end of each week. By monitoring this amount, she can budget their time so that each student earns enough without exceeding the allotted amount.

a. Open the file Work Study Balance on your data disk. The starting amount ($900.00) and hourly rate ($4.75) have been entered in cells B4 and B5 respectively. In cell B10, enter a reference formula that will copy the starting amount for Ed. Keep in mind that you will need to copy that formula to obtain the same starting amount ($900.00) for Carrie Ann, Molly, and Jason. What formula did you use? Copy that formula to cells B11 through B13.

b. There are 15 weeks in a semester. Week 1 has been entered for you in cell C9. Use AutoFill to create the weekly headings in cells C9 through Q9.

c. Open the file Work Study Hours on your data disk. This is a report of the number of hours the students have worked each week from the beginning of the semester through the last full week of classes.

d. Use the logic in step b to enter the column headings Week 1 through Week 15 in cells B5 through P5.

e. Tile the windows. In this portion of the exercise, you will enter an external reference formula that will calculate the amount of money each student has left at the end of each week. (Hint: Since both sheets are visible, you can use pointing to enter the cell references in the formula.) Make the Work Study Balance file active, and go to cell C10. To calculate the amount of money Ed has left after the first week, subtract his Hours Worked*Rate from his Starting Amount. What is the result? Note: It is important that you use cell references and not the numbers they represent in all parts of the formula. Also pay attention to which references should be relative, and which should be absolute.

f. Copy that formula down the column to see how much each student has left at the end of the first week. Maximize the Work Study Balance window.

g. Change the numeric format of the new numbers to match the starting amount. Then copy the Week 1 balances to Week 2 through Week 14, the last week before final exams. Who will be ineligible to work finals week?

h. To keep the row headings in view as you scroll the worksheet, go to column A so you can see all the headings, and then freeze panes at cell C10.

i. What if the students earned $5.00 an hour? Change the rate in cell B5 to $5.00, and scroll to column P. Who will be ineligible to work at the end of the semester? What if the students were allotted $1,000 per semester? Change the starting amount in cell B4 to $1,000. Will everybody be able work the week of final exams? Do you think they will want to?

j. Molly has a lot of money left over. Use Goal Seek to calculate what the hourly rate would have to be before Molly would run out of money by Week 14 if she worked the same number of hours. What is the result? Use The Undo command to reset the values.

k. Unfreeze the panes. Rename the Sheet1 tab Fall 1998.

l. Center the title across the columns. Select a different font, and increase the font size to 16 pt. Draw a bottom border under the column headings in row 9. Draw an outline border around the what-if values and their row labels in cells A4 through B5. Add color to the text and the background within the border. Make whatever other formatting changes you wish using techniques you have learned.

m. Preview the worksheet. Add your name and date to the header. Print the worksheet on one page using landscape orientation. Document the workbook. Save and replace the workbook file Work Study Balance with the new print settings.

n. Close the workbook. The Work Study Hours worksheet should be active. Rename the Sheet1 tab Fall 1998. Use whatever formatting techniques you wish to improve the appearance of the worksheet.

o. Preview the worksheet. Add your name and the date to the header. Remove the page number footer. Print the worksheet on one page using landscape orientation. Document the workbook. Save and replace the workbook file Work Study Hours with the new print settings.

On Your Own

5. To complete this problem, you must have completed Practice Exercise 2 in Lab 2. Open the workbook file Cookie Jar on your data disk. In this exercise you will continue to modify the quarterly sales worksheet for the gourmet cookie shop, The Cookie Jar.

a. Copy Sheet1 as Sheet1 (2) and insert it before Sheet2. Rename the Sheet1 tab 1st Quarter Sales and rename Sheet1 (2) 2nd Quarter Sales.

b. Use the AutoFill feature to replace the months Jan through Mar with Apr through Jun on the 2nd Quarter Sales sheet.

c. Enter the new April sales numbers as follows:

Type	Number
Chocolate Chip	1900
Chocolate Chip w/ Nuts	1425
White Chocolate Macadamia	1300
Butterscotch	750
Peanut Butter	1000
Oatmeal Raisin	350
Gingerbread	525

d. Aggressive advertising should account for a monthly 10 percent increase in sales. Enter formulas to calculate a 10 percent increase over the previous month's sales for May and June (April Sales*1.10 and May Sales*1.10). Copy those formulas down the column.

e. Enter the heading "Projected Sales" over the May month heading. Bold the heading, and center it over the May and June columns.

f. Enter a heading "Projected Sales to Date Total" in cell B14 of the 2nd Quarter Sales sheet. Bold and italicize the entry. In cell E14, calculate a total for the first six months by summing cells E12 on both sheets. Format the new entry to match the rest of the numbers in the workbook.

g. Add a custom header that contains your name and the date right-aligned in both sheets.

h. Preview the workbook. Save and replace the workbook file Cookie Jar. Print the workbook.

You will complete this exercise as Practice Exercise 3 in Lab 4.

6. To complete this problem, you must have completed Practice Exercise 6 in Lab 2. Open the workbook file Time Sheets on your data disk. In this exercise you will continue to modify the time sheet for Ilsa.

Create a second time sheet in a new worksheet. Use last Friday's date as the Sheet1 name, and use this Friday's date as the Sheet1 (2) name. Enter different Total Hours and Regular Hours (8 is the maximum number for regular hours) in the new time sheet. Enter this Monday's date as the Starting Date in B2. Two rows below the Weekly Total amount, enter a formula to calculate the biweekly total as the sum of both weekly totals. Include an appropriate heading.

Add a custom footer that includes your name left-aligned, the date center-aligned, and your class time right-aligned in both worksheets. Document and save the workbook file as Time Sheets. Preview and print both worksheets.

You will complete this exercise as Practice Exercise 1 in Lab 5.

7. To complete this exercise, you must have completed Practice Exercise 3 in this lab. Open the file Grade Report from your disk. Modify this workbook to match your situation. Add or delete sheets as needed. Rename sheet tabs with appropriate semester labels. Save the workbook file as My Grade Report. Print the workbook.

8. To complete this problem, you must have completed Practice Exercise 6 in this lab. Ilsa also wants to create a worksheet to track her earnings using data from the time sheets she maintains each week.

In a new workbook, create the worksheet to track earnings as shown below. Save the workbook file as Earnings Statement.

	A	B	C	D
1				
2	Earnings Statement Of:	[Student's Name]		
3	Period Ending:	[Date]		
4				
5	Earnings:			
6	Rate	Hours		Gross Pay
7	7.5			
8	Deductions	Statutory		
9		Federal Income Tax		
10		State Income Tax		
11		Local Income Tax		
12		Medicare Tax		
13		Social Security Tax		
14		Voluntary		
15		Union Dues		
16		Holiday Club		
17		Total Deductions		
18		Net Pay		

Create a link to calculate the gross pay in the Earnings Statement workbook to the total biweekly hours worked from the Time Sheet workbook. Calculate the gross pay as Rate*Hours.

The statutory deductions will be calculated as follows:
Federal Income Tax = Gross Pay*15%
State Income Tax = Gross Pay*3%
Local Income Tax = Gross Pay*1%
Medicare Tax = Gross Pay*1.5%
Social Security Tax = Gross Pay*7%
The voluntary deductions are:
Union Dues = $10
Holiday Club = $25
Total the deductions and calculate Net Pay (total deductions – Gross Pay).

Apply appropriate number formats and styles to enhance the appearance of the worksheet. Print the Earnings Statement with a custom header and centered horizontally on the page.

You will continue this exercise as Practice Exercise 1 in Lab 5.

SPREADSHEET

Concept Summary

Managing and Analyzing a Complex Workbook

AutoFill

The AutoFill feature makes entering long or complicated headings easier by logically repeating and extending the series.

Referencing Sheets

A formula reference to cells in different worksheets in a workbook allows you to use data from other worksheets and to calculate new values based on this data.

Sheet Names

Each sheet in a workbook can be assigned a descriptive name to identify the contents of the sheet.

Split Windows

A sheet window can be split into sections called panes to make it easier to view different parts of the sheet at the same time.

Freeze Panes

Freezing panes prevents the data in the pane from scrolling as you move to different areas in the worksheet.

Goal Seek

Goal Seek is an Excel tool that is used to find the value needed in one cell to attain a result you want in another cell.

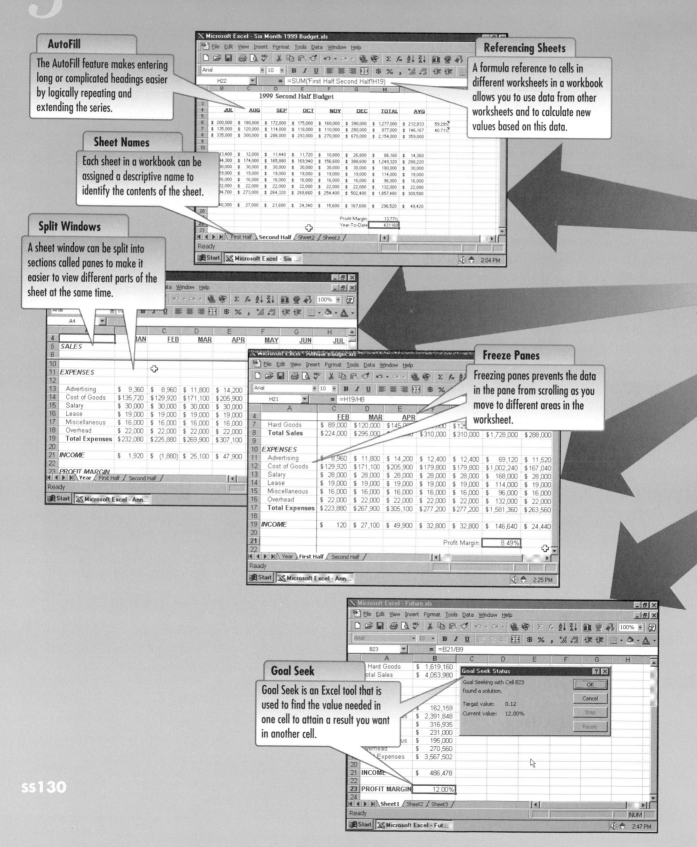

Solver

Solver is an Excel tool that answers what-if problems by determining the value of a cell by changing values in one or more cells in the worksheet.

What-If Analysis

What-if analysis is a technique used to evaluate the effects of changing selected factors in a worksheet.

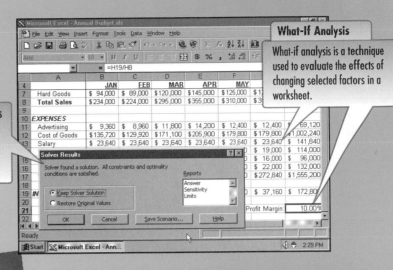

Concepts

Sheet Names
AutoFill
Referencing Sheets

Split Windows
Freeze Panes

What-If-Analysis
Solver

Spelling Checker

Goal Seek

Link Workbooks

Spelling Checker

A spelling checker feature locates misspelled words, duplicate words, and capitalization irregularities and proposes the correct spelling.

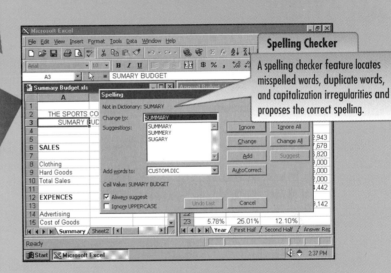

Link Workbooks

A link creates a connection between files that updates the linked data automatically in one file whenever the data changes in the other file.

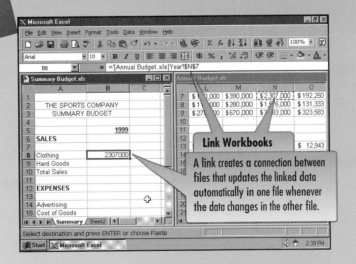

Creating Charts

4

CASE STUDY

You have noticed over the past few months while working at The Sports Company that sales are increasing in some sports and declining in others. While looking through the store sales records, you have found sales data by sport for the past several years. You want to create several charts of this data to make it easier to see the trends and growth patterns over the years.

Excel has the capability to create many types of charts from data in a worksheet. The different chart types emphasize data in various ways. You will create several different charts of the sales data, as shown below.

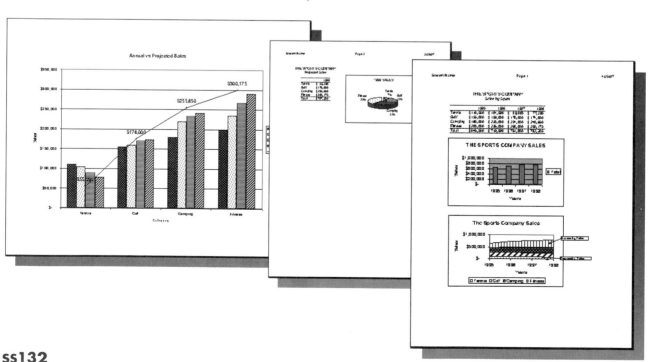

Concept Overview

The following concepts will be introduced in this lab:

1. Autoformat   An autoformat is a built-in combination of formats that can be applied to a range.

2. Types of Charts   Excel 97 can produce 14 basic types of charts with many different formats for each type.

3. Chart Elements   A chart consists of a number of parts or elements that are used to graphically display the worksheet data.

4. Objects   Objects are items that can be added to a worksheet and that can be sized and moved.

Part 1

Using Autoformats

You have created a worksheet of the sales data by sport and will use Excel 97 to create several charts to visually show the sales trends.

- Load Excel 97.

- Put your data disk in drive A (or the appropriate drive for your system).

- Open the workbook file Sales. If necessary, maximize the worksheet window.

Your screen should be similar to Figure 4-1.

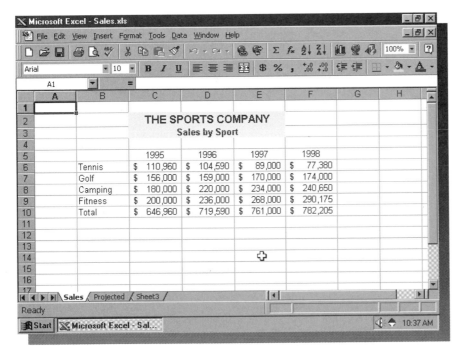

FIGURE 4-1

The Sales sheet displays the sales for the years 1995 through 1998. The worksheet lists four sports categories and a total as row labels in column B. The total is the sum of the sales for the four sports categories for each year. The headings for the four years are displayed in row 5.

You also created a worksheet for the projected sales for 1999.

■ To see this worksheet, make the Projected sheet active.

The data for 1999 projected sales for the four categories is displayed. You will use this worksheet later in this lab.

■ Make the Sales sheet active again.

Before creating the charts, you would like to improve the appearance of the worksheets by applying an autoformat to the worksheet data.

Concept 1: Autoformat

An **autoformat** is a built-in combination of formats that can be applied to a range of cells. There are 16 autoformats from which you can select. The autoformats consist of a combination of number formats, fonts and styles, colors, patterns, borders, and alignment settings.

To use an autoformat, you first specify the range you want affected by the formatting. In this case, you want to apply an autoformat to cells B5 through F10. You can select the range or you can let Excel select the range for you. To have Excel automatically select the range, move the cell selector to any cell in the range. Excel determines that the range you want to apply the autoformat to is the range of cells that includes the active cell and is surrounded by blank cells.

■ Move to B5.

■ Choose F**o**rmat/**A**utoFormat.

Your screen should be similar to Figure 4-2.

FIGURE 4-2

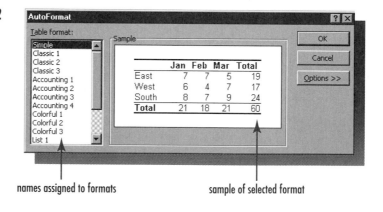

names assigned to formats   sample of selected format

The AutoFormat dialog box displays the names Excel has assigned each of the 16 different formats in the Table Format list box. The Sample box shows how the selected format will look.

- To preview the autoformats, highlight each name in the Table Format list and look at the table layout in the Sample box.

The None autoformat option removes an existing autoformat.

You think the Accounting 2 format would be appropriate for the data in the Sales sheet. To format the worksheet using this layout,

- Select Accounting 2.

- Click [OK].

Your worksheet should be similar to Figure 4-3.

Accounting 2 autoformat applied to selected range

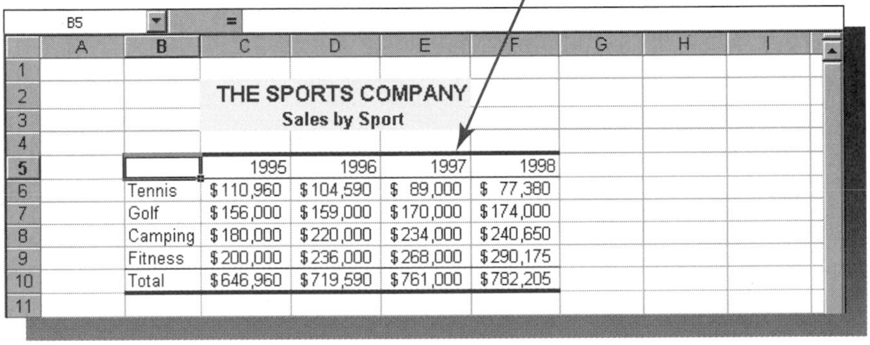

FIGURE 4-3

	A	B	C	D	E	F	G	H	I
1									
2			THE SPORTS COMPANY						
3			Sales by Sport						
4									
5			1995	1996	1997	1998			
6		Tennis	$110,960	$104,590	$ 89,000	$ 77,380			
7		Golf	$156,000	$159,000	$170,000	$174,000			
8		Camping	$180,000	$220,000	$234,000	$240,650			
9		Fitness	$200,000	$236,000	$268,000	$290,175			
10		Total	$646,960	$719,590	$761,000	$782,205			
11									

The Accounting 2 autoformat includes border lines of different weights, color, and accounting number format with no decimal places. You would like to apply this same format to the Projected worksheet.

- Make the Projected sheet active and apply the Accounting 2 autoformat to cells B5 through C10.

- Make the Sales sheet active again.

You can use Edit/Repeat AutoFormat to quickly apply the same autoformat.

About Charts

Although the worksheet shows the sales numbers for each sports category, it is hard to see how the different categories have changed over time. A visual representation of data in the form of a **chart** would convey that information in an easy-to-understand and attractive manner.

Concept 2: Types of Charts

Excel 97 can produce 14 basic types of graphs or charts, with many different formats for each type. The basic chart types are:

Type	Description
	Area charts show the magnitude of change over time by emphasizing the area under the curve created by each data series.
	Bar charts display data as evenly spaced bars. The categories are displayed along the Y axis and the values are displayed horizontally, placing more emphasis on comparisons and less on time.
	Column charts display data as evenly spaced bars. They are similar to bar charts, except the categories are organized horizontally and values vertically to emphasize variation over time.
	Line charts display data along a line. They are used to show changes in data over time, emphasizing time and rate of change rather than the amount of change.
	Pie charts display data as slices of a circle or "pie." They show the relationship of each value in a data series to the series as a whole. Each slice of the pie represents a single value in the series.
	Doughnut charts are similar to pie charts except they can show more than one data series.
	Radar charts display a line or area chart wrapped around a central point. Each axis represents a set of data points.
	XY (scatter) charts are used to show the relationship between two ranges of numeric data.
	Surface charts display values as what appears to be a rubber sheet stretched over a 3-D column chart. These are useful for finding the best combination between sets of data.
	Bubble charts compare sets of three values. It is like a scatter chart with the third value displayed as the size of bubble markers.
	A stock chart is a high-low-close chart. It requires three series of values in this order.
	Cylinder charts display values with a cylindrical shape.
	Cone charts display values with a conical shape.
	Pyramid charts display values with a pyramid shape.

Selecting the Data to Chart

The first chart you want to create will show the total sales pattern over the four years. All charts are drawn from data contained in a worksheet. To create a new chart, you select the worksheet range containing the data you want displayed as a chart plus any row or column headings you want used in the chart. Excel then translates the selected data into a chart based upon the shape and contents of the worksheet selection.

A chart consists of a number of parts or elements, which are important to understand so that you can identify the appropriate data to select in the worksheet. These elements are described in the concept box below and on page SS138.

Concept 3: Chart Elements

The basic elements of a two-dimensional chart are shown in the figure below.

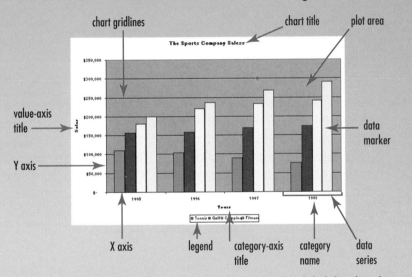

The bottom boundary line of the chart is the **X axis**. It is used to label the data being charted, such as a point in time or a category. The **category names** displayed along the X axis correspond to the headings for the worksheet data that is plotted along the X axis. The left boundary line of the chart is the **Y axis**. This axis is a numbered scale whose numbers are determined by the data used in the chart. Typically the X-axis line is the horizontal line and the Y-axis line is the vertical line.

The selected worksheet data is visually displayed within the X- and Y-axis boundaries. This is called the **plot area**. Each group of related data, such as the numbers in a row or column of the selected area of the worksheet, is called a **data series**. Each number represented in a data series is identified by a **data marker**. A data marker can be a symbol, color, or pattern. To distinguish one data series from another, different data markers are used. In addition, **chart gridlines** are commonly displayed to make it easier to read the chart data. Chart gridlines extend from the Y-axis line across the plot area. A **legend** identifies the chart data series names and data markers that correspond to each data series.

A chart can also contain descriptive **titles** that explain the contents of the chart. The chart title is displayed centered above the charted data. Titles can also be used to describe the X and Y axes. The X-axis title line is called the **category-axis title**, and the Y-axis title is called the **value-axis title**.

In pie charts there are no axes. Instead the worksheet data that is charted is displayed as slices in a circle or pie. Each slice is labeled. In 3-D charts there can also be an additional axis, called the Z axis, which allows you to compare data within a series more easily. This axis is the vertical axis. The X and Y axes delineate the horizontal surface of the chart.

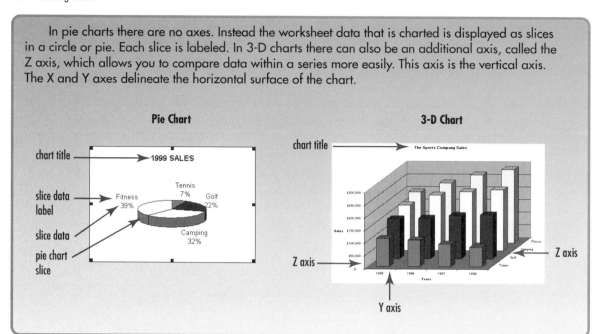

The first chart you will create of the worksheet data will use the year labels in cells C5 through F5 to label the X axis. The numbers to be charted are in cells C10 through F10. In addition, the label "Total" in cell B10 will be used as the chart legend, making the entire range B10 through F10. Notice that the two ranges, C5 through F5 and B10 through F10, are not adjacent and are not the same size. When plotting nonadjacent ranges in a chart, the selections must form a rectangular shape. To do this, the blank cell B5 will be included in the selection. To specify the range and create the chart,

Refer to Lab 1 for a discussion of nonadjacent selections.

- Select B5 through F5.

- Hold down ⌨Ctrl.

- Select B10 through F10.

Your worksheet should be similar to Figure 4-4.

FIGURE 4-4

nonadjacent selections

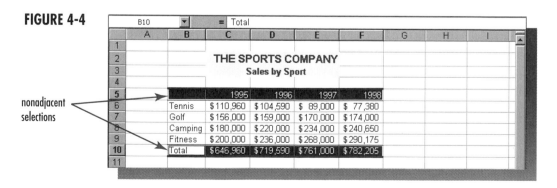

■   Click 🖾 Chart Wizard.

The dialog box on your screen should be similar to Figure 4-5.

You can choose **I**nsert/C**h**art to create the chart.

selected default chart type

FIGURE 4-5

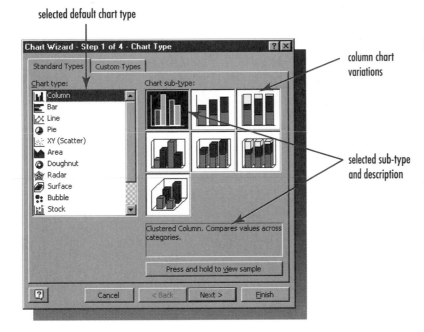

column chart variations

selected sub-type and description

Chart Wizard is an interactive program that guides you through the steps to create a chart. The first step is to select the chart type from the Chart Type list box. The default chart type is a **column chart**. Each type of chart includes many variations. The variations associated with the column chart type are displayed as buttons in the Chart Sub-type section of the dialog box. The default column sub-type is a clustered column. A description of the selected sub-type is displayed in the area below the sub-type buttons. To accept the default settings and move to the next step,

If the Office Assistant is displayed, you are asked if you want help with this feature.

■   Click   Next >   .

Your screen should be similar to Figure 4-6.

sample chart

FIGURE 4-6

selected range

controls chart orientation

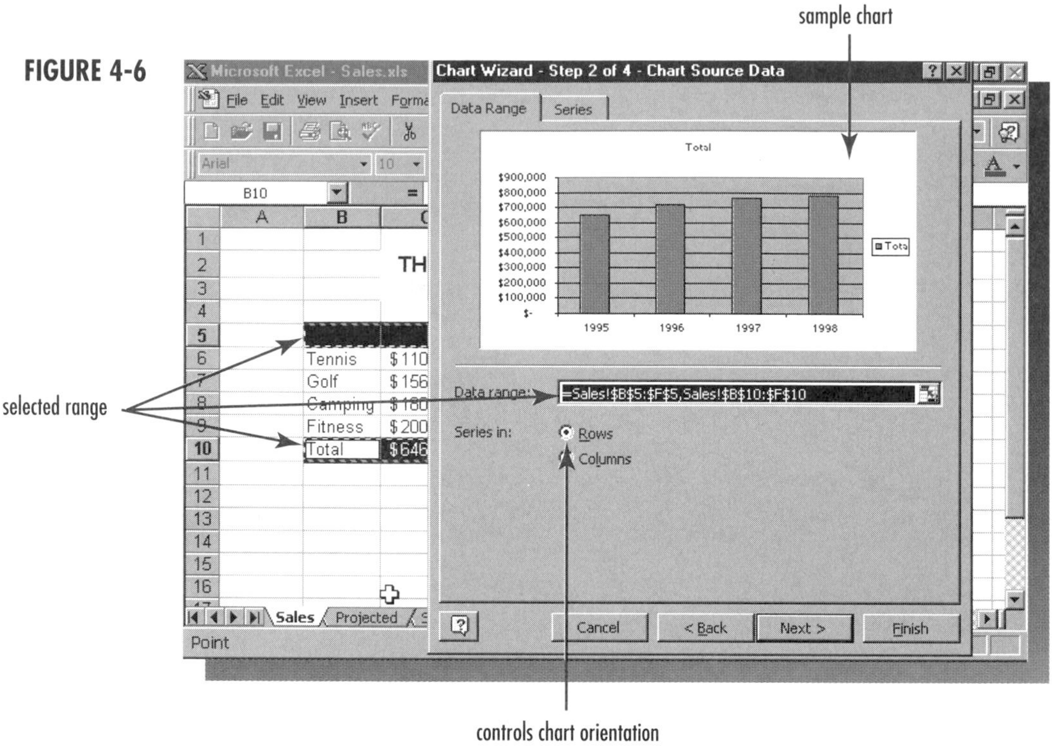

The Chart Wizard Step 2 of 4 dialog box displays a sample of the chart that will be created using the current chart settings and data. The selected range appears in the Data Range text box. You can specify another range in the text box or accept the displayed range.

The two Series In options control how Excel interprets the data series. The interpretation varies depending upon the type of chart selected. In a column chart, the default setting is Rows. In this setting Excel uses the first row as the X-axis category labels and the leftmost column as the legend text. Changing the setting to Columns reverses this, placing the first column of the range along the X axis and the first row of the range as the legend text. To accept the default settings,

- Click Next > .
- If necessary, open the Titles tab.

The dialog box on your screen should be similar to Figure 4-7.

default chart title

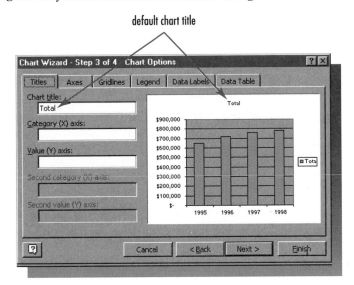

FIGURE 4-7

In the Step 3 dialog box you can change the appearance of chart elements such as a legend and titles. To clarify the chart, you will add a chart title as well as titles along the X and Y axes. As you add the titles, the sample chart will update to display the new settings.

- Replace the default title in the Chart Title text box with **THE SPORTS COMPANY SALES**.

- In the Category (X) Axis text box enter **Years** and in the Value (Y) Axis text box enter **Sales**.

- Click 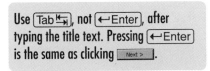 .

Use Tab, not ←Enter, after typing the title text. Pressing ←Enter is the same as clicking Next >.

The dialog box on your screen should be similar to Figure 4-8.

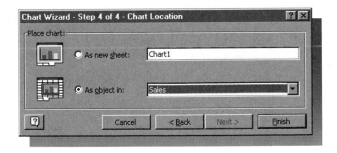

FIGURE 4-8

In the last step you specify where you want the chart displayed in the worksheet. A chart can be displayed in a separate chart sheet or as an object in an existing sheet.

Concept 4: Objects

Objects are items that can be added to a worksheet and that can be sized and moved. A chart that is inserted into a worksheet is one of several different types of graphic objects. A chart is also referred to as a chart object because it is created using the Chart toolbar. Others are comments, text boxes, pictures, and drawing objects created using the Drawing toolbar.

As objects are added to the worksheet, they automatically stack in individual layers. The stacking order is apparent when objects overlap. **Stacking** allows you to create different effects by overlapping objects. Because you can rearrange the stacking order, you do not have to add or create the objects in the order in which you want them to appear.

Objects can also be grouped. A **group** is two or more objects that are combined so you can work with them as a single object. Groups can also be composed of multiple sets of groups.

When a graphic object is selected, it is surrounded by eight black or white boxes, called **selection handles**, and an editing border. Dragging on a handle sizes the object. A selected object is moved by pointing to it and dragging it to a new location. The procedure is very similar to moving and sizing a window.

You would like this chart displayed as an object in the Sales worksheet. This is the default selection. To complete the chart,

■ Click Finish .

Your screen should be similar to Figure 4-9.

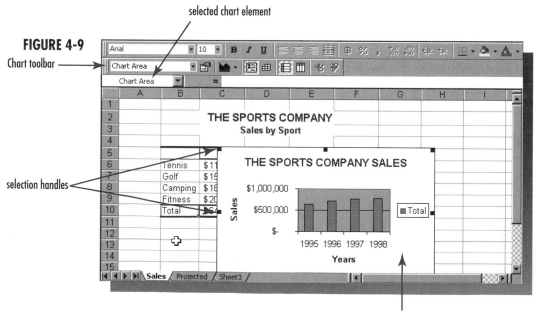

selected chart element

FIGURE 4-9

Chart toolbar

selection handles

embedded chart is a selected object

The chart with the settings you specified using the Chart Wizard is displayed on the worksheet. A chart object that is inserted into a sheet is an **embedded chart**.

Notice that the chart is a selected object, and the name box displays "Chart Area." The Name box identifies the chart element that is selected, in this case the entire chart and all its contents. Also notice that the Chart toolbar is automatically displayed whenever a chart is selected.

- ■ If necessary, move the Chart toolbar below the Formatting toolbar.

- ■ To make more space on the screen to work with the chart, hide the status bar.

Moving and Sizing a Chart

You need to move the chart so that it is displayed below the worksheet data. In addition you want to make the chart object larger. First you will move the chart, then you will increase its size. Notice when you move the mouse pointer into the selected chart object, that it displays Screen Tips to advise you of the chart element that will be affected by your action.

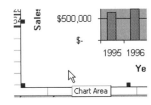

- ■ Point to the chart object and when the Chart Area Screen Tip appears, drag the object so that it covers the worksheet range B13 through F24.

- ■ Point to the lower right corner selection handle and drag the chart box down and to the right until it is displayed over cells B13 through G27.

Your screen should be similar to Figure 4-10.

> Move toolbars by dragging the title bar of a floating toolbar or the move handle ‖ of a docked toolbar.

> Use View/Status Bar to hide and display the status bar.

> The mouse pointer appears as a ↔ while dragging to move an object.

> The mouse pointer appears as a ↖ while sizing an object.

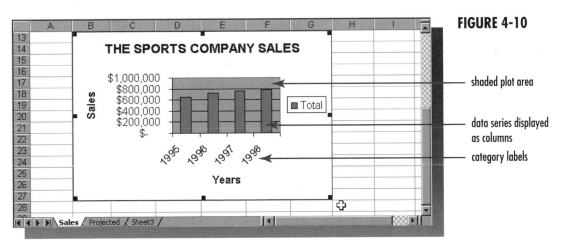

FIGURE 4-10

shaded plot area

data series displayed as columns

category labels

With the chart larger, there are now values along the Y axis, making the data in the chart easier to read. Each column represents the total for that year. The chart includes standard formats that are applied to the selected chart sub-type, such as a shaded background in the plot area and blue columns.

Changing the Type of Chart

Next you would like to see how the same data displayed in the column chart would look as a line chart. A **line chart** displays data as a line and is used to show trends. This is easily done by changing the chart type using the 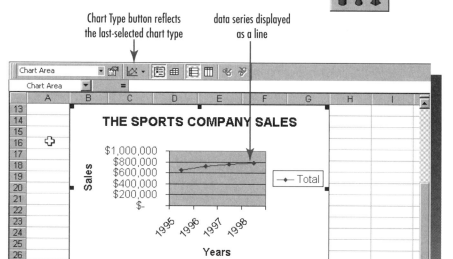 Chart Type button on the Chart toolbar.

> The ⬛- button initially displays an area chart. Subsequently it will display the last-selected chart type.

- Open the ⬛- Chart Type drop-down list.

- Click ⬚ Line Chart.

Your chart should be similar to Figure 4-11.

FIGURE 4-11

Chart Type button reflects the last-selected chart type   data series displayed as a line

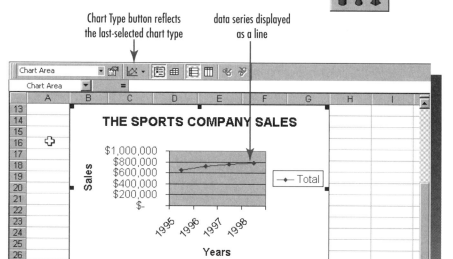

The data for the total sales for each year is now displayed as a line. Although the line chart shows the trend in sales over time, because it contains only one data series, it is not as interesting as the column chart.

> You could also click ↶- Undo to change the chart type back to the previous type.

- Change the chart type back to Column Chart.

Creating a Chart with Multiple Data Series

Now you are ready to continue your analysis of sales trends. You want to create a second chart to display the sales data for each sports category for the four years. You could create a separate chart for each category and then compare the charts; however, to make the comparisons between the categories easier, you will display all the categories on a single chart.

The data for the four years for the four categories is in cells C6 through F9. The year headings (X-axis data series) are in cells C5 through F5, and the legend text is in the range B6 through B9. To specify the chart data series,

■ Select B5 through F9.

■ Click 📊 Chart Wizard.

The Chart Wizard - Step 1 dialog box is displayed. You think a line chart would be an appropriate chart type. From the Chart Type options list,

■ Select 📈 Line.

To preview how this default line chart sub-type will look using the selected data series,

■ Click and hold [Press and hold to view sample].

The dialog box on your screen should be similar to Figure 4-12.

FIGURE 4-12

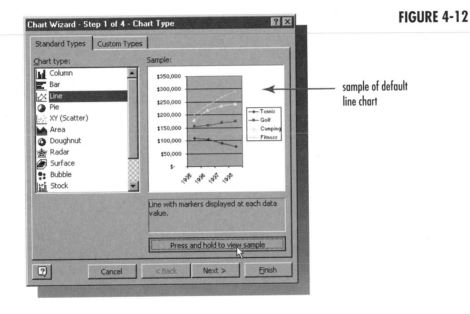

sample of default line chart

You like how it looks.

■ Release the [Press and hold to view sample] button.

■ Click [Next >].

Again Excel selects Rows as the default orientation. To confirm the data series range and move to the next box,

■ Click [Next >].

■   Enter the following titles:

Title	Entry
Chart title	**The Sports Company Sales**
Category-axis title	**Years**
Value-axis title	**Sales**

■   Click Next > .

You would also like this chart embedded in the Sales worksheet.

■   Choose Finish .

■   Move and size the chart until it covers cells B29 through G44.

Your screen should be similar to Figure 4-13.

FIGURE 4-13

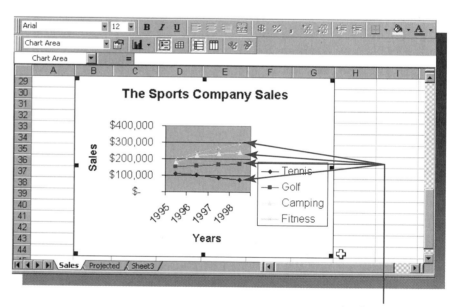

four data series as lines

The line chart clearly shows that sales in fitness and camping are increasing, sales in tennis are decreasing, and golf sales are steady.

Although the line chart shows the sales trends for the four years for the four sports categories, it does not give you a feeling for the magnitude of the change. You feel that a stacked-column chart or an area chart may better represent the data. First you will change the type to a stacked-column chart. In a **stacked-column chart** the columns are stacked upon each other rather than displayed side by side. Unfortunately, this type of chart is not an option in the Chart Type palette. It is, however, available from the Chart menu.

When a chart is selected, the Data menu changes to the Chart menu. In addition, many of the commands under the other menus have changed to commands that apply to charts only. The Chart menu contains commands that can be used to modify the chart.

■ Choose **C**hart/Chart **T**ype.

The Chart Type dialog box contains the same options as the Chart Wizard - Step 1 dialog box. The current chart type, line, is the preselected option. To select a column chart,

■ Select 📊 Column.

■ Select 📊 Stacked column with 3-D visual effect.

■ Click and hold [Press and hold to **v**iew sample].

The sample chart is redrawn. A stacked-column chart shows the proportion of each type of sport to the total sport sales in each year. The stacked-column chart shows the amount of change better, but it is still difficult to see trends.

■ Release the mouse button.

Next you would like to see the data represented as an area chart. An **area chart** represents data the same as a line chart, but in addition it shades the area below each line to emphasize the degree of change.

■ Select 📈 Area.

■ Click and hold [Press and hold to **v**iew sample].

The area chart shows the magnitude of change and the trend from year to year better than the other types of charts. To apply this chart type,

■ Click [OK].

Your chart should be similar to Figure 4-14.

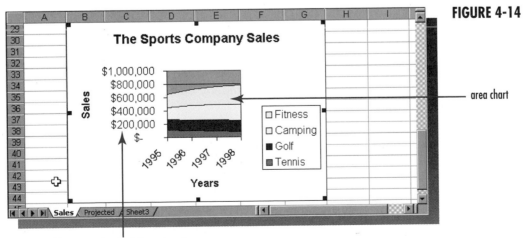

FIGURE 4-14

area chart

Y-axis range is sum of four categories

SPREADSHEET

The Y-axis scale has changed to reflect the new range of data. The new Y-axis range is the sum of the four categories, or the same as the total number in the worksheet. It is now easy to see the magnitude of change each category contributes to the total sales in each year.

As you can see, it is very easy to change the chart type and format once the data series are specified. The same data can be displayed in many different ways. Depending upon the emphasis you want the chart to make, a different chart style can be selected.

Note: If you are ending your lab session now, add your name as a header and print the Sales sheet. Save the file as Sales Charts. When you begin Part 2, load Excel, open Sales Charts, and select the area chart.

Part 2

Moving the Legend

After looking at the area chart, you decide to modify several other chart features. First you want to move the legend below the X axis.

A chart is a grouped object made up of many separate elements. Each object in the group can be individually selected and then formatted or edited. Some of the objects in a chart are also groups that consist of other objects. For example, the legend is a group object. Each item in the legend is a separate object that can be manipulated. Other chart objects are the axis lines, a data series, a data marker, the entire plot area, or the entire chart. You can also select chart objects from the Chart Objects button drop-down list or click on the object to select it.

■   Click on the legend to select it.

> **If the wrong item is selected, reposition the mouse pointer and click again.**

Your screen should be similar to Figure 4-15.

Clear Objects button   Name box   Format Object box   selected object

FIGURE 4-15

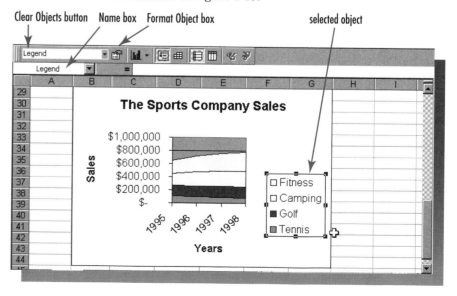

The legend box is surrounded by selection handles, indicating that it is the selected object and will be affected by any changes you make. In addition, the Name box and Chart Objects button display "Legend" as the selected chart object.

■   To identify the objects within the Legend group, point to each line in the legend to see the Screen Tip.

As different objects in the chart are selected, the commands on the Format menu change to commands that can be used on the selected object. In addition, the ⬚ Format Object button to the right of the [Legend ▾] Chart Object button can be used to format the selected object.

■   Click ⬚ Format Legend.

The dialog box on your screen should be similar to Figure 4-16.

The menu equivalent is Format/ Selected Legend, and the shortcut key is ⌷Ctrl⌷ + 1.

FIGURE 4-16

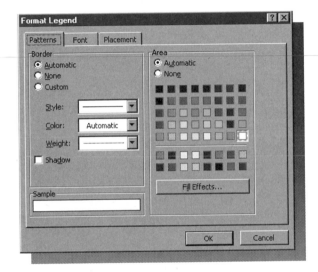

The Format Legend tab dialog box is used to change the patterns, font, and placement of the legend. To change the legend placement to below the plot area,

■   Open the Placement tab.

■   Choose **B**ottom.

■   Click [OK].

You can also move the legend by dragging it, and then you can resize it to fit the new location.

Your chart should be similar to Figure 4-17.

FIGURE 4-17

legend placed at bottom of chart

The legend object is centered below the chart and resized to fit below the axis title.

Adding Patterns

The next change you would like to make is to add patterns to the chart data series. If you have a color monitor, the data series are automatically displayed in different colors. If you have a monochrome monitor, they are displayed as varying shades of gray. You want to change the default display to black-and-white patterns to make it easier to distinguish one series from the other. Adding black-and-white patterns is particularly important if you do not have a color printer. Without black-and-white patterns, the colors are printed as shades of gray and may be difficult to distinguish.

To add black-and-white patterns, you need to select each data series object and use the Format command to change the color and pattern settings. The Shortcut menu also contains a Format option. You can quickly select a chart object and open the related Shortcut menu by right-clicking directly on the object.

■   Right-click the Fitness series chart object.

Your screen should be similar to Figure 4-18.

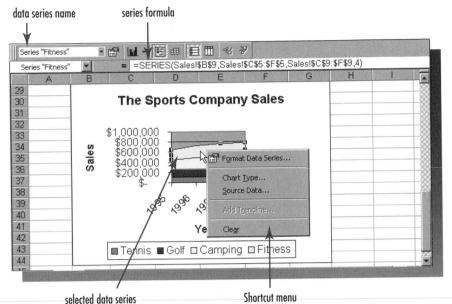

FIGURE 4-18

The Shortcut menu is displayed, and handles appear around the selected series only. Also notice that the formula bar displays a **series formula**. This formula links the chart object to the source worksheet, Sales. The formula contains four arguments: a reference to the cell that includes the data series name (used in the legend), ref-

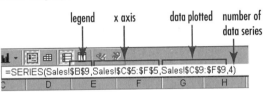

erences to the cells that contain the categories (X-axis numbers), references to the numbers plotted, and an integer that specifies the number of data series plotted.

Now you can use the Format menu to change the pattern used in the selected series. From the Shortcut menu,

■   Choose F**o**rmat Data Series.

■   If necessary, open the Patterns tab.

> The menu equivalent is F**o**rmat/S**e**lected Data Series, and the shortcut key is
> (Ctrl) + 1.

The dialog box on your screen should be similar to Figure 4-19.

FIGURE 4-19

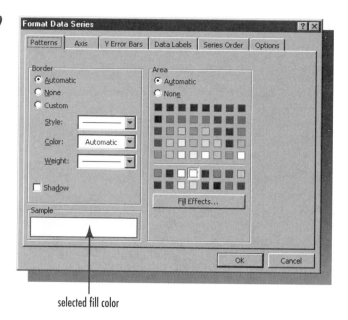

selected fill color

The options available in the Patterns tab vary depending upon the type of data marker that is selected. In this case, because an area data marker is selected, the options let you change the border and the background area of the selected series. The current setting for the selected series is displayed in the sample area. To change the area color to black, and to add a pattern,

■ Click [Fill Effects...].

The Fill Effects tab dialog box is displayed.

■ Choose Pattern.

■ Change the foreground color to black.

■ From the Pattern palette, select a pattern of your choice.

■ Click [OK] (twice).

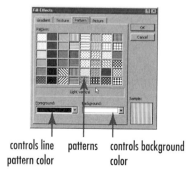

controls line   patterns   controls background
pattern color   color

The chart is redrawn with the Fitness area of the chart displaying the black-and-white pattern. The legend has also been updated to reflect the new pattern and color selection.

■   In the same manner, select the other three data series and apply a different black-and-white pattern to each.

Your chart should be similar to Figure 4-20.

You can double-click the data series to both select it and open the Format dialog box.

FIGURE 4-20

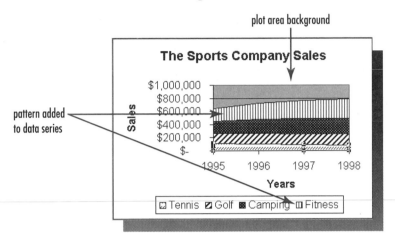

The chart displays the selected black-and-white patterns for the four data series.

The last change you would like to make is to remove the shading from the plot area background. The only background visible is above the Fitness data area.

■   Double-click the plot area.

■   Click None (in the Area section).

■   Click   OK   .

Adding a Text Box

The last item you want to add to the area chart is a text box. A **text box** is a rectangular object in which you type text. Text boxes can be added to a sheet or a chart. You will add a text box containing the text "Increasing Sales" to the worksheet to draw attention to the Fitness area of the chart. A text box is created using the 📧 Text Box button on the Drawing toolbar. To display the Drawing toolbar,

■   Click 🔧 Drawing.

■   Click 📧 Text Box.

■   Move the mouse pointer to the blank area to the right of the chart and drag to create a text box that is approximately 1/4 inch by 2 inches.

The mouse pointer appears as ↓, indicating a text box will be created as you drag the mouse.

If a chart is selected when you create a text box, it is added to the chart object.

Your screen should be similar to Figure 4-21.

FIGURE 4-21

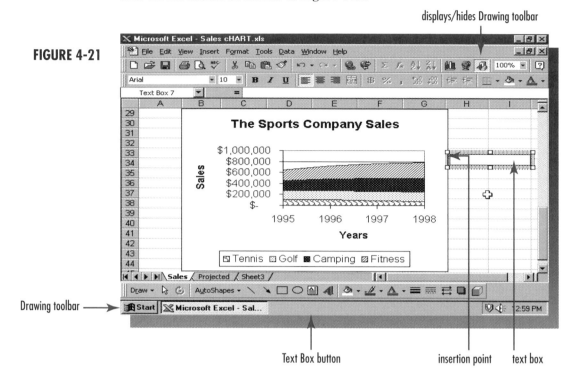

displays/hides Drawing toolbar

Drawing toolbar →

Text Box button   insertion point   text box

The text box displays an insertion point and is waiting for you to enter the text. As you type the text below, do not be concerned if all the text is not visible within the text box. As you type, the text will automatically begin on the next line when the right edge of the text box is reached. This feature is called **word wrap**. You should not press ⏎Enter to move to the next line.

- Type **Increasing Sales**.

- If necessary, adjust the size of the text box until it is just large enough to fully display the text on one line.

You want to make the text font smaller and bold.

> You can also choose F**o**rmat/Text B**o**x to modify the format settings.

- Select the text by highlighting it and choose 8 pt from the ⟨10 ▾⟩ Font Size button drop-down list.

- Click **B** Bold.

- Readjust the size of the text box and move it to the position displayed in Figure 4-22.

Your screen should be similar to Figure 4-22.

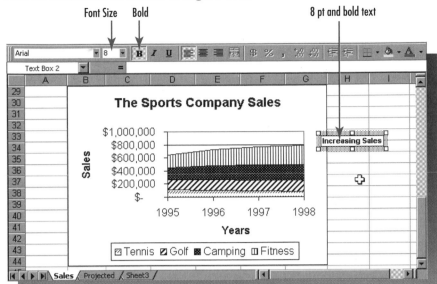

FIGURE 4-22

Adding Arrows

Next you want to draw an arrow from the text box to the Fitness area of the chart.

- ■ Click [▼] Arrow.

- ■ To draw the arrow, click on the left edge of the text box and drag to the Fitness area.

A line with an arrowhead at the end is displayed in the worksheet. The arrow is automatically a selected object. The handles at both ends of the arrow let you adjust its size and location.

- ■ If necessary, move and size the arrow to adjust its position as in Figure 4-23. Deselect the arrow.

- ■ In the same manner, add a text box with the text "**Decreasing Sales**" and an arrow pointing to the Tennis area of data.

- ■ Close the Drawing toolbar.

> The mouse pointer appears as a +.

> If you hold down ⬆Shift while dragging, a straight horizontal line is drawn.

Your screen should be similar to Figure 4-23.

FIGURE 4-23

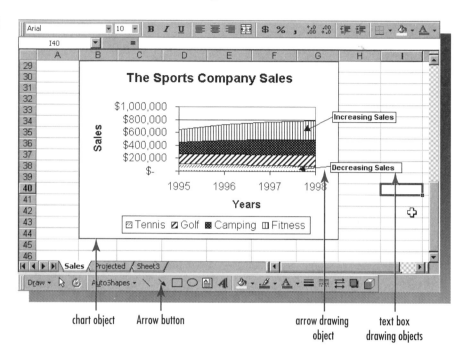

chart object   Arrow button   arrow drawing   text box
                                 object   drawing objects

Creating a Combination Chart

The next chart you want to create will show data from both the Sales and Projected sheets. You want to display the past four years' sales numbers as columns and the 1999 projected sales as a line. This type of chart is called a **combination chart**. It uses two or more chart types to emphasize that the chart contains different kinds of information. First you will create a column chart of the sales data for the four years. Then you will add the projected sales data as a line. You want to create this chart in its own sheet.

- ■ Select B5 through F9.

- ■ Click ▥ Chart Wizard.

- ■ Click Next > .

- ■ Choose Columns.

- ■ Click Next > .

- ■ Add the chart title **Annual vs Projected Sales**. Enter **Category** as the category-axis title and **Sales** as the value-axis title.

- ■ Click Next > .

- ■ Choose As new sheet.

- ■ Click Finish .

Your screen should be similar to Figure 4-24.

FIGURE 4-24

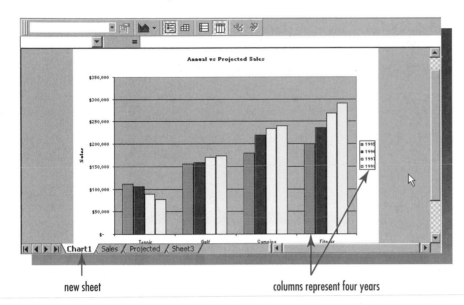

new sheet   columns represent four years

The column chart is displayed in a new sheet named Chart1. The sheet is inserted to the left of the active sheet. A chart that is not embedded in a worksheet as an object is displayed in a chart sheet. Generally, you display a chart in a chart sheet when you want the chart displayed separately from the associated worksheet data. The chart is still automatically linked to the worksheet data from which it was created.

Next you need to add the projected sales data series to the chart. To add a data series,

- Select **C**hart/**A**dd Data.

- Click the Projected sheet tab.

- Select C5 through C9.

- Click [OK].

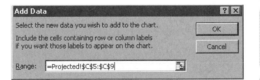

The Paste Special dialog box is displayed. By default Excel appropriately applies the same orientation, Column, as in the existing chart. To identify the first row of data in the range to be used as the legend label,

- Select Series **N**ames in First Row.

- Click [OK].

The new data series is added to the chart as a column. To change it to a line,

- Select 1999 data series.

- Open the Chart Type drop-down list.

- Choose [⟋] Line.

> If the chart was embedded in the worksheet, you could use "drag and plot" to drag data from the worksheet to add a data series to a chart.

> When a chart is displayed in a chart sheet, the chart does not need to be selected before it is modified.

> The Add Data dialog box automatically shrinks while you select the worksheet data.

Your chart should be similar to Figure 4-25.

FIGURE 4-25

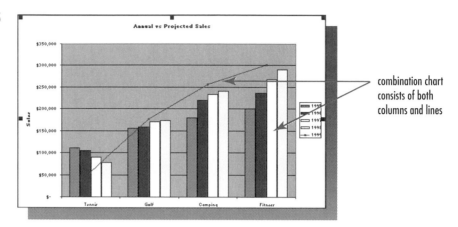

combination chart consists of both columns and lines

A combination chart makes it easy to see comparisons between groups of data or to show different types of data in a single chart. In this case you can easily see how the sales for each category are changing compared to projected sales for each category.

Adding Data Labels

You would also like to display on the combination chart the actual numbers plotted for the projected sales. These are called **data labels**. The numbers you want to use as data labels are in cells C6 through C9 in the Projected sheet.

■   Switch to the Projected worksheet and select cells C6 through C9.

■   Make the Chart1 sheet active and display the Shortcut menu for the 1999 data series line.

■   Choose Format Data Series/Data Labels/Show Value/ OK .

Your chart should be similar to Figure 4-26.

data labels

FIGURE 4-26

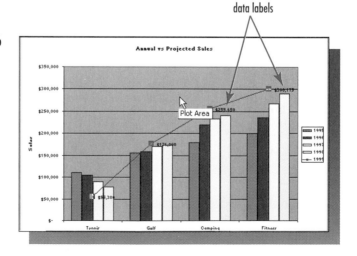

The data labels for the 1999 projected sales are displayed next to the data points on the line in the chart. They are selected objects.

- ■ Zoom the window to 75 percent to see the data labels better.

The data labels are difficult to see because the numbers are small. To make them more obvious, you will change the font size of the data labels and make them bold. You also want the labels to be displayed above their data points on the line.

- ■ Display the Data Labels Shortcut menu.

- ■ Choose Format Data Labels.

- ■ Open the Font tab.

- ■ Select 12 from the Size list box and Bold from the Font Style list box.

- ■ Open the Alignment tab.

- ■ Select Above from the Label Position drop-down list.

- ■ Choose [OK].

> You could also individually format the data labels using the [10 ▾] Font Size and [B] Bold toolbar buttons.

The data labels are now easier to see.

- ■ Apply different black-and-white patterns to each column data series.

- ■ Change the plot area background to None.

Creating a Pie Chart

The last chart you will make will use the Projected worksheet data. The sales of fitness items have been increasing and you are particularly interested in next year's sales projections.

- ■ Make the Projected sheet active.

You want to see what proportion fitness sales are of all sales for the projected year. The best chart for this purpose is a pie chart. A **pie chart** compares parts to the whole, in a similar manner to a stacked-column chart. However, each value in the range is a slice of the pie displayed as a percentage of the total.

The use of X (category) and data series settings in a pie chart is different from their use in a column or line chart. The X series labels the slices of the pie rather than the X axis. The data series is used to create the slices in the pie. Only one data series can be specified in a pie chart.

- ■ Select B6 through C9.

Another way to create a chart is to use the [📊 ▾] Chart Type toolbar button.

- ■ Display the Chart toolbar.

- ■ Click [📊 ▾] Chart Type.

- ■ Click [◐] Pie Chart.

A basic pie chart is drawn in the worksheet. It does not include a chart title or labels to clarify the slices of the pie.

■ Move and expand the chart to be displayed over cells E4 through I16.

Your screen should be similar to Figure 4-27.

FIGURE 4-27

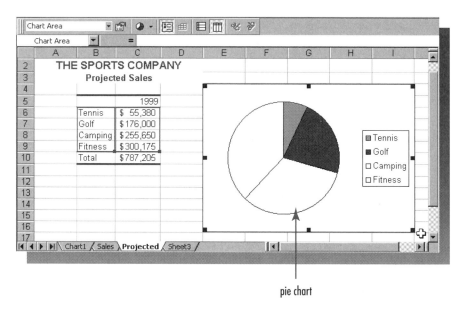

pie chart

Each value in the data series is displayed as a wedge of the pie chart. However, because the chart does not contain a title or labels, the meaning of the chart is unclear. First you will add a chart title. A pie chart can have only a main title because it does not contain axis lines.

■ Choose **C**hart/Chart **O**ptions.

■ In the Chart Title text box of the Titles tab enter the title **1999 SALES**.

The sample chart shows the title displayed centered in the chart area. Now you want to add labels for the wedges to help clarify the information in the chart.

■ Choose Data Labels/Show Label **a**nd Percent.

The sample pie chart is redrawn again to show the data label and percents. Because the category labels display the same information as the legend, you can turn off the display of the legend.

■ Choose Legend/**S**how legend.

■ Click OK .

The Pie Chart does not look very attractive. You want to see if the chart would look better as a three-dimensional pie chart.

■ Change the chart type to a 3-D Pie chart.

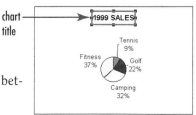

Your worksheet should be similar to Figure 4-28.

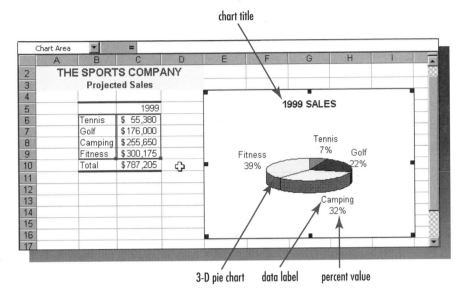

FIGURE 4-28

chart title

3-D pie chart   data label   percent value

The chart looks much better.

Finally, you want to add black-and-white patterns to the wedges.

■ Select each wedge and apply a black-and-white pattern to each.

Now that the pie chart is formatted as you want it to appear, you want to separate slightly or **explode** the Fitness wedge of the chart to emphasize the data.

■ Select the Fitness wedge and, to explode the selected wedge, drag it away from the pie.

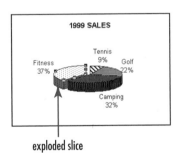

exploded slice

> To select an object within a group, select the group first, then select the object.

Changing Worksheet Data

As you look at the chart, you notice that the Tennis category represents 9 percent of the total. You think this figure is a little high. After checking your records, you find that you entered the data in cell C6 incorrectly. It should be 55380.

■ Enter the value **55380** in cell C6.

The worksheet has been recalculated, and the pie chart has been redrawn to reflect the change in the 1998 data for the Tennis category. Tennis now accounts for 7 percent of total sales for the projected year. Since the chart document is linked to the source data, changes to the source data are automatically reflected in the chart.

Printing Charts

- Update the file properties summary information with your name and applicable comments.

- Move to cell A1 of the Sales sheet and save the workbook file as Sales Charts.

Use **F**ile/**P**rint/**E**ntire Workbook/
[Previe**w**].

- Preview all sheets in the workbook.

Because the combination chart is on a separate sheet, it is displayed on a page by itself.

- Add a header to the combination chart sheet to display your name, page number, and date.

- Preview the Sales sheet containing the column and area charts.

- Add a header as in the combination chart.

- Center the page horizontally.

Your screen should be similar to Figure 4-29.

FIGURE 4-29

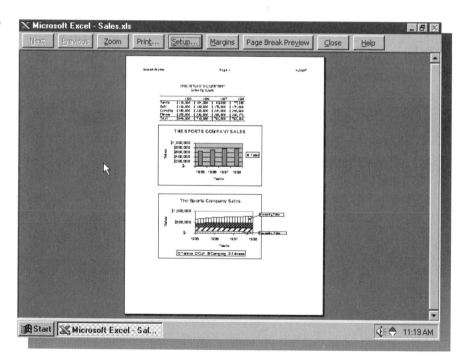

- Preview the Projected worksheet containing the pie chart.

- Add a header as you did the others.

Printing a worksheet that includes charts requires a printer with graphics capability. However, the actual procedure to print is the same as printing a worksheet that does not include charts.

- Click Print... .
- Close the Chart toolbar.
- Redisplay the status bar.
- Exit Excel, saving the workbook again if necessary.

> If you need to specify a different printer, use the Print command on the File menu to print the workbook.

Lab Review

Key Terms

area chart (SS147)	data label (SS158)	object (SS142)	title (SS137)
autoformat (SS134)	data marker (SS137)	pie chart (SS159)	value-axis title (SS137)
category-axis title (SS137)	data series (SS137)	plot area (SS137)	word wrap (SS154)
category name (SS137)	embedded chart (SS142)	selection handle (SS142)	X axis (SS137)
chart (SS135)	explode (SS161)	series formula (SS151)	Y axis (SS137)
chart gridlines (SS137)	group (SS142)	stack (SS142)	
column chart (SS139)	legend (SS137)	stacked-column chart (SS146)	
combination chart (SS156)	line chart (SS144)	text box (SS153)	

Command Summary

Command	Shortcut	Toolbar	Action
Insert/**C**hart		📊	Inserts chart into worksheet
F**o**rmat Data Series/ Data Labels			Inserts data labels into chart
F**o**rmat/**A**utoFormat			Applies one of 16 built-in table formats to the worksheet range
F**o**rmat/S**e**lected Legend	Ctrl + 1		Changes legend
F**o**rmat/S**e**lected Data Labels	Ctrl + 1		Changes format of selected data labels
F**o**rmat/S**e**lected Data Series	Ctrl + 1		Changes format of selected data series
F**o**rmat/Text B**o**x			Changes format of text box
Chart/Chart **T**ype		📈 ▾	Changes type of chart
Chart/Chart **O**ptions			Adds options to chart
Chart/ **A**dd Data			Inserts new data into chart

Matching

1. chart gridlines   _____
2. data marker   _____
3. stacked-column   _____
4. X axis   _____
5. explode   _____
6. plot area   _____
7. category-axis   _____
8. Y axis   _____
9. legend   _____
10. pie chart   _____

a. left boundary of chart
b. bottom boundary of chart
c. design or color assigned to each data range in chart
d. area of chart bounded by X and Y axes
e. makes chart data easier to read
f. displays symbols and descriptive labels of data
g. clarifies values displayed along X axis
h. shows proportion of each value
i. to separate wedge slightly from other wedges of pie
j. compares parts to the whole

Fill-In Questions

1. Complete the following statements by filling in the blanks with the correct terms.

a. A visual representation of data in an easy-to-understand and attractive manner is called a(n) _____.

b. A(n) _____ describes the symbols used within the chart.

c. The bottom boundary of a chart is the _____ and the left boundary is the _____.

d. A chart that is not embedded in a worksheet is displayed in a(n) _____ sheet.

e. A(n) _____ chart and a(n) _____ chart both display data as a set of evenly spaced bars.

f. A(n) _____ and a(n) _____ compare parts to the whole.

g. The _____ toolbar contains commands that let you add text boxes and arrows to a chart.

h. _____ can be added to a chart to identify the actual data values.

i. When a chart is printed in black and white, _____ can be added to the data series to make it easier to read.

j. When a wedge of a pie chart is separated from the other wedges, the wedge has been _____.

Discussion Questions

1. Discuss how the autoformat feature can be use to enhance the appearance of a worksheet. What types of formats are associated with autoformats?

2. Discuss how column and bar charts represent data. How do they differ from pie charts?

3. What type of information would best be represented by a line chart?

4. Describe how a 3-D column chart differs from a 2-D column chart.

Hands-On Practice Exercises

■ ■ ■ ■ ■ ■ ■ ■ ■ ■

Step by Step

Rating System		
☆	Easy	
☆☆	Moderate	
☆☆☆	Difficult	

1. WonderWord is a popular word processor available in DOS, Windows, and Macintosh formats. Below is a table that represents sales of this program over the past several years.

	1992	1993	1994	1995	1996	1997
DOS	200000	105330	97350	57830	24560	13687
MAC	94000	75320	64320	74780	74380	84260
WIN	82350	105150	193260	214940	285350	378330

a. Create a worksheet based on this data. Add a title, and use the formatting techniques you learned to enhance the appearance of the worksheet. Make sure that the data you will chart does not contain blank columns or rows. Enter your name and date below the worksheet.

b. Use the Chart Wizard to create a stacked area chart with 3-D visual effect. Add appropriate titles and add patterns. Size the chart so all axis labels are displayed. Center the chart below the worksheet. Enlarge the chart title and choose a different font.

c. Rename the Sheet1 tab WonderWord Sales.

d. Update the document summary properties. Save the workbook file as Wonderword Area. Preview the worksheet and select a header that displays the sheet name and the page number. Print the worksheet with the chart centered horizontally on the page.

e. Change the area chart to a default column chart. Add titles to the chart. Save the workbook as Wonderword Column. Print the worksheet with the chart.

f. Change the column chart to a line chart. Display the legend below the chart. You want to draw attention to increased Windows and declining DOS sales. Add text boxes with appropriate comments, and draw arrows to the Windows and DOS lines. Save the workbook as Wonderword Line. Print the worksheet with the chart.

g. Using the line chart settings, experiment with different chart types, and select one that appeals to you. Format the chart using any techniques you wish. Save the workbook using an appropriate name, and print the worksheet with the chart.

h. Use the three format headings and the corresponding 1997 sales figures to create a 3-D pie chart as a new sheet. Add the title "1997 SALES." Explode the wedge representing the lowest sales value. Add patterns to the wedges. Increase the font size of the wedge labels. Increase the font size of the title, and add a second line that displays your name and the current date.

i. Add a header that displays your name, the date, and the page number. Document the workbook. Save the workbook as Wonderword Pie. Print the pie chart sheet.

2. In May of 1995, *Advertising Age* listed the top 100 advertising companies for 1994. The first five are listed in the table below.

Top 5 Advertisers	
Company	**$ Spent**
AT&T Corp.	698.6
Ford Motor Co.	549.3
Sears, Roebuck & Co.	491.7
Kellogg Co.	483.7
McDonald's Corp.	425.8

a. Create a worksheet of this data. Use the formatting techniques you have learned to enhance the appearance of the worksheet.

b. Use the data to create a default 3-D bar chart. Turn the legend off, and add appropriate titles.

c. Size the chart so all axis labels can be displayed. Below the value axis, add a text box that displays the comment "In Millions of Dollars." Draw an arrow from the text box to the value axis. Edit the title to include your name and the current date.

d. Update the summary properties and save the workbook as Top 5 Advertisers. Print the worksheet with the chart centered horizontally on the page.

3. To complete this exercise, you must have completed Practice Exercise 2 in Lab 2. Open the file Cookie Jar on your data disk.

a. Use the column A row headings and the corresponding first-quarter total numbers to create an embedded 3-D pie chart. Add an appropriate title. Remove the legend and add to the slices of the pie data labels that display the different types of cookies and the percents. Size the chart so all labels can be displayed. If necessary, reduce the font size of the labels. Explode the chocolate chip cookie wedge, and add patterns to the slices. Add a text box and an arrow that draws attention to the two wedges that represent the lowest sales.

b. The chart you just created shows a part-to-whole relationship between each cookie type and the total cookie sales for the first quarter. On a new sheet, create a chart that shows a part-to-whole relationship between each cookie type and each monthly value. (Hint: The data will be in rows, not columns.)

c. Add appropriate titles and add patterns to each data series. Size the chart so the legend information can be displayed. Add patterns to each data series, and display the legend below the chart.

d. Update the summary properties for the workbook. Preview the workbook and add headers to both sheets that display your name, the date, and the page number. Print the worksheet. Save and replace the workbook file.

4. As part of a freshman orientation survey, Luzerne University students were asked how many hours a day they expected to spend on school work. The choices were: Less than 1 hour, 1–2 hours, 2–3 hours, and More than 3 hours. Below is a table of the results.

Choice	# Responses
Less than 1 hour	87
1–2 hours	404
2–3 hours	475
More than 3 hours	123

a. Use the table information to create a worksheet, and make any formatting changes you wish.

b. Create an embedded chart that will show a part-to-whole relationship for the four categories of responses. Format the chart as desired.

c. Create a header that displays your name and the current date.

d. Update the summary properties for the workbook. Save the workbook file as Student Survey. Print the worksheet with the chart centered horizontally on the page.

e. At the end of the first semester, the students were again surveyed. This time they were asked how many hours a day they actually spent on school work. The table below shows the results from those who responded.

Choice	# Responses
Less than 1 hour	15
1–2 hours	101
2–3 hours	592
More than 3 hours	246

f. Replace the original values with the new values. Save and replace the workbook Student Survey. Print the worksheet with the chart. Can you relate to the differences in the results?

On Your Own

⭐⭐☆

5. Sadie Jacobs, owner of Jacobs Furniture Galleries, likes to have her sales staff close a sale with at least 35 percent of the customers with whom they come in contact. The worksheet below displays this month's results.

	A	B	C	D	E	F	G
1		**Jacobs Furniture Galleries**					
2		**Monthly Sales Report**					
3							
4		Ron	Charmaine	Michael	Polly	Al	Mary Claire
5	Contacts	113	127	95	129	113	135
6	Sales	26	49	42	19	43	54
7	% of Closings						
8							

Create the worksheet shown above and calculate the percent of Closings. Create an embedded chart that best compares customer contacts to sales for each employee. Add appropriate titles, and format as desired.

Create a header and footer that displays your name and the current date. Print the worksheet with the chart. Update the summary properties for the workbook. Save the workbook file as Sales Report.

Use Goal Seek to determine how many sales would be needed to increase the percent of Closings to 35 percent for those who do not meet that goal. Save and replace the workbook file Sales Report. Print the worksheet with the chart.

⭐⭐⭐

6. According to "The College Savings Bank," the 1995 cost of a four-year education was approximately $35,000 and $72,000 respectively for public and private colleges.

	A	B	C	D	E	F	G	
1				**College Costs**				
2								
3		1995	1996	1997	1998	1999	2000	
4	Public	35,000						
5	Private	72,000						
6								

Create the worksheet shown above and, using an annual inflation rate of 7.5 percent, complete the worksheet to calculate the cost of a college education for each type of school from 1995 to the year 2000. Add the following comment in a text box below the worksheet:

Note: **The above costs include tuition, room, board, books, and other expenses and fees.**

Create an embedded chart that will compare private and public school costs annually. Add appropriate titles, and format as desired. Rename the sheet tab.

Create a chart as a new sheet that will show the change in cost from 1995 to 2000. Add appropriate titles, and format as desired. Rename the chart sheet tab.

Create a header to display your name and the current date. Print the workbook.

Update the summary properties for the workbook. Save the workbook as College Costs.

⭐⭐⭐

7. Create a worksheet that tracks your grades. It can be a record of the test scores you received this semester, or it can be a record of your GPA each semester. Create an embedded chart that best represents your grade trends. Use the formatting techniques you have learned to change the appearance of the worksheet and the chart. Save the workbook as Grades. Print the worksheet with the chart.

⭐⭐⭐

8. Create a worksheet that displays a list of your monthly expenses (rent, car payment, food, day care, utilities, insurance, credit cards, etc.). Total the expenses. Create a chart that best shows a part-to-whole relationship between each expense and total expenses. Using the formatting techniques you have learned, change the appearance of the worksheet and the chart. Save the workbook as Expenses. Include your name and the date in a header. Print the worksheet and the chart.

SPREADSHEET

■ ■ ■ ■ ■ ■ ■ ■ ■ ■ ■ ■ ■

Creating Charts

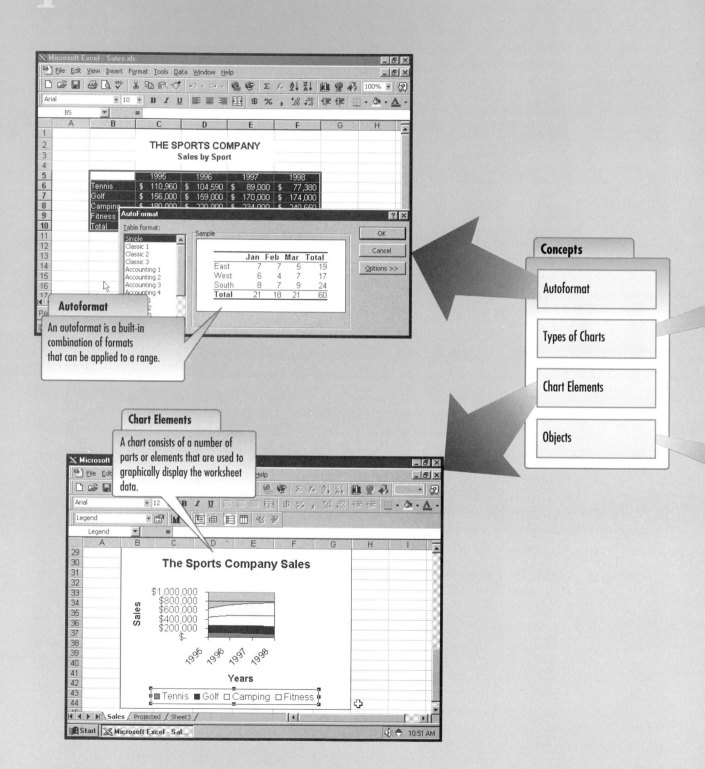

Autoformat

An autoformat is a built-in combination of formats that can be applied to a range.

Chart Elements

A chart consists of a number of parts or elements that are used to graphically display the worksheet data.

Concepts

- Autoformat
- Types of Charts
- Chart Elements
- Objects

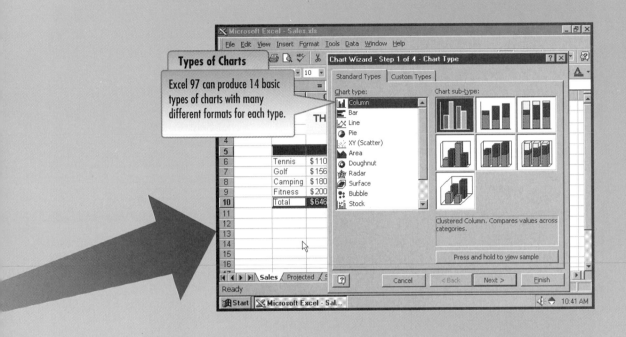

Types of Charts

Excel 97 can produce 14 basic types of charts with many different formats for each type.

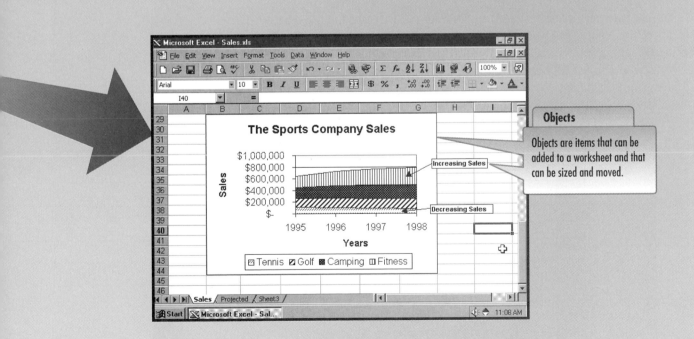

Objects

Objects are items that can be added to a worksheet and that can be sized and moved.

ss169

Creating a Form Template

5

CASE STUDY

As you have used Excel to create more complex worksheets and workbooks for The Sports Company, you have seen how the program makes it easier and faster to produce an accurate, attractive, and useful worksheet. Your next project with The Sports Company is to create a form to be used to track the monthly new charge card enrollments and to calculate the employee bonuses. While using Excel to create the form (shown below), you will use many advanced features.

Among the many features are the hundreds of functions included with Excel that are designed to perform complex financial and statistical analysis of data. Specifically you will learn about the IF function, which is used to perform conditional tests on data. In addition, you will learn how to create forms and templates, to add controls, and to protect your worksheets so that their contents cannot be changed.

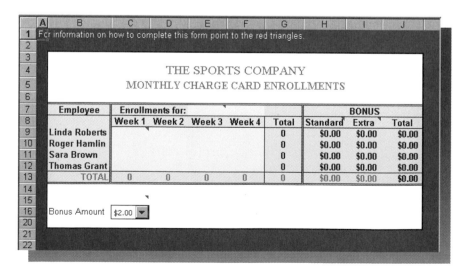

> **Concept Overview**
>
> The following concepts will be introduced in this lab:
>
> **1. Range Name**   Adding a descriptive range name to a cell or range of cells makes formulas easier to read and understand.
>
> **2. IF Function**   The IF function checks to see if certain conditions are met and then takes action based upon the results of the check.
>
> **3. Controls**   Controls are graphic objects that are designed to automate the process of filling out the form. Controls include property settings that affect how they behave and work.
>
> **4. Worksheet Protection**   To prevent others from changing a sheet's contents, you can protect the entire worksheet or specified areas of the worksheet. When you protect a sheet, all cells and graphic objects on the sheet are locked.
>
> **5. Workbook Template**   A workbook template is a workbook file that contains predesigned sheets that can be used as a pattern for creating other similar worksheets in new workbooks.

Naming a Range

The Sports Company has decided to offer its own charge card. As an incentive to apply for a card, customers receive 15 percent off any purchases made using the card for the first time. As an incentive to employees to promote the charge card, they earn a bonus for each credit card application they process. The store manager has asked you to create a form to track the enrollments and bonuses each month.

A **form** is a formatted worksheet that is designed to be completed by filling in data in the blank spaces. Forms can be used online on an individual computer or on a network, or can be printed to be completed on paper. The steps in creating a form are the same for both purposes. However, the different elements are more appropriate for one than the other. For example, color and shading are more effective on online forms, while simplicity of design and layout are very important in printed forms. In addition, online forms can contain formulas that immediately calculate results such as totals, whereas printed forms would need to include blank spaces where the calculations would be entered manually.

The first step when creating a form is to decide what information is to be entered on the form and what questions need to be asked. You also need to decide if the form will be computerized or printed. The form to monitor employee bonuses will be used online. You have already started designing the form by entering much of the text, many of the formulas, some formatting to improve the appearance, and some sample data.

■   To see what has been done so far, load Excel and open the workbook file Enrollment Bonus. If necessary, maximize the worksheet.

Your worksheet should be similar to Figure 5-1.

FIGURE 5-1

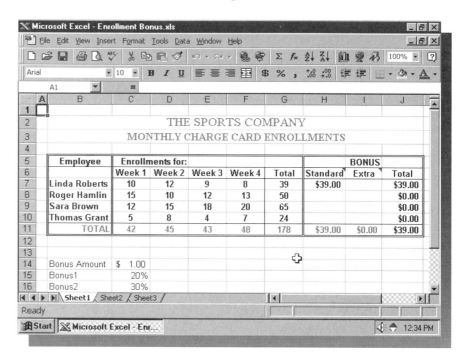

This worksheet displays the names of four salespeople as row headings in column B. The enrollments for each week of the month are entered in columns C through F for each salesperson. The monthly enrollment total is displayed in column G. The worksheet contains some sample enrollment data for each salesperson. The sample data for Linda shows that she enrolled ten charge card applicants in week 1, twelve in week 2, nine in week 3, and eight in week 4, for a monthly total of 39 enrollments.

The three columns to the right of the enrollment data are where the bonus will be calculated. The Sports Company is awarding a standard bonus of $1.00 for each credit card application signed up. Additionally, if a salesperson files 25 applications or more, an extra bonus equal to 20 percent of the standard bonus is awarded. If they file more than 50 applications, the extra bonus amount is increased to 30 percent. The formulas that will be used to calculate the bonus are described below:

Standard	The total number of enrollments times $1.00
Extra	The Standard bonus times 20 percent if total enrollments are 25 or more, or times 30 percent if the total is 50 or more
Total	The sum of the Standard and Extra bonuses

Notice that cells H6 and I6 indicate they contain cell comments.

■ Display the cell comments for cells H6 and I6.

The comments help clarify the meaning of the data that will be entered in these columns.

The formula to calculate the Standard bonus for Linda Roberts has already been entered.

■ Move to H7.

Your worksheet should be similar to Figure 5-2.

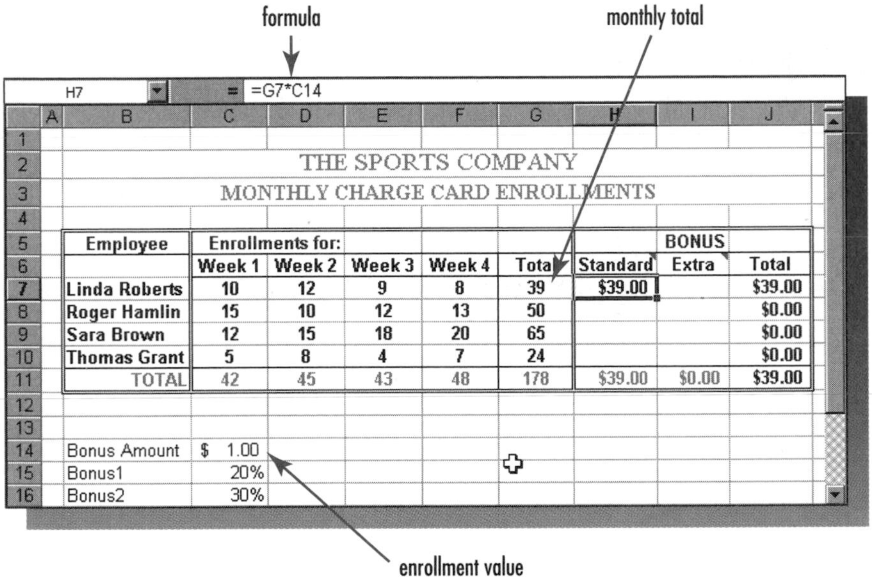

FIGURE 5-2

The formula references cell C14. This cell contains the bonus amount of $1.00. To make the formula easier to read and understand, you will assign a descriptive name to this cell reference.

Concept 1: Range Name

A descriptive **range name** can be assigned to a cell or range of cells and used in place of cell references. The name can be used any time a cell or range is requested as part of a command or in a formula or function.

Excel automatically proposes a name for the cell or range using the contents of the active cell if it contains text, or the cell above or to the left of the active cell if the active cell does not contain text. If the active cell or the cells above or to the left of the active cell do not contain text, or if you do not want to use the proposed name, you can type in a name of your choice. The name can be up to 255 characters. It can include letters, numbers, underlines, periods, backslashes, and question marks. It cannot contain spaces. The first character must be a letter, underline, or backslash. A name that resembles a cell reference is not allowed.

To see how this works, you will assign the name "Bonus Amount" to cell C14.

■ Move to C14.

■ Choose <u>I</u>nsert/<u>N</u>ame/<u>D</u>efine.

Your screen should be similar to Figure 5-3.

FIGURE 5-3

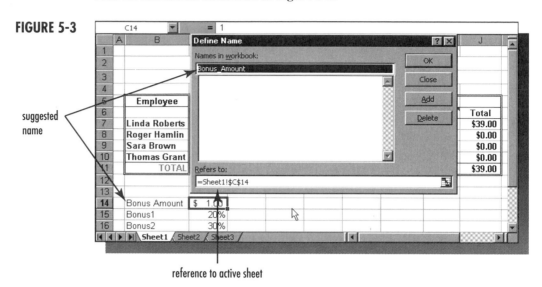

suggested name

reference to active sheet

In the Names in Workbook text box, Excel has proposed the name Bonus_Amount. The proposed name is the contents of the cell to the left of the active cell. Excel replaced the blank space between the words with an underline character because a name cannot contain spaces.

The Refers To text box displays the reference for the active cell. The reference includes the sheet name and cell reference. By default Excel makes named cell references absolute. The Names in Workbook list box is empty because this worksheet does not contain any names yet. Since both the name and the cell reference are acceptable, to complete the command,

■ Click   OK   .

> You can also name a range by selecting the range and typing the name into the Name box.

In place of the cell reference in the Name box of the formula bar, the name is displayed. Now you can replace the cell reference in the formula in cell H7 with the name. To do this,

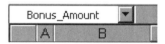

> You can toggle between displaying the cell reference and the name by clicking on the cell.

■ Move to H7.

■ Change to Edit mode and select (highlight) the cell reference C14 in the formula.

■ Choose Insert/Name/Paste.

> Notice that Range Finder has highlighted the cells in the formula.

■ Select Bonus_Amount.

■ Click   OK   .

Your worksheet should be similar to Figure 5-4.

cell name is used in place of reference

FIGURE 5-4

AVERAGE ▼	✗ ✓ =	=G7*Bonus_Amount							

	A	B	C	D	E	F	G	H	I	J
1										
2				THE SPORTS COMPANY						
3				MONTHLY CHARGE CARD ENROLLMENTS						
4										
5		Employee	Enrollments for:						BONUS	
6			Week 1	Week 2	Week 3	Week 4	Total	Standard	Extra	Total
7		Linda Roberts	10	12	9		=G7*Bonus_Amount			$39.00
8		Roger Hamlin	15	10	12	13	50			$0.00
9		Sara Brown	12	15	18	20	65			$0.00
10		Thomas Grant	5	8	4	7	24			$0.00
11		TOTAL	42	45	43	48	178	$39.00	$0.00	$39.00
12										
13										
14		Bonus Amount	$ 1.00							
15		Bonus1	20%							
16		Bonus2	30%							

Sheet1 / Sheet2 / Sheet3 /

The name Bonus_Amount has replaced the reference to cell C14 in the formula. Using a name makes the formula easier to understand. To complete the edit,

■ Press ⏎Enter.

Next you will name the bonus percent values in cells C15 and C16 that will be used in the formula to calculate the bonus. You will name both cells at the same time using the headings in B15 and B16 as the names. To create names using headings in a selected range, you specify the location of the headings in relation to the cells to be named. In this case the headings are located in the column to the left of the cells to be named.

■ Select B15 through C16.

■ Choose Insert/Name/ Create.

■ Click OK.

■ Move to C15.

labels to be used as names are in column to left of cells to be named

The name assigned to this cell, Bonus1, is displayed in the Name box.

Using the IF Function

Now you are ready to enter a formula in cell I7 to calculate the extra bonus earned. The store awards an extra bonus equal to 30 percent of the Standard bonus if total enrollments are 50 or more, and a 20 percent extra bonus if total enrollments are 25 or more. To calculate this value, you will use the IF function.

Concept 2: IF Function

The IF function checks to see if certain conditions are met and then takes action based upon the results of the check. The syntax for this function is:

IF(logical_test,value_if_true,value_if_false)

This function contains three arguments: logical_test, value_if_true, and value_if_false. The logical_test argument is an expression that makes a comparison using logical operators. **Logical operators** are used in formulas and functions that compare numbers in two or more cells or to a constant. The result of the comparison is either true (the conditions are met) or false (the conditions are not met).

The logical operators are:

Symbol	Meaning	Symbol	Meaning
=	Equal to	<>	Not equal to
<	Less than	NOT	Logical NOT
>	Greater than	AND	Logical AND
<=	Less than or equal to	OR	Logical OR
>=	Greater than or equal to		

The logical test argument asks the question, Does the entry in this cell meet the stated conditions? The answer is either True (Yes) or False (No). The second argument, value_if_true, provides directions for the function to follow if the logical test result is true. The third argument, value_if_false, provides directions for the function to follow if the logical test result is false.

First you will enter the formula to calculate the bonus earned for enrollments of 50 or more. Then you will modify the function to include the other conditions. You will enter the IF function using the Paste Function feature.

The menu equivalent is **I**nsert/**F**unction.

If the IF function name is not listed in the Most Recently Used category, switch to the Logical category to select it.

■ Move to I7.

■ Click f_x Paste Function.

■ Select IF.

■ Click OK .

Your screen should be similar to Figure 5-5.

text boxes

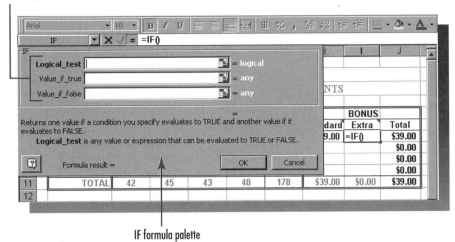

FIGURE 5-5

IF formula palette

The IF formula palette contains three text boxes, one for each IF statement argument. The logical test is whether the total monthly enrollment (G7) is greater than (>) or equal to (=) 50. The logical_test argument will be G7>=50. In the logical_test text box,

- Type **G7>=50**

- Press Tab.

The value_if_true argument contains the instructions that are executed if the condition is true. In this case if the number in cell G7 is greater than or equal to 50 (true), then H7 is multiplied by 30 percent (H7*30%). Instead of entering the bonus amount (30%) to complete the argument, you will reference the named cell, B16, that contains the bonus number. This way, if the bonus changes, the function will not need to be changed. The value_if_true argument then will be: G7*Bonus2. To enter the value_if_true argument,

- Type **G7***

- Choose Insert/Name/Paste.

- Select Bonus2.

- Click OK.

The value_if_false argument contains instructions that are executed if the condition is not true, or false. If the number in cell G7 is less than 50 (false), then the bonus is 0. To enter the last argument,

- Click the dialog box to make it active again.

- Press Tab.

- Type **0**.

- Click OK.

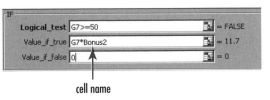

cell name

Your worksheet should be similar to Figure 5-6.

FIGURE 5-6

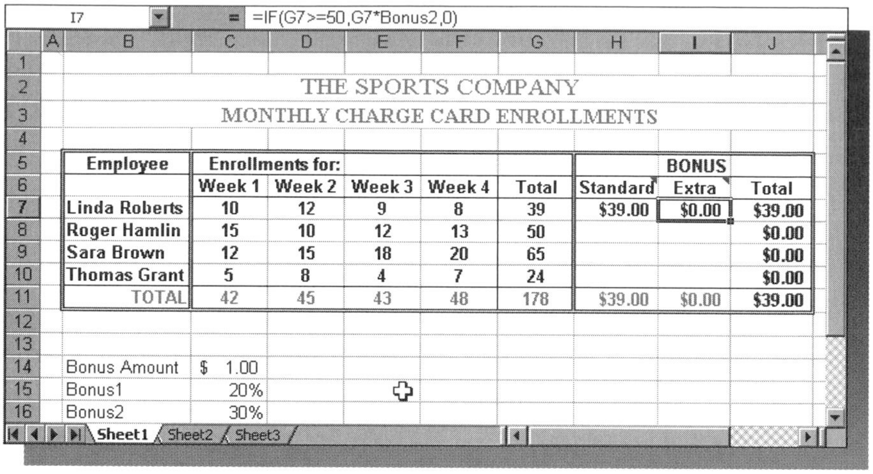

| | I7 | | = =IF(G7>=50,G7*Bonus2,0) | | | | | | |

	A	B	C	D	E	F	G	H	I	J
1										
2				THE SPORTS COMPANY						
3				MONTHLY CHARGE CARD ENROLLMENTS						
4										
5		Employee	Enrollments for:						BONUS	
6			Week 1	Week 2	Week 3	Week 4	Total	Standard	Extra	Total
7		Linda Roberts	10	12	9	8	39	$39.00	$0.00	$39.00
8		Roger Hamlin	15	10	12	13	50			$0.00
9		Sara Brown	12	15	18	20	65			$0.00
10		Thomas Grant	5	8	4	7	24			$0.00
11		TOTAL	42	45	43	48	178	$39.00	$0.00	$39.00
12										
13										
14		Bonus Amount	$ 1.00							
15		Bonus1	20%							
16		Bonus2	30%							

Sheet1 / Sheet2 / Sheet3

The Extra bonus is calculated for Linda using the sample data. The Extra bonus is $0.00 because the number in cell G7 is less than 50.

Now you need to modify this function to include a second IF statement that will apply the bonus of 20 percent to total enrollments that are greater than or equal to 25. The new IF statement will be IF(G7>=25,G7*Bonus1,0). The arguments for the second IF statement are enclosed in their own set of parentheses within the existing formula. This is called a **nested function**. The new function will be:

IF(G7>=50,G7*Bonus2,IF(G7>=25,G7*Bonus1,0))

second IF statement

To edit the formula using the Paste Function feature,

- Click [=] Edit Formula.

- In the value_if-false text box enter **IF (G7>=25,G7*Bonus1,0)**

- Click [OK].

> You can also add the second IF function directly by editing it in the cell or formula bar.

Your worksheet should be similar to Figure 5-7.

FIGURE 5-7

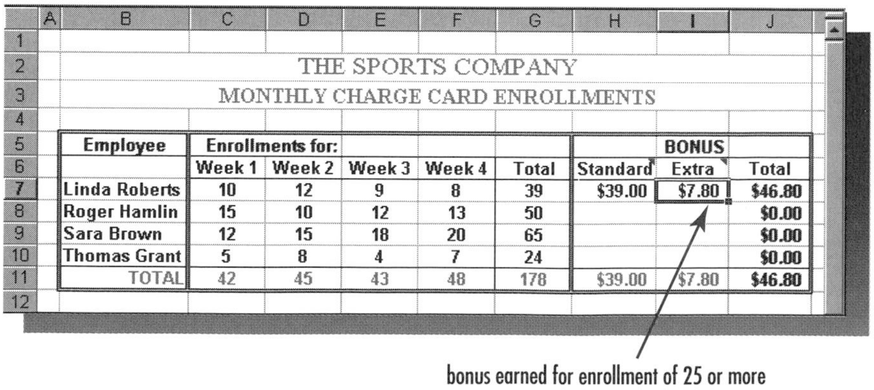

	A	B	C	D	E	F	G	H	I	J
1										
2				THE SPORTS COMPANY						
3				MONTHLY CHARGE CARD ENROLLMENTS						
4										
5		Employee	Enrollments for:						BONUS	
6			Week 1	Week 2	Week 3	Week 4	Total	Standard	Extra	Total
7		Linda Roberts	10	12	9	8	39	$39.00	$7.80	$46.80
8		Roger Hamlin	15	10	12	13	50			$0.00
9		Sara Brown	12	15	18	20	65			$0.00
10		Thomas Grant	5	8	4	7	24			$0.00
11		TOTAL	42	45	43	48	178	$39.00	$7.80	$46.80
12										

bonus earned for enrollment of 25 or more

The Extra bonus for Linda is now $7.80. The formula determined that the number in cell G7 was 25 or more and calculated a 20 percent bonus on the number in cell G7.

■ Copy the formulas in cells H7 and I7 to cells H8 through I10 to complete the columns.

■ Move to I8.

Your worksheet should be similar to Figure 5-8.

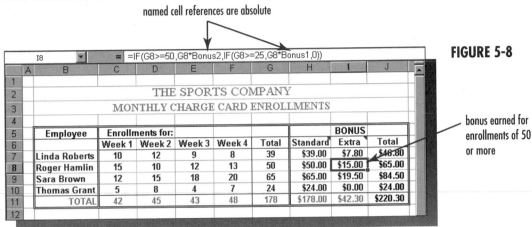

named cell references are absolute

FIGURE 5-8

bonus earned for enrollments of 50 or more

The cell names in the copied formula appear exactly as they did in the formula in cell I7. You did not need to change the names to absolute because named cell references can only be absolute.

The Extra bonus in cell I8 is $15.00. The function calculated the 30 percent bonus because the number in G8 is equal to 50. The bonus in cell I9 is $19.50 because the number in cell G9 is greater than 50. Finally, the function calculated the bonus of $0.00 in cell I10 because the number in cell G10 is less than 25. The IF function is operating correctly.

Adding Controls

Your manager really likes the layout of the form. One change that needs to be made, however, is to the bonus amount. During some months the bonus amount may be raised to $2.00 or $3.00. The formulas to calculate the bonus will need to be adjusted to use the other two bonus amounts during those months. You could create two additional forms that would each have a different bonus amount in cell C14. This would require that the correct form be used for that month's input based on the bonus award for that month. A simpler way to deal with this problem is to add a control element to the form.

Concept 3: Controls

Controls are graphic objects that are designed to automate the process of filling out the form. Controls include property settings that affect how they behave and work. The properties associated with many controls can be changed to customize the control for your own use. Examples of controls include text boxes, list buttons, scroll bars, and option buttons.

Check box   Combo box   List box   Option box

Using controls makes it easier to fill out a form and increases the accuracy of the information entered in it. This is because many of the controls can include a list of options from which the user selects.

Although controls are most effectively used in online forms, they can also be used in printed forms. For example, controls such as buttons and check boxes can be printed blank and then filled in by the user.

The Forms toolbar is used to add controls. The procedure is similar to adding a text box.

- Display the Forms toolbar.

- If necessary, move the toolbar to the right side of your screen.

- Display the Tooltips.

You will add a combo box control to the form. This control creates a text box and button that will display a drop-down list with the three bonus amounts as options that can be selected. Then the selected option is displayed in the combo text box, which can then be linked to cell C14 to be used in the computation of the bonus.

First you need to enter the three bonus amount values in a columnar range.

- In cells E15 through E17 enter the numbers **1**, **2** and **3**.

- Format the range to currency with two decimal places.

- Click 🔲 Combo Box.

- Move the mouse pointer into the worksheet and drag to create a combo box the approximate size of a single cell.

> The mouse pointer appears as a + to indicate you can drag to create the control.

Your screen should be similar to Figure 5-9.

FIGURE 5-9

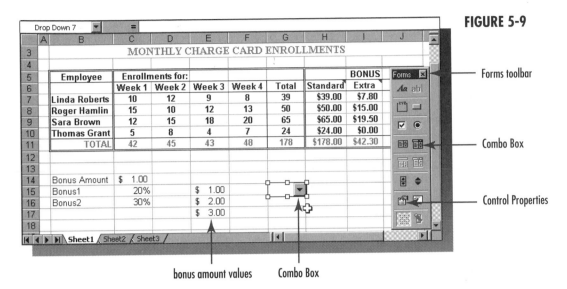

Forms toolbar

Combo Box

Control Properties

bonus amount values   Combo Box

The combo box is a selected object that can be sized or moved like any other object. Next, you need to specify the information to be displayed in the drop-down list and the location of the cell to link the selection to. Modifying the control's properties makes these changes.

> You can also select Format Control from the object's Shortcut menu to modify the properties.

- Click 🔲 Control Properties.

- If necessary, open the Control tab.

- Specify cells E15 through E17 as the Input Range.

- Specify cell C14 as the Cell Link.

- Click ▢ OK ▢ .

- Click outside the control to deselect it.

enter location of data to appear in drop-down list

enter location of cell to link selection to

Notice that the bonus amount in cell C14 is empty and the standard bonus formulas have been recalculated. This is because the combo box is blank. You need to select a bonus amount from the combo box drop-down list.

- Open the combo box drop-down list and select $2.00.

> The mouse pointer changes to a 🖑 when pointing to a control.

Your worksheet should be similar to Figure 5-10.

FIGURE 5-10

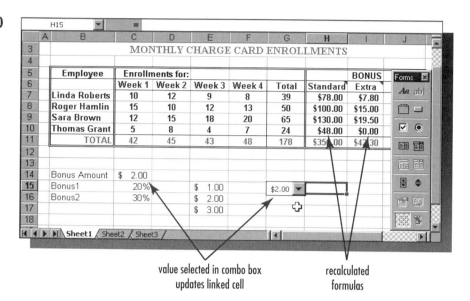

value selected in combo box
updates linked cell

recalculated
formulas

The standard bonus amount has been updated to reflect the selection in the combo box, and the formulas have been appropriately recalculated.

- Double right-click the control to select it and move it over cell C14.

- Close the Forms toolbar.

- Move to cell A1.

Improving the Appearance of the Form

Now that the text and formulas for the form are complete, the next step is to improve its appearance. A form usually takes advantage of border lines, white space, color, and shading to identify areas of the form. Some of this has already been completed. When improving the appearance of a form, a prime consideration should be simplicity. Although there are many format features that can be used, too many tend to complicate and confuse. This form will probably be used by the department managers to input the enrollment data. To make it easier for them to use, you want to remove any unnecessary information and screen distractions and to include instructions and procedures on how to use the form.

First you want to identify the area of the form where data will be entered by adding one fill background color to the entire form and another to the input area.

- Apply a light green fill color to cells B5 through J11.

- Apply a light yellow fill color to cells C7 through F10 and to cells E5 and F5.

- Move to cell A1.

Your worksheet should be similar to Figure 5-11.

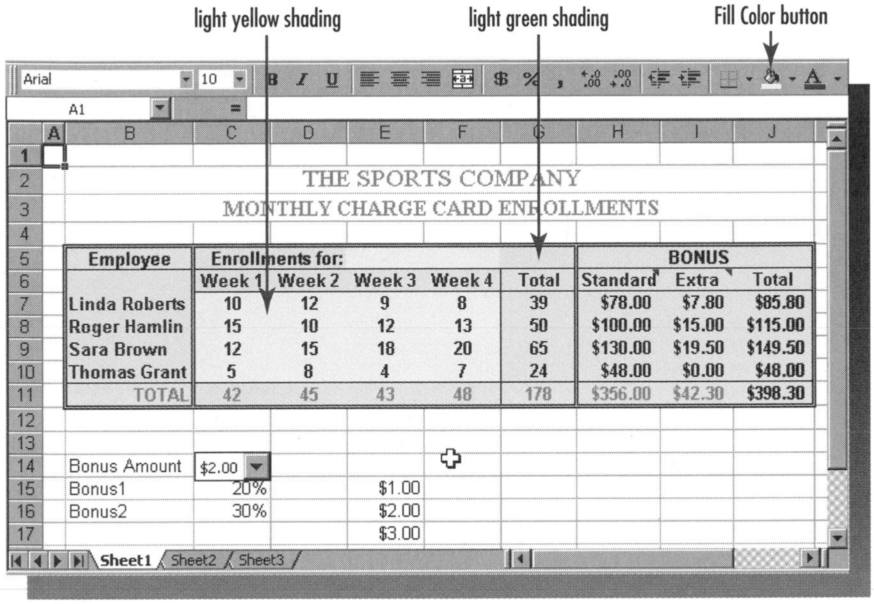

light yellow shading   light green shading   Fill Color button

FIGURE 5-11

Hiding Rows

Next you want to clean up the appearance of the form in the window by removing information that is not needed by the user. You do not want the Bonus1 and Bonus 2 labels and values or the combo box input range visible in the window. You could move them to another area of the sheet or to another sheet in the workbook. Instead you will simply hide the rows containing this information.

- Select rows 15 through 17.

- Choose F**o**rmat/**R**ow/**H**ide.

Your worksheet should be similar to Figure 5-12.

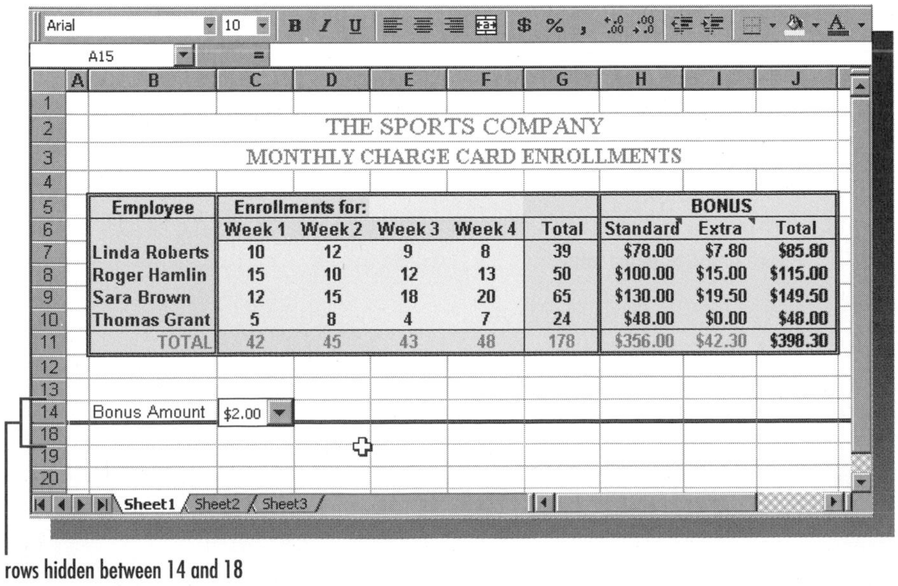

> Click the row number to select the entire row quickly.

> To redisplay hidden rows, select the row above and below the hidden rows and use F**o**rmat/**R**ow/**U**nhide.

rows hidden between 14 and 18

FIGURE 5-12

Hiding Window Elements

Now you will turn off the display of several other window elements to simplify the appearance of the online form.

■ Choose: <u>T</u>ools/<u>O</u>ptions/View.

The dialog box on your screen should be similar to Figure 5-13.

FIGURE 5-13

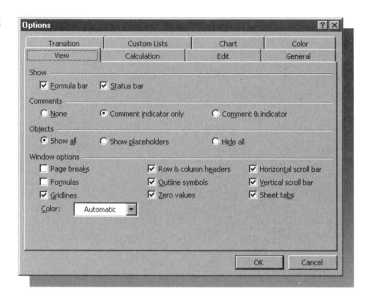

■ Clear the following settings: Formula bar, Status bar, Gridlines, Horizontal scroll bar, Vertical scroll bar, and Sheet tabs.

■ Click [OK].

■ Press [Ctrl] + [Home].

Although the screen is much simplified, it looks very plain. To define the edge of the form area, you will add an outline border around the form and a dark color of your choice around the entire edge of the form that is visible in the window space.

■ Add two additional blank rows above the title to better center the form in the window.

■ Add an outline border around cells B3 through J20.

■ Highlight the appropriate rows and columns on your screen and select a fill color of your choice to surround the form.

Your screen should be similar to Figure 5-14.

FIGURE 5-14

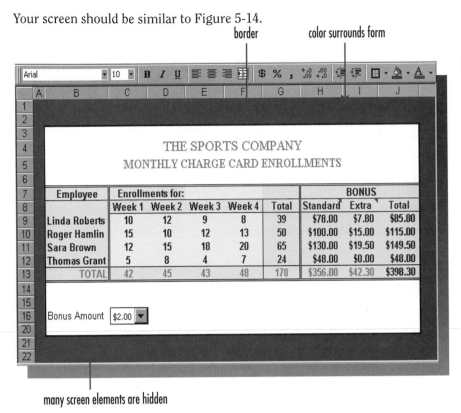

border — color surrounds form

many screen elements are hidden

Documenting a Form

Finally, it is good procedure when creating a form for others to use to include documentation within the form. The documentation should be brief and may include the following:

Purpose	Briefly describes what information is needed to complete the form and what output is generated from the form.
Instructions	Discusses the steps for completing the form.
Procedures	Explains how to move to different areas of the form, enter data, and how to name and save the form.

Some documentation needs to be entered in the form as text entries. Others can be entered as cell comments. Using cell comments is a good method of adding documentation that does not interfere with the appearance of the form. You will add one text entry and several cell comments that will provide the documentation for this form. To make it easier to see your location in the sheet, you will first turn on the display of the row and column headings again.

- In cell A1 enter the following text in white letters and bold: **For information on how to complete this form point to the red triangles.**

Since you will be inserting several cell comments next, you will display the Reviewing toolbar (shown at right) to make it easier to work with comments.

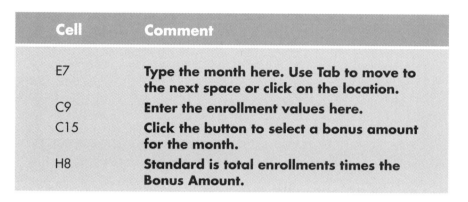

■ Display the Reviewing toolbar.

■ Using the appropriate Reviewing toolbar buttons, enter or edit the comments shown in the table below in the cells indicated.

■ Adjust the size of the comment boxes appropriately.

Cell	Comment
E7	Type the month here. Use Tab to move to the next space or click on the location.
C9	Enter the enrollment values here.
C15	Click the button to select a bonus amount for the month.
H8	Standard is total enrollments times the Bonus Amount.

To see all the comments at once to check them,

■ Click 🔲 Show All Comments.

Your screen should be similar to Figure 5-15.

FIGURE 5-15

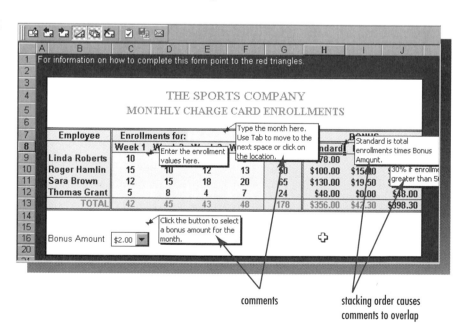

comments

stacking order causes comments to overlap

Comments are also graphic objects and may overlap each other.

- Move and resize the comments so they do not overlap.

- Edit any comments as needed.

- Click ⬚ Hide All Comments.

- Close the Reviewing toolbar.

Protecting a Worksheet

Now that the form is complete, you want to prevent changes to the worksheet that would cause headings and formulas in the worksheet to be altered or cleared. To do this, you can protect the worksheet.

Concept 4: Worksheet Protection

To prevent others from changing a sheet's contents, you can **protect** the entire worksheet or specified areas of the worksheet. When you protect a sheet, all cells and graphic objects on the sheet are locked. The contents of a **locked** cell cannot be changed. If you want to leave some cells unlocked for editing, such as in a worksheet you use as an entry form, you can lock cells containing labels and formulas but unlock the entry fields so that others can fill them in. This type of protection prevents you from entering or changing an entry in any locked cells.

An entire workbook can also be protected from unauthorized changes in two ways. The structure of a workbook can be protected so that sheets cannot be moved or deleted or new sheets inserted. A workbook's windows can also be protected. This prevents changes to the size and position of windows and ensures they appear the same way each time the workbook is opened.

In addition, you can include a **password** that prevents any unauthorized person from turning off protection and changing the worksheet. If you use a password, you must remember the password in order to turn protection off in the future.

Initially all cells in a worksheet are locked. However, you can enter data in the cells because the worksheet protection feature is not on. When protection is turned on, all locked cells are protected. Therefore, before protecting this sheet, you need to unlock the range of cells where the data will be entered.

- Select C9 through F12.

- Choose F_ormat/C_ells.

- Open the Protection tab in the Format Cells dialog box.

> Format Cells is also on the Shortcut menu.

The dialog box on your screen should be similar to Figure 5-16.

FIGURE 5-16

cells are locked
by default ————

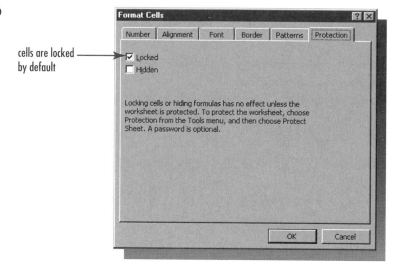

■ To allow changes to the selected range of cells, clear the Locked option box.

■ Click [OK].

Use the arrow keys to move to cell C16.

■ In a similar manner, unlock cell C16 where the selected Bonus Amount is entered.

Now you are ready to turn on worksheet protection. To prevent unauthorized users from removing the sheet protection, you will require a password. A password can be a maximum of 15 characters and can contain any combination of letters, numbers, and symbols. It is also case sensitive, so you must remember the exact combination of uppercase and lowercase letters you used in your password.

■ Choose **T**ools/**P**rotection/**P**rotect Sheet.

■ Type **secret**.

As you enter the password, asterisks are displayed in place of the characters you type to prevent anyone from seeing the password as it is entered.

■ Click [OK].

Next, you are asked to verify the password by reentering it.

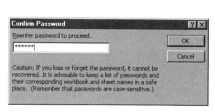

If the entry you type does not exactly match the original password entry, a warning appears. Click [OK] and try again.

■ Type **secret**.

■ Read the Caution in this box.

■ Click [OK].

Now all locked cells in the worksheet are protected. Any cells you unlocked prior to turning protection on can be changed. To show the effect of trying to enter data into a protected cell, you will try to enter the month in cell E7.

■ Move to cell E7 and type any character.

A warning dialog box is displayed, informing you that you cannot change entries in locked cells. To clear the message,

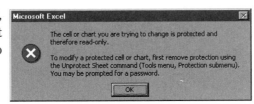

■ Click  OK .

You need to change this cell to unprotected so you can edit it to display the month. To do this, you first need to turn off worksheet protection and then unlock the cell and turn on protection again.

■ Choose <u>T</u>ools/<u>P</u>rotection/Un<u>p</u>rotect Sheet.

■ Type **secret**.

■ Click OK .

■ Choose F<u>o</u>rmat/C<u>e</u>lls.

■ Clear the Locked option in the Protection folder.

■ Click OK .

■ Choose <u>T</u>ools/<u>P</u>rotection/<u>P</u>rotect Sheet.

■ Enter and verify the password "secret."

■ To verify that cell E7 can now accept data, enter **October** in the cell.

Likewise you will be able to enter the data in cells C9 through F12 because they were unlocked before protecting the worksheet.

Creating a Template File

Each time you use this form, you will be entering data for a new month. Therefore, you want to clear the sample data from the form before saving it.

■ Clear the data in cell E7 and in cells C9 through F12.

■ Update the file's property summary information with the following documentation:

Title:	**Monthly Charge Card Enrollment**
Subject:	**Monthly report of charge card enrollments and employee bonuses.**
Author:	**[your name]**
Comments:	**Point to the red triangles for information on how to use this form. Enter the report month in cell E7. Enter the enrollment values in cells C9 through F12. Use the print button to print the form. Save the workbook as XXX Bonus, replacing XXX with the month.**

You also want to specify the area to print and to add a header to the printed output before saving the form. Then these settings will be saved with the workbook also.

When the form is printed, you only want the information in cells B4 through J20 to print. To specify this range as the area to print,

> **The dotted line surrounding the form identifies the print area.**

■ Select B3 through J20.

■ Choose: <u>F</u>ile/Prin<u>t</u> Area/<u>S</u>et Print Area.

■ Preview the workbook.

■ Add a header to the worksheet that displays your name and date only.

■ If you have a black-and-white printer and do not want the colored areas of your form to print in shades of gray, select Black and White from the Sheet tab of the Page Setup dialog box.

■ Center the form horizontally on the page.

Your screen should be similar to Figure 5-17.

header   preview of form

FIGURE 5-17

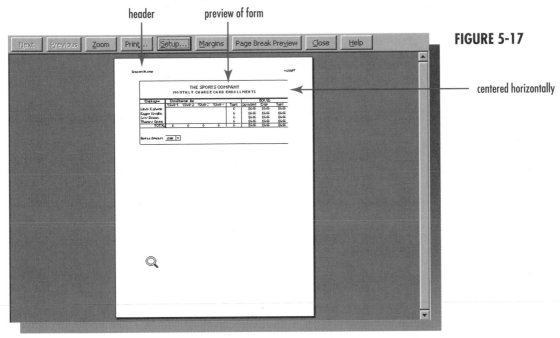

centered horizontally

- Print the form.

- To hide the dotted lines showing the print area, use Tools/Options to turn off the display of page breaks.

- Move to E7.

Because this information will be entered in a different workbook file for each month's data, you will save it as a workbook template.

Concept 5: Workbook Template

A workbook **template** is a workbook file that contains predesigned sheets that can be used as a pattern for creating other similar sheets in new workbooks. Templates are useful in any application where input and output are required using the same format. The template saves the user time by not having to redesign the same worksheet form each time the report is needed. The original design can be used repeatedly by saving the workbook containing the data using a different file name than the file name used to save the workbook template.

Excel saves a workbook template using a special file format with the file extension .xlt. Workbook templates are also stored in a special Templates folder. To use a workbook template, you select the template file name from the General tab of the New File dialog box. When you save the workbook after entering data in the template, Excel automatically displays the Save As dialog box so you can specify the new file name. It also changes the file type to an Excel workbook file (.xls). This ensures that you do not save over the template file unintentionally.

- Choose File/Save As.

- Enter the new file name, **Bonus Form**, in the File Name text box.

- Open the Save As Type list box.

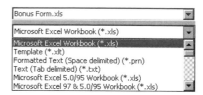

To set the file format to template, you need to specify the type of file from the Save As Type drop-down list box. Your selection from this list determines the way information in a document is stored in a file. Many of the file formats make it easier to use Excel documents with other applications. You need to save the workbook as an Excel template file.

- Select Template.

Notice that the Save In box now displays the Templates folder as the location where the file will be saved.

> If you are prompted to replace a file with the same file name, select Yes.

- Click [Save].

- Close the Bonus Form template file.

Now you want to create a new workbook file to record the enrollment data for the month of November using the Bonus Form template.

- Choose File/New.

- If necessary, display the General tab of the New dialog box.

> If you save a workbook template to a location other than the Templates folder, the file icon will not appear in the General tab.

The Bonus Form template file appears in the General tab as an icon.

- Select [Bonus Form.xlt icon].

- Click [OK].

The workbook template is opened and appears just as it did when you saved it.

- Enter **November** as the month.

> Use Tab to quickly move from one unlocked cell to another.

- Then enter the following data for each salesperson:

	Week 1	Week 2	Week 3	Week 4
Linda Roberts	23	15	22	20
Roger Hamlin	12	11	10	13
Sara Brown	14	12	10	10
Thomas Grant	18	25	18	14

■ Select $3.00 as the Bonus Amount.

When you are done, your screen should be similar to Figure 5-18.

FIGURE 5-18

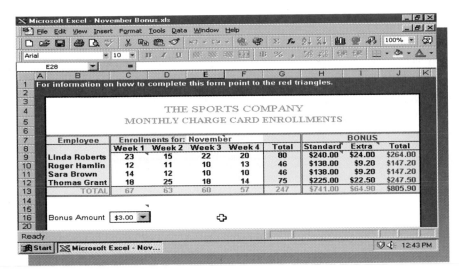

Now you are ready to save the workbook. You want to use a file name that reflects the month the data represents.

Click 💾 Save.

The Save As dialog box is displayed whenever you use a template file. This prevents you from accidentally overwriting the template file with the changes you have made. Excel proposes a file name of Bonus Form1. Notice that the Save As Type text box automatically displays "Microsoft Excel Workbook [*.xls]" as the type of file. Again, this prevents you from accidentally creating another template file.

■ Specify the drive containing your data disk as the location to save the file.

■ Change the proposed file name to **November Bonus**.

■ Click Save.

■ Close the November Bonus file.

■ Use the View menu to turn on the display of the formula bar and status bar again.

■ Exit Excel.

LAB REVIEW

■ ■ ■ ■ ■ ■ ■ ■ ■ ■

Key Terms

control (SS180)   password (SS187)
form (SS171)   protect (SS187)
lock (SS187)   range name (SS173)
logical operator (SS176)   template (SS191)
nested function (SS178)

Command Summary

Command	Action
File/Save As/Save As Type	Sets file format for document
File/Print Area/Set print area	Sets a range as area to print
Edit/Delete Sheet	Removes sheet from workbook
Insert/Name/Define	Assigns a name you specify to a cell or range of cells
Insert/Name/Paste	Places name in formula bar or lists names in worksheet
Insert/Name/Create	Creates range name using text in cells
Format/Cells/Protection	Changes protection of selected cells to locked or unlocked
Format/Row/Hide	Hides selected rows in worksheet
Tools/Protection/Protect Sheet	Turns on protection for all locked cells
Tools/Protection/Unprotect Sheet	Turns off protection for all locked cells
Tools/Options/View	Turns on/off display of window elements

Matching

1. template   _____   a. information supplied to a function for calculation
2. <   _____   b. workbook that contains predesigned sheets to be used as patterns
3. IF   _____   c. keeps worksheet data from being altered
4. protection   _____   d. logical operator
5. arguments   _____   e. evaluates condition and takes one of two actions
6. nested function _____   f. function within another function

Fill-In Questions

1. Complete the following statements by filling in the blanks with the correct terms.

a. _____ are used in formulas and functions that compare values in two or more cells.

b. A(n) _____ is a workbook that contains predesigned sheets.

c. A range _____ can consist of any combination of 255 characters.

d. The _____ feature is used to keep parts of the worksheet from being accidentally altered or erased.

e. _____ is important when creating a template so that others will know how the worksheet functions.

Discussion Questions

1. Discuss range names and when it is appropriate to use them. Give some examples.

2. What are logical operators used for? Describe five logical operators and give examples of their use.

3. Discuss why you would want to save a workbook as a template and give several examples of where a template would be useful. Why would you want to protect the cells of a template?

Hands-On Practice Exercises

■ ■ ■ ■ ■ ■ ■ ■ ■ ■ ■ ■ ■

Step by Step

Rating System		
☆	Easy
☆☆	Moderate
☆☆☆	Difficult

1. To complete this problem, you must have completed Practice Exercises 6 and 8 in Lab 3.

a. Open the workbook files Earnings Statement and Time Sheets (in that order) from your data disk. Close both files without saving. Now, open the same files in the reverse order (Time Sheets first). Is there a difference between the two procedures? What might that be? In this exercise you will use an IF function to calculate Regular Hours on the time sheet, and you will protect the worksheets.

b. In the Time Sheets file rename the sheet tabs Week 1 and Week 2 so they will apply to any biweekly period.

c. The Regular Hours column will be calculated by a formula, so all you have to do is enter the Total Hours, and the remaining columns will be calculated for you. Enter an IF function in the cell that displays Monday's Regular Hours in the Week 1 sheet. The IF function will determine if Monday's Total Hours are greater than or equal to 8 and will enter the number 8, otherwise it will enter Monday's Total Hours. What was the function you used?

d. Copy the IF function down the column and to the corresponding cells in column C of the Week 2 sheet. What was the function you used?

e. Unlock the Total Hours and cells that display the "Week of" information on both sheets. Protect both sheets.

f. In the Earnings Statement file notice that the formula in B7 has adjusted so that it now refers to the Biweekly Total in the Week 2 sheet of the Time Sheets file. Erase and unlock the period-ending date and protect the worksheet.

g. In the Time Sheets file, erase the starting dates and total hours from both sheets. Update the documentation and save the file.

h. In the Earnings Statement file notice the hours are zero, and the statutory deductions are blank. The only values displayed are the rate and the fixed voluntary deductions. Document the worksheet and save the file.

i. Enter new starting dates and total hours of your choosing in both worksheets of the Time Sheets file. Save the file as Current Time Sheet and print the worksheets.

j. In the Earnings Statement file notice that the hours have changed, and the file is linked to the Current Time Sheet file. Modify the period-ending date appropriately. Save the file as Current Earnings Statement and print the worksheet.

From now on, if you remember to save the original files with new names when the variable information changes, you can use the originals over and over again. Using templates with linked files is difficult because the dependent worksheet is always looking for the original source template (.xlt file), and you must redefine the link to the temporary copy that the template has loaded.

2. To complete this problem, you must have completed Practice Exercise 4 in Lab 2. Open the workbook file Invoice on your data disk. In this exercise you will continue to modify the worksheet.

   a. Draw an outline border around the invoice number and date information. Add color to the text and background. Remove the underlines from the column headings and replace them with a bottom border. Enhance the appearance of the worksheet by adding lines and/or color in other locations.

   b. A 15 percent discount is given to customers who purchase more than 12 items. Insert a column after the Price column and enter the column heading Discount. In the cell below the heading, enter an IF function that will calculate a 15 percent discount if the quantity for Pentium Computers exceeds 12. Otherwise the cell will display zero. Copy the function down the column. Note: When this formula is copied, cells with a zero in them will display "$-" or "-" if the cells are formatted with the Currency or Comma format.

   c. Modify the formula in the Total column so the total will be calculated as Quantity times the difference between the Price and the Discount. Copy the new Total formula down the column.

   d. Save and replace the workbook file Invoice. Print the workbook.

   e. You want to use this invoice over again. Erase and unlock the entries in the Qty, Description, and Price columns. Erase and unlock the invoice number and the date. Erase and unlock the cells that contain the customer's name and address. Protect the worksheet.

   f. Update the documentation. Save the workbook as a template file named Invoice Template. If necessary,

respond yes to the prompt to replace existing file. Close the template file.

   g. Use the template to enter the following information:

Heading	Entry
Invoice #	**12345**
Date	**current date**
Customer	**your name and address**
Qty	**20**
Description	**Highlighters**
Price	**.99**

   h. Unprotect the worksheet and delete the blank rows above the Subtotal. Delete your address information at the top of the worksheet.

   i. Save the file as an Excel workbook file named My Invoice. Print the worksheet.

On Your Own

3. In this lab you learned to create templates that can be the basis of future workbooks. Excel comes with several workbook templates called Spreadsheet Solutions. Included are an invoice, a loan manager, and a purchase order.

To access the Excel templates, open the Spreadsheet Solutions tab of the New dialog box. The invoice and loan manager operate in much the same way as the templates you created. The purchase order is very similar to the invoice. Select one of these templates.

Once the template you selected is loaded, click the Customize sheet tab once. You can now enter personalized information such as the name of the company, your tax rate, and so on in the form. Add information to complete the template. If you use the invoice or purchase order, you can enter information from the invoice exercise (Practice Exercise 2). If you need help, each template displays a toolbar that contains a Help button.

Note: Once you have customized your template and have returned to the worksheet, the Customize tab will no longer be displayed. However, you can click the Customize button in the upper right corner if you need to return. Update the summary properties for the workbook. Save the file and print the worksheet.

4. Colin Call enjoys keeping track of game statistics for his favorite baseball team. If necessary, refer to your local paper for baseball game statistics. Use the concepts presented in the lab to create a template to keep track of a baseball team.

Your template should contain the team name as a heading, the opponent, and date played. Create a drop-down button that contains all the teams in your team's league. The body of the template should contain the names of the players, number of at bats (AB), runs scored (R), hits (H), runs batted in (RBI), base on balls (BB), and strike outs (SO). Total the columns to produce team statistics.

Protect the appropriate parts of your template. Save the template using the team name. Close the template. Open the template and enter statistics for a game. Print and save the worksheet.

5. Use the concepts presented in the lab to create a template to keep track of your monthly expenses. Format the worksheet appropriately and protect it. Include your name and the date in a header. Print and save the blank template. Use the template to add data for the current month. Save and print the worksheet containing your monthly expenses.

Concept Summary

Creating a Form Template

Range Name

Adding a descriptive range name to a cell or range of cells makes formulas easier to read and understand.

IF Function

The IF function checks to see if certain conditions are met and then takes action based upon the results of the check.

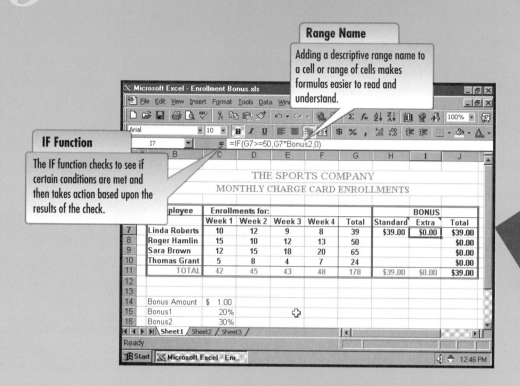

Controls

Controls are graphic objects that are designed to automate the process of filling out the form. Controls include property settings that affect how they behave and work.

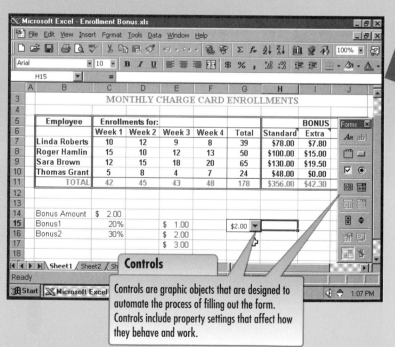

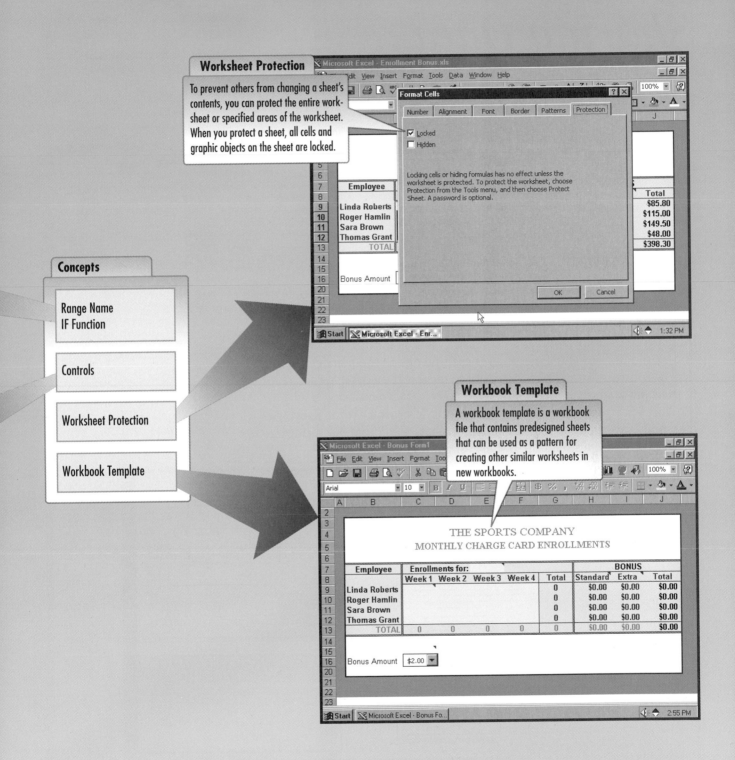

Concepts

Range Name
IF Function

Controls

Worksheet Protection

Workbook Template

Worksheet Protection

To prevent others from changing a sheet's contents, you can protect the entire worksheet or specified areas of the worksheet. When you protect a sheet, all cells and graphic objects on the sheet are locked.

Workbook Template

A workbook template is a workbook file that contains predesigned sheets that can be used as a pattern for creating other similar worksheets in new workbooks.

Sharing Data Between Applications

COMPETENCIES

After completing this lab, you will know how to:

1. Copy between applications.
2. Link objects.
3. Embed objects.
4. Update linked and embedded objects.
5. Decide when to use linking or embedding.

CASE STUDY

Your analysis of sales data for the past four years has shown a steady increase in total sales. However, the analysis of sales in four main categories of sporting goods has shown that sales in fitness and camping are increasing, sales in tennis are decreasing, and golf sales remain steady. You would like to send a memo of these findings to the manager of The Sports Company. In addition, you want to include the worksheet and chart of the sales analysis in the memo.

You have probably noticed while using Microsoft Word, Excel, Access, and PowerPoint that the applications have a common user interface such as similar commands and menu structures. In addition to these obvious features, they have been designed to work together, making it easy to share and exchange information between applications.

Note: This lab assumes that you have completed Lab 2 of Word and Lab 4 of Excel. You will need the data file Sales Charts you created in Lab 4 of Excel.

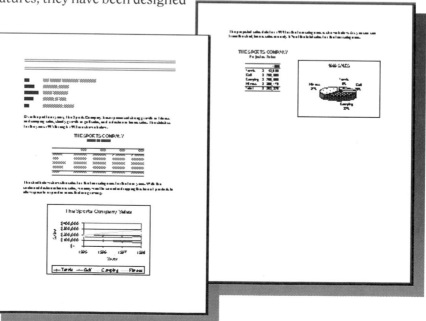

Concept Overview

The following concepts will be introduced in this lab:

1. Copy Between Applications   Information can be copied between applications and, if possible, inserted in the document in a format the document can edit.

2. Linked Object   Information that is copied from one file to another as a linked object maintains a connection between the two files, allowing the linked object to automatically update when the source file changes.

3. Embedded Object   Information that is copied as an embedded object to a file created by a different application becomes part of the file and can be updated using the server application from within the document in which it is inserted.

Copying Between Applications

The memo to the manager about the analysis of the sales data has already been created using Word 97. However, you still need to add the Excel worksheet data and charts to the memo.

- Start Word and open the file Sales Analysis Memo on your data disk.

- In the memo header, replace the Student Name with your name and the Professor's Name with your instructor's name.

- Scroll the window to view the three paragraphs in the body of the memo.

Your screen should be similar to Figure 6-1.

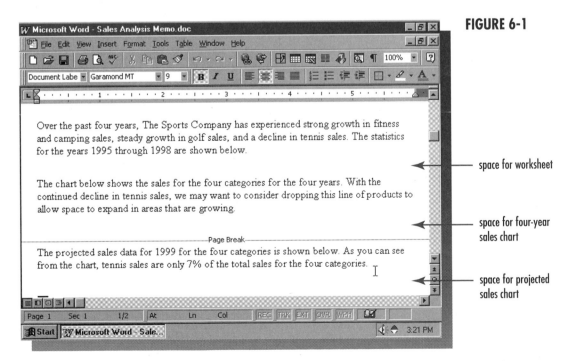

FIGURE 6-1

space for worksheet

space for four-year sales chart

space for projected sales chart

You will insert the data from the Sales sheet of the Sales Charts workbook below the first paragraph. Below the second paragraph, you will display a chart of The Sports Company sales. The second page of the memo will display a chart of the projected sales data for 1999 below the paragraph.

Now you are ready to insert the information from the Excel workbook file into the Word memo.

- ■ Load Excel and open the workbook file Sales Charts on your data disk.

- ■ If necessary, move the cell selector to cell A1 of the Sales sheet.

Your screen should be similar to Figure 6-2.

FIGURE 6-2

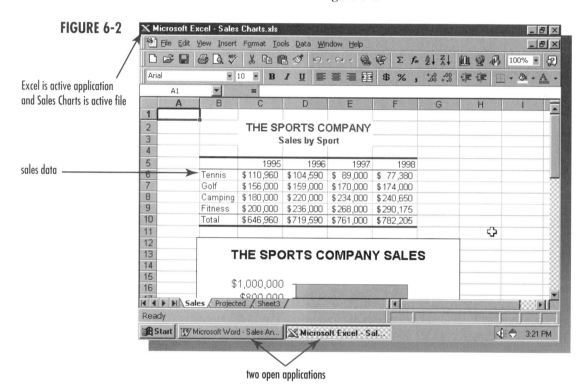

Excel is active application and Sales Charts is active file

sales data

two open applications

There are now two open applications, Word and Excel. Word is open in a window behind the Excel application window. Both application buttons are displayed in the taskbar. There are also two open files, Sales Charts in Excel and Sales Analysis Memo in Word. Excel is the active application, and Sales Charts is the active file.

First you will copy the worksheet data in the Sales sheet and paste it into the Word memo.

Concept 1: Copy Between Applications

While using the Excel application, you have learned how to use cut, copy, and paste to move or copy information within the same document and between documents in the same application. You can also perform these same operations between applications. For example, you can copy information from a Word document and paste it into an Excel worksheet. The information is pasted in a format that the application can edit, if possible.

- Select and copy the contents of cells B2 through F10.

- Click [W Microsoft Word - Sales An...] in the taskbar.

- Move to the second blank line below the first paragraph of the memo.

- Paste the contents of the Clipboard into the memo.

Your screen should be similar to Figure 6-3.

> If both program windows are displayed on the screen, you can drag data between applications using the right mouse button. Then select Move Here or Copy Here from the Shortcut menu.

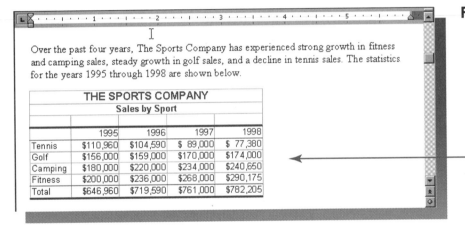

FIGURE 6-3

Excel worksheet inserted into Word document as a table

The worksheet data has been copied into the Word document as a table that can be edited and manipulated within Word. Much of the formatting associated with the copied information is also pasted into the document. However, you think the memo would look better if the table was centered between the margins.

- Select the entire table.

- Click [≡] Center.

- Clear the selection.

> To select the table, drag or use **T**able/ Select T**a**ble.

Linking an Object to Another Application

Next you want to display the area chart of sales trends for the four categories below the second paragraph in the memo.

> Click on the chart to select it.

- Switch to the Excel application and select the area chart.

- Copy the selected chart object to the Clipboard.

- Switch to the Word application and move to the second blank line below the second paragraph of the memo.

You will insert the chart object into the memo as a linked object.

Concept 2: Linked Object

Information created in one application can also be inserted as a **linked object** into a document created by another application. When an object is linked, the data is stored in the **source file** (the document it was created in). A graphic representation or picture of the data is displayed in the **destination file** (the document in which the object is inserted). A connection between the information in the destination file to the source file is established by the creation of a link. The link contains references to the location of the source file and the selection within the document that is linked to the destination file.

When changes are made in the source file that affect the linked object, the changes are automatically reflected in the destination file when it is opened. This is called a **live link**. When you create linked objects, the date and time on your machine should be accurate. This is because the program refers to the date of the source file to determine whether updates are needed when you open the destination file.

By making the chart a linked object, it will be automatically updated if the source file is edited. To create a linked object,

> To link an entire file, use **I**nsert/**O**bject.

- Choose **E**dit/Paste **S**pecial.

- Select Paste **L**ink.

The Paste Special dialog box on your screen should be similar to Figure 6-4.

type of object stored in Clipboard

FIGURE 6-4

creates a linked object

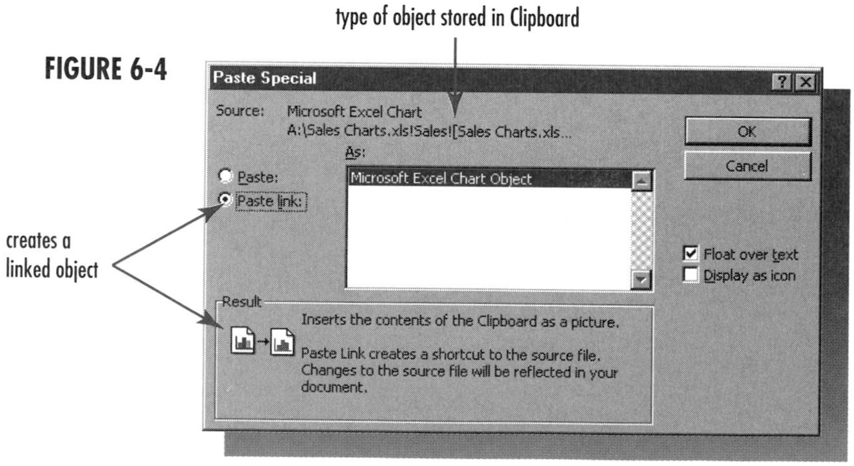

The Source area displays the type of object contained in the Clipboard and its location. From the As list box you select the type of format in which you want the object inserted into the destination file. The only available option for this object is as a Microsoft Excel Chart Object. The Result area describes the effect of your selections. In this case, the object will be inserted as a picture and a link will be created to the chart in the source file.

The last two options in this dialog box allow you to control how the object is inserted and displayed. Float Over Text adds the object to the drawing layer. It can then be positioned anywhere in the document and manipulated using the Draw menu. If this option is cleared, the object is inserted in-line where it behaves like regular text. Selecting the Display as Icon option changes the display of the object from a picture to an icon. Double-clicking the icon displays the object picture. The default selection for both options is appropriate.

■ Click [OK].

Word changes to Page Layout view and displays the picture of the area chart.

■ Set the Zoom to 50%.

■ Scroll the window so you can see both the worksheet and the chart on the page.

Your screen should be similar to Figure 6-5.

> If both program windows are displayed on the screen, you can drag data between applications using the right mouse button. Then select Insert Object Here from the Shortcut menu to create a linked object.

FIGURE 6-5

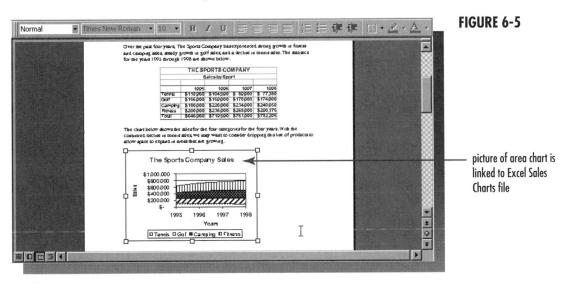

picture of area chart is linked to Excel Sales Charts file

The chart object is displayed at the location of the insertion point aligned with the left margin. The object has been scaled to fit in the document.

■ Move the chart object so it is centered horizontally on the page.

Updating a Linked Object

While reading the text and looking at the chart, you decide to change the chart type from an area chart to a line chart. You feel a line chart will show the sales trends more clearly. To change the type of chart, you need to switch back to Excel. Double-clicking on a linked object quickly switches to the open source file. If the source file is not open, it opens the file for you. If the application is not loaded, it will both load the application and open the source file.

■   Double-click the chart object.

■   Click [📈 ▼] Chart Type.

■   Click [📉] Line.

■   Adjust the placement of the text box and arrows.

You will also make another change while in Excel. You will change data in the worksheet to verify that the worksheet data that is pasted into the memo is not linked to Excel.

■   Edit the value in cell F6 to 177380.

■   View the line chart to verify that the chart was automatically updated to reflect this change in data.

■   To see the changes made in the memo, switch to Word.

Your screen should be similar to Figure 6-6.

FIGURE 6-6

inserted worksheet ——

linked chart ——

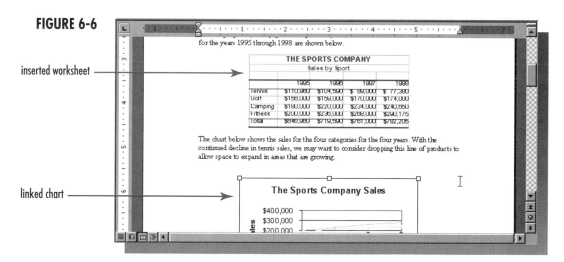

The chart in the memo reflects the change in both chart type and the change in data for the tennis sales. This is because any changes you make in the chart in Excel will be automatically reflected in the linked chart in the Word document.

Because the table is not a linked object, it does not reflect the change in data made in Excel. However, normally you would want to link both the worksheet and the related chart so both would reflect the changes made to the data.

Whenever a document is opened that contains links, the application looks for the source file and automatically updates the linked objects. If there are many links, updating can take a lot of time. Additionally, if you move the source file to another location, or perform other operations that may interfere with the link, your link will not work. To help with situations like these, you can edit the settings associated with links. To see how you do this,

■   Choose E̲dit/Lin̲ks.

The dialog box on your screen should be similar to Figure 6-7.

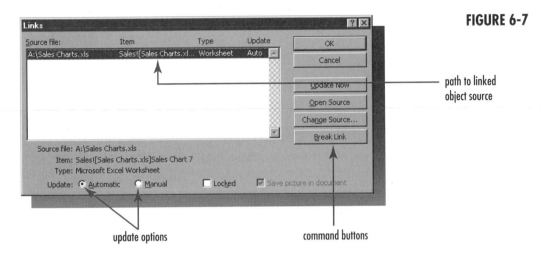

FIGURE 6-7

path to linked object source

update options   command buttons

The Links dialog box displays the object path for all links in the document in the list box. The field code specifies the path and name of the source file, the range of linked cells or object name, the type of file, and the update status. Below the list box the details for the selected link are displayed. The two update option buttons, Automatic and Manual, are used to change how the object is updated. The default option, Automatic, updates the linked object whenever the destination document is opened or the source file changes. If you change to Manual, the destination document is not automatically updated and you must use the Update Now command button to update the link. The Open Source command button will open the source document for the selected link, and the Change Source button allows you to modify the path to the source document.

To return to Excel and change the value in cell F6 back to its original value,

Because the workbook and Excel application were already open, using the Open Source command button simply switched to the application window.

- ■ Click Open Source .

- ■ Change the value in cell F6 back to 77380.

- ■ Switch to Word and view the chart object to verify that it updated automatically and reflects the change in data.

- ■ Return the zoom to Page Width.

Embedding an Object in Another Application

On the second page of the memo, you want to show the projected sales data for 1999 and the pie chart.

- ■ Move to the second blank line immediately below the paragraph on the second page of the memo.

- ■ Switch to Excel and make the Projected sheet active.

- ■ Copy the range A1 through I20.

- ■ Switch to Word.

This time you will embed this selection in the memo.

Concept 3: Embedded Object

Information can also be inserted into another application document as an embedded object. An object that is embedded is stored in the destination file and becomes part of the document. The entire file, not just the selection that is displayed in the destination file, becomes part of the document. This makes a document containing an embedded object much larger than a document containing the same object using linking.

If the user has access to the application that created the embedded document, called the **server**, the embedded object can be edited or updated from within the destination document. The connection to the server is established through the use of a field code that identifies the server associated with the object. Double-clicking on an embedded object starts the server application within the destination document. Any changes you make to the embedded object are not reflected in the original source file, however.

Object Linking and Embedding, or **OLE**, is the program-integration technology that makes it possible to share data between applications. All Office 97 programs support OLE.

A document that contains a linked or embedded object is called a **container file** or **compound document**.

To embed an entire file use Insert/ Object.

- ■ Choose Edit/Paste Special.

The dialog box on your screen should be similar to Figure 6-8.

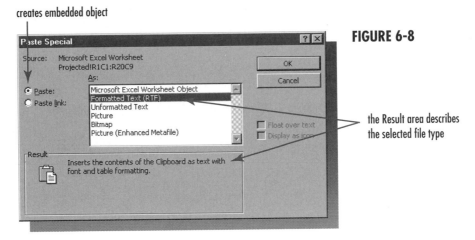

FIGURE 6-8

creates embedded object

the Result area describes the selected file type

The Paste option creates an embedded object. This is the preselected option. The As list box displays six file format types that can be used to embed the object. To embed the contents of the Clipboard into a document so it can be edited using the server application, select the option that displays the server name.

■ Select Microsoft Excel Worksheet Object.

■ Click [OK].

Your screen should be similar to Figure 6-9.

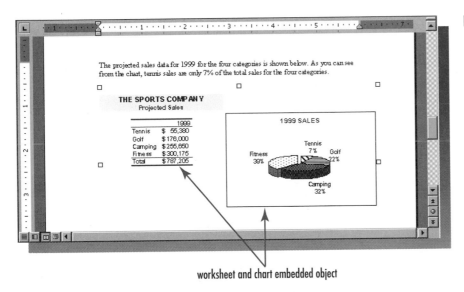

FIGURE 6-9

worksheet and chart embedded object

The entire worksheet selection including the chart is displayed in the memo at the location of the insertion point. When an object is embedded, the entire selection is pasted and displayed in the destination document as a single object.

If you linked this selection, only the worksheet data would appear and be linked in the destination. The chart would not be included in the link. To link the chart, you would need to select the chart object separately and establish a separate link and a separate object.

Updating an Embedded Object

To demonstrate how an embedded object works, you will close the source file and application and edit the worksheet from within the Word document.

- Switch to Excel and move to cell A1 in both sheets.

- Save the workbook file as 1995-1999 Sales Charts.

- Exit the program. If Excel asks if you want to save the Clipboard contents to a file, choose No.

The server application is used to edit data in an embedded object. To open the server, simply double-click on the embedded object.

- Double-click the embedded object.

Your screen should be similar to Figure 6-10.

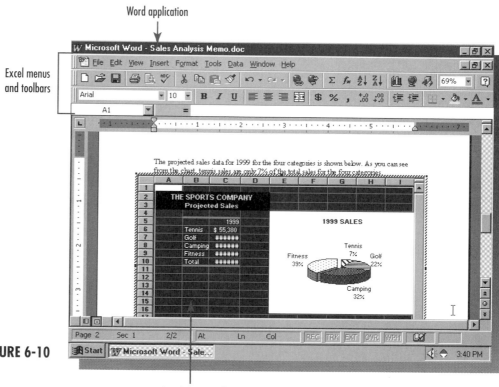

FIGURE 6-10

The server application, in this case Excel, is opened. The Excel menus and toolbars replace some of the menus and toolbars in the Word application window. The selected embedded object is displayed in an editing worksheet window. Now you can use the server commands to edit the object.

■ If necessary, expand the column width of column C to fully display the values.

■ Reduce the tennis projection value to 48,000 and increase the golf projection to 200,000.

The chart is updated to reflect the change in data. The new projection has decreased the tennis percentage to 6 percent and increased golf to 25 percent. The original Excel file, 1995–1999 Sales Charts, has not been affected by these changes.

■ After editing is complete, close the server application by clicking anywhere outside the object.

The embedded object in the memo is updated to reflect the changes you made. It now also displays gridlines. To turn off the display of the cell gridlines,

■ Open the server application.

■ Choose **T**ools/**O**ptions/View/**G**ridlines/ OK .

■ Close the Server application.

■ Edit the lead-in sentence in the memo to reflect the new tennis value (6%).

■ Save the memo as 1995-1999 Sales Analysis.

■ Preview both pages of the memo in the Preview screen.

Your screen should be similar to Figure 6-11.

> Use the ⊞ Multiple Pages button to view both pages of the document.

FIGURE 6-11

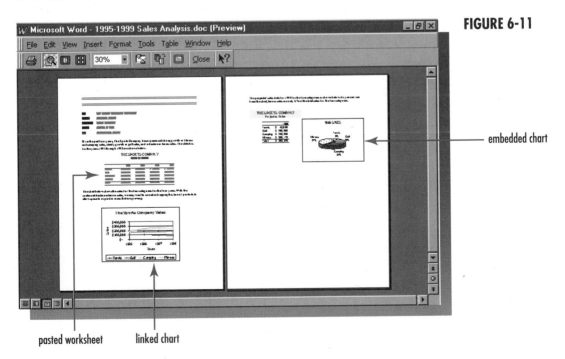

embedded chart

pasted worksheet   linked chart

■   Print the memo.

Note: Do not set the printer to draft quality. If you do, the charts will not print.

■   Exit Word.

Deciding When to Link or Embed Objects

Most documents would not include both linked and embedded objects. This is because the reasons for using each are different.

Use linking when:	Use embedding when:
File size is important	File size is not important
Users have access to the source file and application	Users have access to the application but not to the source file
The information is updated frequently	The data changes infrequently

LAB REVIEW

■ ■ ■ ■ ■ ■ ■ ■ ■ ■

Key Terms

compound document   (SS208)
container file   (SS208)
destination file   (SS204)
linked object (SS204)
live link   (SS204)
Object Linking and Embedding (OLE)   (SS208)
server   (SS208)
source file   (SS204)

Command Summary

Command	Action
Edit/Paste **S**pecial/Paste **L**ink	Links a selection
Edit/Linked Worksheet **O**bject/**E**dit Link	Allows you to modify path for a link
Edit/Paste **S**pecial/Paste	Embeds a selection
Edit/Lin**k**s	Edits settings associated with a link

Matching

1. destination file	_____	**a.**	a link that automatically updates when the document is opened
2. live link	_____	**b.**	file in which object is inserted
3. source file	_____	**c.**	application that created embedded document
4. server	_____	**d.**	the document in which the linked or embedded object was created
5. OLE	_____	**e.**	the program integration technology that makes linking and embedding possible

Discussion Questions

1. Describe how a linked object is created and edited.
2. Describe how an embedded object is created and edited.
3. Explain when you would use linking rather than embedding.

Hands-On Practice Exercises

■ ■ ■ ■ ■ ■ ■ ■ ■ ■

Step by Step

Rating System ☆ Easy
☆☆ Moderate
☆☆☆ Difficult

1. Karen works for a large hotel chain in the marketing department. She has recently researched hotel occupancy rates for the Phoenix area and has created a worksheet and stacked-column chart of the data. Now Karen wants to send a memo containing the chart to her supervisor.

a. Open a new Word document using the Professional template.

b. Delete the Company Name Here text box. In the header, replace the placeholder information in brackets with the following:

TO:	**Brad Wise**
FROM:	**Karen Howard**
CC:	**[your name]**
RE:	**Hotel Occupancy**

c. Replace the body placeholder text with the following:

Below is a column chart showing the percent of hotel occupancy rates in the Phoenix area for the years 1994 to 1999.

d. Enter two blank lines below the paragraph.

e. Load Excel and open the workbook file Hotel. Link the stacked-column chart to below the paragraph in the Word memo. Center the chart in the memo.

f. Change the stacked-column chart to a side-by-side column chart.

g. You would like to add another sentence to the memo. Enter the following sentence below the chart:

The chart shows that the resort occupancy rate is consistently slightly higher than the overall occupancy rate.

h. Save the Word document as Hotel Occupancy. Preview and print the document. Resave the Excel file.

SPREADSHEET

2. Sean Rees has a summer internship with a local car dealership. He has researched changes in new and used car prices and created a worksheet and line chart of the data. Now Sean wants to send a memo containing the worksheet and chart to his supervisor.

a. Open a new Word document using the Contemporary Memo template. Select and remove the faint gray circle element below and to the left of the How to Use the Memo Template information.

b. Replace the placeholder information in the memo heading with the following information:

TO:	**Supervisor**
CC:	**[your name]**
FROM:	**Sean Rees**
DATE:	**[current date]**
RE:	**Changes in Car Prices**

c. Replace the body placeholder text with the following two paragraphs. Separate the paragraphs with two blank lines.

Below is the data you requested showing the percent change in new vs used car prices. I have embedded the Excel worksheet in this Word document file so you can make changes to it if necessary.

d. Enter two blank lines below the last paragraph.

e. Load Excel and open the workbook file Car Analysis. Below the first paragraph of the Word memo, embed the worksheet and line chart from the workbook Car Analysis. Add a border around the entire embedded object. If necessary, adjust the placement of the object so it appears centered under the paragraph.

f. Exit Excel. Do not resave the workbook.

g. The supervisor wants to change the chart to a column chart. Change the embedded line chart to a column chart.

h. Using Word add a text box and arrow identifying the increasing car sales.

i. Save the Word document as New and Used Car Comparison. Preview and print the document.

3. After completing the first and second half budget for The Sports Company, you want to give the manager the Excel file. You would like to include a memo on a separate sheet of this file to briefly explain the worksheet contents.

a. Open the workbook file 1999 Budget that you created at the end of Lab 3. Insert a new sheet before the Annual sheet and change the sheet tab name to Memo.

b. Open Word and create the following memo to the store manager.

TO:	**Sports Company Store Manager**
FROM:	**[your name]**
DATE:	**[current date]**

The 1999 Annual budget data is contained on the following three sheets. To view the budget worksheets click on the appropriate tab.

If you have any changes or suggestions about the budget, I have scheduled time to work on the budget again next week.

c. Save the memo as Budget Memo. Link the memo to the Memo sheet in the Excel file.

d. After inserting the memo, you decide to add a sentence about the year-to-date income total. Switch back to Word and add the following after the first sentence:

Please note that the profit margin in all three worksheets reflect the industry standard's profit margins for the same time periods.

e. Resave the memo and switch to Excel. Save the Excel file as Sports Company Budget.

f. Print the Word memo document and the Excel Memo sheet only.

On Your Own

4. Dave Robson has gathered population statistics on several Native American tribes for a report and has created a worksheet and pie chart of this data. Now Dave wants to include the worksheet and chart as a separate page in his report. Create a new Word document using the Elegant Report template. Replace the Company Name placeholder with your name. Replace the other placeholder text with an appropriate title and subtitle.

Below the titles, copy and paste the worksheet data from the Excel workbook file Tribe Populations. Center the table and remove the gridlines. Copy and link the chart to the document below the table. Center, and size the pie chart. Unexplode the Apache slice. Resave the workbook file. Delete pages 2 and 3 of the template. Save the Word document as Tribal Populations. Preview and print the document.

5. Each week you see tables of data in publications such as newspapers and magazines. Find a table of interest to you and create a worksheet and chart of the data. Use Word to create a brief report summarizing the data. Embed the chart and worksheet into the Word document. Change the type of chart in the Word document. Include your name and the date as a header in both documents. Print both the Word and Excel documents.

Concept Summary

Sharing Data Between Applications

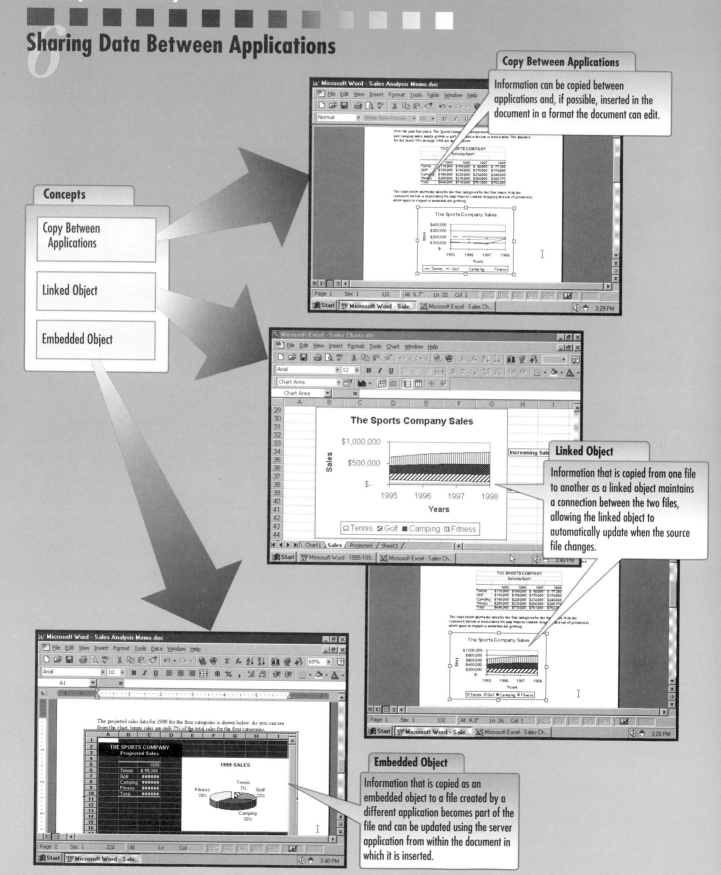

Concepts

- Copy Between Applications
- Linked Object
- Embedded Object

Copy Between Applications

Information can be copied between applications and, if possible, inserted in the document in a format the document can edit.

Linked Object

Information that is copied from one file to another as a linked object maintains a connection between the two files, allowing the linked object to automatically update when the source file changes.

Embedded Object

Information that is copied as an embedded object to a file created by a different application becomes part of the file and can be updated using the server application from within the document in which it is inserted.

Case Project

Introduction

This project is designed to reinforce your knowledge of the worksheet features used in the Excel labs. You will also be expected to use the Help feature to learn more about advanced features available in Excel.

Case

Marianne Virgili is the Director of the Glenwood Springs Chamber Resort Association. Each quarter the Chamber sends a newsletter called *Trends* to all Chamber members. The Director has asked you to create the end-of-year balance sheet, tables, and graphs to be included in the first-quarter issue of *Trends*. The first-quarter issue will contain the end-of-year balance sheet for the previous year.

Part 1

Open the file Glenwood Springs 1999 Balance. This file contains the Glenwood Springs Chamber Resort Association's 1999 balance sheet.

   a. Change the width of columns A and B to fully display the headings. Change the width of column C to 4. Delete column D.

   b. Enter the formulas and functions in column D needed to complete the totals for the balance sheet. The Total Assets number should equal the Total Liabilities plus Capital numbers.

   c. Format the numbers to be displayed with commas and two decimal places. Format the first number in each group and all totals as currency with two decimal places.

   d. Delete all blank rows above each subtotal and grand total.

   e. Add a bottom-line border under the last number in each group above a subtotal and under subtotals immediately above the grand total. Add a double-line border under the grand total of each group.

f. Change the size of the main title to be displayed larger than the rest of the text. Italicize and bold the headings in cells A4 and A25.

g. Insert three blank rows above the main title. Enter your name and the date in a header. Save and replace the workbook.

h. Preview the worksheet before printing. Print the worksheet.

Part 2

This issue of *Trends* will contain two tables. The first table will provide employment information for 1998 to 1999 for Garfield county. The second table will provide information on gross sales.

a. The employment information is shown below. Create a worksheet from this data.

Job Category	1998	1999
Agr., For., Fish.	174	197
Mining	813	920
Construction	1171	1593
Manufacturing	327	652
Trans., Comm., Util.	504	551
Wholesale Trade	410	466
Retail Trade	2859	3170
Fin., Ins., Real Est.	601	684
Services	2767	2841
Non-classified	15	18
Government	2328	2521

b. Format the two columns of data to display commas with no decimal places. Add an appropriate title to the worksheet.

c. Add a third column of data to show the percent change from 1998 to 1999. Enter the column heading % Change above the new column. Enter the formula to calculate the percent change from 1998 to 1999. Format the column as percent with two decimal places.

d. Add a row to show the total for the two columns of data and the percent change. Enter a row heading and the formulas to make these calculations. Format the data appropriately.

e. Enhance the appearance of the worksheet by adding such features as bold, bottom borders, different fonts, colors, and so on.

f. Put your name and the date in a header. Save and print the worksheet.

The second table will display the percent of gross sales for the second half of 1998 for the five major cities in the county.

g. Open a new worksheet file. Create a worksheet from the following data.

City	Sales	% of Total
Glenwood Springs	172.3	
Silt	4.1	
Rifle	39.7	
Carbondale	22.3	
Parachute	3.0	
Remainder of County	47.2	

h. Add a row to show the total sales. Enter a row heading and formula to make this calculation.

i. Enter the following worksheet title: TOTAL GROSS SALES for JUNE-SEPT. 1999 (in millions of dollars).

j. Enter formulas to calculate the percent of total sales for each city. Display the numbers as percents with one decimal place. Include an appropriate column heading.

k. Enhance the appearance of the worksheet using such features as bottom borders, bold, colors, and font changes.

l. Enter your name and the current date in the worksheet.

m. Save and print the worksheet.

Part 3

This issue of *Trends* will also include two charts. The first chart will be a visual representation of the gross sales table you created in Part 2.

a. Open the file you created containing the gross sales data. Create a 3-D pie chart of the gross sales data below the worksheet.

b. Add an appropriate title to the chart. Increase the font size of the title. Display the legend labels next to the percent values.

c. Add patterns and explode the Carbondale wedge of the pie.

d. Save and replace the worksheet. Print the worksheet.

The second chart included in this issue of *Trends* will display the gross sales for each quarter of 1999 and the last two quarters of 1998 for Garfield county and the two surrounding counties, Eagle and Pitkin.

e. Open the file County Gross Sales.xls. Enter your name in cell A1 and the date in cell A2.

f. Create a 3-D column chart of the data displayed in the worksheet in a new sheet.

g. Enter an appropriate title. Add X-axis and Y-axis titles.

h. Add patterns to the columns.

i. Create a header that contains your name and the current date centered over the chart.

j. Save and replace the worksheet. Print the chart only.

Glossary of Key Terms

3-D reference: A reference to the same cell or range on multiple sheets in the same workbook.

Absolute reference: A cell or range reference in a formula whose location remains the same (absolute) when copied. Indicated by a $ character entered before the column letter or row number or both.

Active cell: The cell displaying the cell selector and which will be affected by the next entry or procedure.

Active pane: The pane that contains the cell selector.

Active sheet: A sheet that contains the cell selector and that will be affected by the next action.

Adjacent range: A rectangular block of adjoining cells.

Alignment: The vertical or horizontal placement and orientation of an entry in a cell.

Area chart: A chart that shows trends by emphasizing the area under the curve.

Argument: The data the function uses to perform a calculation. It can be a number, a cell address, a range of cells, or a formula.

Autoformat: A built-in combination of formats that can be applied to a range.

Automatic recalculation: The recalculation of a formula within the worksheet whenever a value in a referenced cell in the formula changes.

Category-axis title: A label that describes the X axis.

Category name: Labels displayed along the X axis in a chart to identify the data being plotted.

Cell: The space created by the intersection of a vertical column and a horizontal row.

Cell selector: The heavy border surrounding a cell in the worksheet that identifies the active cell.

Chart: A visual representation of data in a worksheet.

Chart gridlines: Lines extending from the axis lines across the plot area that make it easier to read and evaluate the chart data.

Column: A vertical block of cells one cell wide in the worksheet.

Column chart: A chart that displays data as vertical columns.

Column letters: The border of letters across the top of the worksheet that identifies the columns in the worksheet.

Combination chart: A chart type that includes mixed data markers, such as both columns and lines.

Compound document: A document that contains a linked or embedded object.

Constant: A value that does not change unless you change it directly by typing in another entry.

Container file: A file that contains a linked or embedded object.

Control: A graphic object designed to automate the process of filling out a form.

Copy area: The cell or cells containing the data to be copied.

Custom dictionary: An additional dictionary you create to supplement the main dictionary.

Data labels: Labels for data points or bars that show the values being plotted on a chart.

Data marker: Represents a data series on a chart. It can be a symbol, color, or pattern, depending upon the type of chart.

Data series: The numbers to be charted.

Date numbers: The integers assigned to the days from January 1, 1900 through December 31, 2099 that allow dates to be used in calculations.

Dependent workbook: The workbook file that receives linked data.

Destination: The cell or range of cells that receives the data from the copy area or source.

Destination file: A document in which a linked object is inserted.

Docked: A toolbar or menu bar that is fixed to the edge of the window.

Embedded chart: A chart that is inserted into another file.

Embedded object: Information inserted into a destination file of another application that becomes part of this file but can be edited within the destination file using the server application.

Explode: To separate a wedge of a pie chart slightly from the other wedges in the pie.

External reference formula: A formula that creates a link between workbooks.

Fill handle: A small black square located in the lower right corner of the selection that is used to create a series or copy to adjacent cells with a mouse.

Floating: A toolbar or menu bar that appears in its own window.

Font: The typeface, type size, and style associated with a worksheet entry that can be selected to improve the appearance of the worksheet.

Footer: A line of text printed just above the bottom margin on each page.

Form: A formatted worksheet that is designed to be completed by filling in data in the blank spaces.

Format: Formats are settings that affect the display of entries in a worksheet.

Formatting toolbar: A toolbar that contains buttons used to change the format of a worksheet.

Formula: An entry that performs a calculation.

Formula bar: The bar near the top of the Excel window that displays the cell contents.

Freeze: To fix in place on the screen specified rows or columns or both when scrolling.

Function: A prewritten formula that performs certain types of calculations automatically.

Group: An object that contains other objects.

Header: A line of text printed just below the top margin on each page.

Heading: Row and column entries that are used to create the structure of the worksheet and describe other worksheet entries.

Landscape: The orientation of the printed document so it prints sideways across the length of the page.

Legend: A brief description of the symbols used in a chart that represent the data ranges.

Line chart: A chart that represents data as a set of points along a line.

Link: A relationship created between files that allows data in the destination file to be updated automatically when changes occur in the source file.

Linked object: Information created in a source file from one application and inserted into a destination file of another application while maintaining a link between files.

Live link: A linked object that automatically reflects in the destination document any changes made in the source document when the destination document is opened.

Lock: Cells whose contents cannot be changed when a worksheet is protected.

Logical operators: Symbols used in formulas that compare values in two or more cells.

Main dictionary: The dictionary included with Office 97.

Merged cell: A cell made up of several selected cells combined into one.

Minimal recalculation: The recalculation of only the formulas in a worksheet that are affected by a change of data.

Mixed reference: A cell address that is part absolute and part relative.

Name box: The area located on the left side of the formula bar that provides information about the selected item such as the reference of the active cell.

Nested function: A second argument in a function that is enclosed within its own set of parentheses.

Nonadjacent range: Cells or ranges that are not adjacent but are included in the same selection.

Number: A cell entry that contains any of the digits 0 to 9, and any of the special characters + = ( ) , . / $ % E e.

Object: An element such as a text box that can be added to a workbook and that can be selected, sized, and moved.

Office Assistant: A feature that is used to get Help on features specific to the Office application you are using.

OLE: Object Linking and Embedding is the program integretion technology that makes it possible to share data between applications.

Operand: A value on which a numeric formula performs a calculation.

Pane: A division of the worksheet window, either horizontal or vertical, through which different areas of the worksheet can be viewed at the same time.

Password: Prevents unauthorized users from turning off protection.

Paste area: The cells or range of cells that receives the data from the copy area or source.

Pie chart: A chart that compares parts to the whole. Each value in the data range is a wedge of the pie (circle).

Plot area: The area of the chart bounded by the axes.

Portrait: The orientation of the printed document so it prints across the width of a page.

Protection: A worksheet feature that prevents changes to data and formats.

Range: A selection consisting of two or more cells in a worksheet.

Range name: A descriptive name assigned to a cell or range of cells.

Reference: The column letter and row number of a cell.

Relative reference: A cell or range reference that automatically adjusts to the new location in the worksheet when the formula is copied.

Row: A horizontal block of cells one cell high in the worksheet.

Row numbers: The border of numbers along the left side of the worksheet that identifies the rows in the worksheet.

Selection handles: Small boxes surrounding a selected object that are used to size the object.

Series formula: A formula that links a chart object to the source worksheet.

Server: The application in which an embedded object is created.

Sheet: A division of a workbook that is used to display different types of information in Excel.

Sheet tab: On the bottom of the workbook window, the tabs where the sheet names appear.

Source: The cell or range of cells containing the data you want to copy.

Source file: The document that stores the data for the linked object.

Source workbook: The workbook file that supplies linked data.

Spreadsheet: A rectangular grid of rows and columns used to enter data.

Stack: The order in which objects are added in layers to the worksheet.

Stacked-column chart: A chart that displays the data values as columns stacked upon each other.

Standard toolbar: A toolbar that contains buttons used to complete the most frequently used menu commands.

Style: A named combination of formats that can be applied to a selection.

Syntax: Rules of structure for entering all functions.

Tab scroll buttons: Located to the left of the sheet tabs, they are used to scroll sheet tabs right or left.

Template: A workbook file that contains predesigned worksheets that can be used as a pattern for creating other similar sheets in new workbooks.

Text: A cell entry that contains text, numbers, or any other special characters.

Text box: A rectangular object in which you type text.

Title: In a chart, descriptive text that explains the contents of the chart.

Typeface: The appearance and shape of characters. Some common typefaces are Roman and Courier.

Value-axis title: A label that describes the values on the Y axis.

Variable: The resulting value of a formula that changes if the data it depends on changes.

What-if analysis: A technique used to evaluate what effect changing one or more values in formulas has on other values in the worksheet.

Word wrap: Feature that automatically determines when to begin the next line of text.

Workbook: The file in which you work and store sheets created in Excel.

Workbook window: A window that displays an open workbook file.

Worksheet: Similar to a financial spreadsheet in that it is a rectangular grid of rows and columns used to enter data.

Workspace: The area of the Excel application window where workbook windows are displayed.

X axis: The bottom boundary line of a chart.

Y axis: The left boundary line of a chart.

Command
Summary

Command	Shortcut	Toolbar	Action
File/**O**pen <file name>	Ctrl + O		Opens an existing workbook file
File/**C**lose			Closes open workbook file
File/**S**ave <file name>	Ctrl + S		Saves current file on disk using same file name
File/Save **A**s <file name>			Saves current file on disk using a new file name
File/Save **A**s/Save As **T**ype			Sets file format for document
File/Propert**i**es			Displays information about a file
File/**P**rint	Ctrl + P		Prints a sheet
File/Page Set**u**p/Header/Footer			Adds header and/or footer
File/Page Set**u**p/**L**andscape			Prints worksheet across length of paper
File/Prin**t** Area/**S**et Print Area			Sets a range as area to print
File/Print Pre**v**iew			Previews worksheet as it will be printed
File/E**x**it			Exits Excel
Edit/**U**ndo	Ctrl + Z		Undoes last editing or formatting change
Edit/**R**epeat	Ctrl + Y		Repeats last-used command
Edit/**C**opy	Ctrl + C		Copies selected data to Clipboard
Edit/**P**aste	Ctrl + V		Pastes selected data from Clipboard
Edit/Paste **S**pecial/Paste **L**ink			Creates a link to the source document
Edit/Paste **S**pecial/Paste			Embeds a selection
Edit/F**i**ll			Fills selected cells with contents of source cell
Edit/Cle**a**r/**C**ontents	Delete		Clears cell contents
Edit/Cle**a**r/Co**m**ments			Removes comment from cell
Edit/**D**elete/Entire **R**ow			Deletes selected rows
Edit/**D**elete/Entire **C**olumn			Deletes selected columns

Command	Shortcut	Toolbar	Action
Edit/De**l**ete Sheet			Removes sheed from workbook
Edit/**M**ove or Copy Sheet			Moves or copies current sheet
Edit/Lin**k**s			Edits settings associated with a link
View/**T**oolbars			Displays/hides selected toolbars
View/**F**ormula Bar			Displays/hides formula bar
View/**S**tatus Bar			Display/hides status bar
View/**Z**oom		100%	Changes magnification of window
Insert/**R**ows			Inserts a blank row
Insert/**C**olumns			Inserts a blank column
Insert/**W**orksheet			Inserts a new blank worksheet in workbook
Insert/C**h**art			Inserts chart into worksheet
Insert/**F**unction	⇧Shift + F3	f_*	Inserts a function
Insert/**N**ame/**D**efine			Assigns a name you specify to a cell or range of cells
Insert/**N**ame/**P**aste			Places name in formula bar or lists names in worksheet
Insert/**N**ame/**C**reate			Creates names using text in cells
Insert/Co**m**ment			Inserts a comment to a cell
F**o**rmat/C**e**lls	Ctrl + 1		Applies formats to selected cells
F**o**rmat/C**e**lls/**P**rotection			Changes protection of selected cells to locked or unlocked
F**o**rmat/C**e**lls/Number/Currency			Applies Currency format to selection
F**o**rmat/C**e**lls/Number/Accounting			Applies Accounting format to selection
F**o**rmat/C**e**lls/Font			Changes font and attributes of cell contents
F**o**rmat/C**e**lls/Font/**C**olor		A	Adds color to text
F**o**rmat/C**e**lls/Alignment/ Horizontal/Left, Center, or Right		≡, ≡, ≡	Aligns data left, center, or right in cell space
F**o**rmat/C**e**lls/Alignment/Center Across Selection			Centers cell contents across selected cells
F**o**rmat/C**e**lls/Alignment/Horizontal/Left/Indent 1			Indents cell entry one space
F**o**rmat/C**e**lls/Border/**O**utline			Adds border around selection
F**o**rmat/C**e**lls/Border			Adds border to selected edge of selection
F**o**rmat/C**e**lls/Patterns			Adds shading to selection
F**o**rmat/**R**ow/**H**ide			Hides selected rows
F**o**rmat/**R**ow/**U**nhide			Displays hidden rows
F**o**rmat/**C**olumn/**W**idth			Changes width of columns

Command	Shortcut	Toolbar	Action
Format/Column/Autofit Selection			Changes column width to match widest cell entry
Format/AutoFormat			Applies one of 16 built-in table formats to the worksheet range
Format/Style			Applies selected style to selection
Format/Sheet/Rename			Renames sheet
Tools/Spelling	F7	ᵃᵇᶜ✓	Spell-checks worksheet
Tools/Protection/Protect Sheet			Turns on protection for all locked cells
Tools/Protection/Unprotect Sheet			Turns off protection for all locked cells
Tools/Goal Seek			Adjusts value in specified cell until a formula dependent on that cell reaches specified result
Tools/Solver			Calculates a formula to achieve a given value by changing one of variables that affects formula
Tools/Options/View			Changes worksheet view options
Tools/Options/View/Gridlines			Turns on/off display of cell gridlines
Window/Arrange/Tiled			Arranges open windows side by side
Window/Split			Divides window into four panes at active cell
Window/Remove Split			Removes split bar from active worksheet
Window/Freeze Panes			Freezes top and/or leftmost panes
Window/Unfreeze			Unfreezes window panes

Charts

Command	Shortcut	Toolbar	Action
Format/Selected Data Series/ Data Labels	Ctrl + 1		Inserts data labels into chart
Format/Selected Legend	Ctrl + 1		Changes legend
Format/Selected Data Labels	Ctrl + 1		Changes format of data labels
Format/Selected Data Series/ Patterns	Ctrl + 1		Applies color and patterns to selected data series
Format/Text Box			Changes format of text box
Chart/Chart Type		◪ ▾	Changes type of chart
Chart/Chart Options			Adds or modifies chart elements
Chart/ Add Data			Inserts new data into chart

Index

ABS function, SS54
Absolute references, SS60-62
Accounting format for numbers, SS69-71
Active cell, SS10
Active pane, SS100
Active sheet, SS10
Addition, in formulas, SS30
Adjacent range, SS17
Alignment:
    changing, in cells, SS32-34
    defined, SS3, SS32
    right-aligning, SS33-34
AND function, SS54
Area charts, SS136, SS147
Arguments:
    for functions, SS54
    for IF functions, SS176
Arial typeface, SS75
Arithmetic operators, SS30
Arrows, adding to charts, SS155-156
AutoCorrect feature, SS111
AutoFill, using, SS92-94
AutoFit feature, SS70-71
Autoformats, using, SS133-135
Automatic recalculation, SS31
AutoSum, using, SS55-57
AVERAGE function, SS54, SS58

Bar charts, SS136
Bold, formatting as, SS76-77
Borders, adding to worksheets, SS119-120
Bubble charts, SS136
Buttons:
    Align Left, Align Right, SS33-34
    Arrow, SS155
    AutoSum, SS55
    Bold, SS76
    Cancel, SS16
    Center, SS33
    Chart Wizard, SS139

Buttons (continued):
    Close, SS8, SS9
    Control-menu, SS8
    Copy, SS26
    Enter, SS16
    Fill Color, SS118
    Italic, SS76
    Merge and Center, SS74
    Minimize, SS8, SS9
    Paste, SS27
    Paste Function, SS57
    Preview, SS38
    Redo, SS66-67
    Restore, SS8, SS9
    Save, SS36
    Spelling, SS111
    tab scroll, SS10
    Text Box, SS153
    toolbar, SS11
    Underline, SS77
    Undo, SS66

Category-axis title, SS137
Category names, on charts, SS137
Cell selector, SS10
Cells:
    active, SS10
    alignment of data in, SS32-34
    clearing data from, SS17-18
    comments in, SS63-64
    defined, SS3, SS10
    locking, SS187-189
    moving contents of, SS74
    selecting, SS10
Centering, across columns, SS74-75
Chart toolbar, SS142
Chart Wizard, using, SS139-143
Charts:
    adding arrows to, SS155-156
    adding patterns to, SS150-153

ss229

SPREADSHEET

Notes

Appendix A

Additional Microsoft Excel 97 User Specialist Certification Topics

- Sort Data
- Clear Formats
- Save Spreadsheets as HTML Documents
- Create and Modify 3D Shapes
- Delete Worksheets

Sorting Data

Often the data in a worksheet consists of rows that contain related data. For example, in the worksheet shown below of a grade book for an introductory computer class each row in column A contains the last name of each student in the class. Data organized in this fashion can be rearranged or sorted to make it easier to locate information. In this case, the instructor wants the information in alphabetical order by name for his/her own use when entering the grades.

This file can also be downloaded from www.mhhe.com/cit/apps/oleary.

- Create the worksheet of student grades shown in Figure A-1 below.
- Save it as Grades.

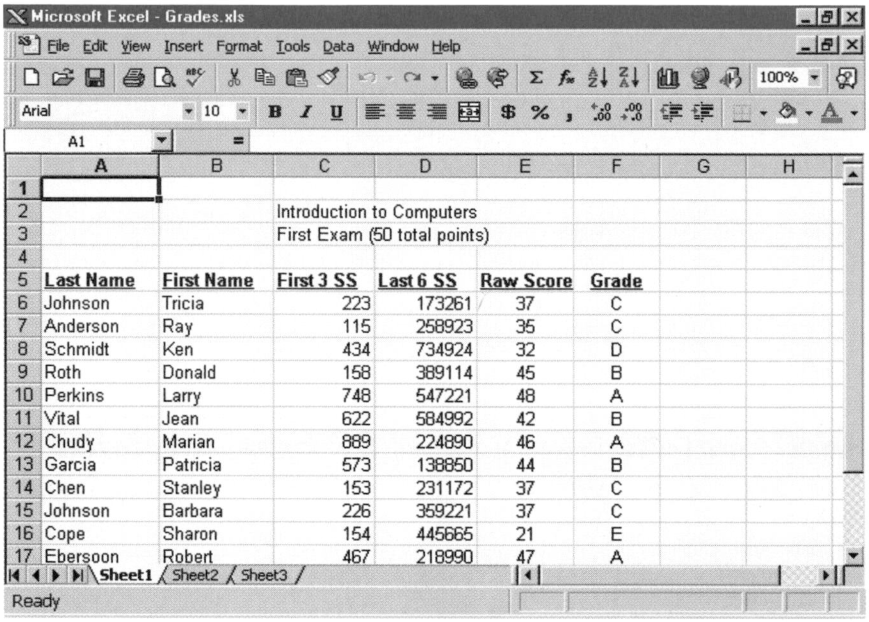

	A	B	C	D	E	F
1						
2			Introduction to Computers			
3			First Exam (50 total points)			
4						
5	Last Name	First Name	First 3 SS	Last 6 SS	Raw Score	Grade
6	Johnson	Tricia	223	173261	37	C
7	Anderson	Ray	115	258923	35	C
8	Schmidt	Ken	434	734924	32	D
9	Roth	Donald	158	389114	45	B
10	Perkins	Larry	748	547221	48	A
11	Vital	Jean	622	584992	42	B
12	Chudy	Marian	889	224890	46	A
13	Garcia	Patricia	573	138850	44	B
14	Chen	Stanley	153	231172	37	C
15	Johnson	Barbara	226	359221	37	C
16	Cope	Sharon	154	445665	21	E
17	Ebersoon	Robert	467	218990	47	A

FIGURE A-1

You can also sort data by date. Excel sorts lists alphabetically by default.

The data in a worksheet can be rearranged by sorting the information into ascending (1 to 9, A to Z) or descending (9 to 1, Z to A) sort order. When you sort, Excel rearranges the rows, columns, or individual cells according to the sort order you specify.

You want the worksheet to appear in ascending alphabetical order by last name. To indicate which column to sort on you first position the cell pointer in any cell of the column to be sorted.

The menu equivalent is Data/Sort.

- Move to any cell that contains a name in column A.
- Click 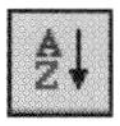.

Your screen should be similar to Figure A-2.

FIGURE A-2

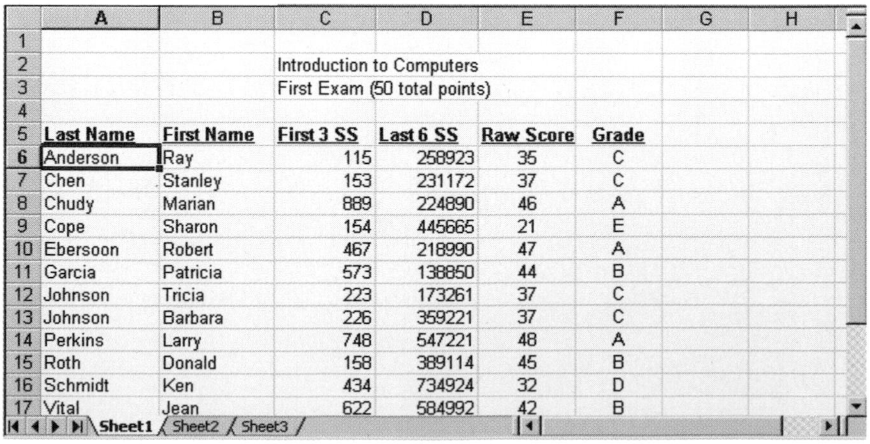

	A	B	C	D	E	F
1						
2			Introduction to Computers			
3			First Exam (50 total points)			
4						
5	Last Name	First Name	First 3 SS	Last 6 SS	Raw Score	Grade
6	Anderson	Ray	115	258923	35	C
7	Chen	Stanley	153	231172	37	C
8	Chudy	Marian	889	224890	46	A
9	Cope	Sharon	154	445665	21	E
10	Ebersoon	Robert	467	218990	47	A
11	Garcia	Patricia	573	138850	44	B
12	Johnson	Tricia	223	173261	37	C
13	Johnson	Barbara	226	359221	37	C
14	Perkins	Larry	748	547221	48	A
15	Roth	Donald	158	389114	45	B
16	Schmidt	Ken	434	734924	32	D
17	Vital	Jean	622	584992	42	B

The worksheet data is rearranged to display in ascending alphabetical order by last name. However, notice that although the records for Tricia and Barbara Johnson are sorted correctly by last name, they are not by first name. You want the records that have the same last name to be further sorted by first name. To do this, you will perform a sort on the contents of more than one column. This is called a **multilevel sort**.

■ Choose <u>D</u>ata/<u>S</u>ort.

The Sort dialog box on your screen should be similar to Figure A-3.

FIGURE A-3

The Sort by text box correctly displays the column header of the column containing the cell pointer on which the sort will be performed. Additionally, because the default setting is ascending sort order, this option does not need to be changed. A multilevel sort uses the first column selected in Sort by as the primary sort column; all other sort columns are sorted in order after the primary sort is performed. You need to specify the second column, First Name, in the first Then by box, as the second column to be sorted.

■ Select First Name from the first Then by drop down list.

When a sort is performed, Excel assumes that you want all data except the uppermost row contained in contiguous rows and columns surrounding the selected cell to be sorted. The first row is not included in the sort range because the default setting assumes that the first row contains headers that you do not want included in the sort. If your data did not include a header row as the first row in the range, you would need to choose the No Header Row option to change the setting to include this row in the sort. Since this worksheet includes a header row as the first row, the Header row option is correctly specified already.

■ Click  .

Your screen should be similar to Figure A-4.

FIGURE A-4

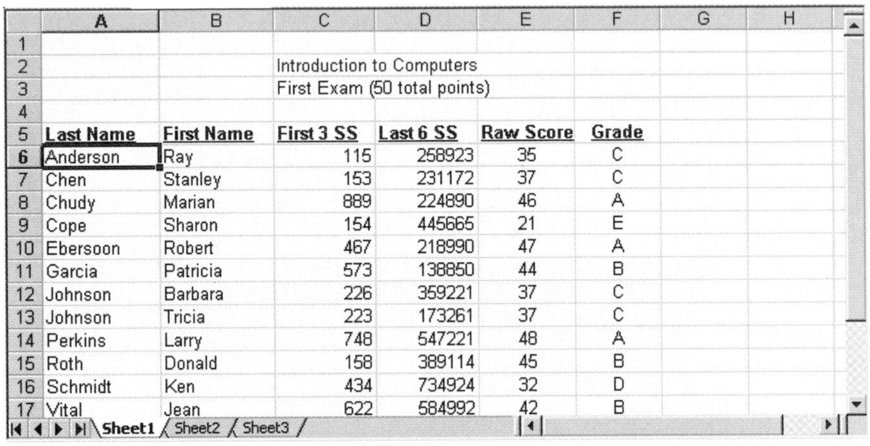

	A	B	C	D	E	F	G	H
1								
2			Introduction to Computers					
3			First Exam (50 total points)					
4								
5	**Last Name**	**First Name**	**First 3 SS**	**Last 6 SS**	**Raw Score**	**Grade**		
6	Anderson	Ray	115	258923	35	C		
7	Chen	Stanley	153	231172	37	C		
8	Chudy	Marian	889	224890	46	A		
9	Cope	Sharon	154	445665	21	E		
10	Ebersoon	Robert	467	218990	47	A		
11	Garcia	Patricia	573	138850	44	B		
12	Johnson	Barbara	226	359221	37	C		
13	Johnson	Tricia	223	173261	37	C		
14	Perkins	Larry	748	547221	48	A		
15	Roth	Donald	158	389114	45	B		
16	Schmidt	Ken	434	734924	32	D		
17	Vital	Jean	622	584992	42	B		

Sheet1 / Sheet2 / Sheet3 /

The worksheet has been sorted first by last name and second by first name wherever a duplicate occurred in the primary sort column.

- Add a header that displays your name and the current date to the worksheet.

- Print the worksheet.

- Save the worksheet as Sorted Grades to your data disk.

Clearing Formats and Saving Spreadsheets as HTML Documents

All Office 97 programs include the capability to convert documents to HTML format.

Excel worksheet data can also be saved in HTML (Hypertext Markup Language) format so it can be posted on the World Wide Web (WWW). The WWW is a part of the Internet that consists of information containing text and graphic images and hypertext links. The information must be written using the HTML programming language so that a browser program, such as Internet Explorer, can display it. To demonstrate this feature, you will use the Sorted Grades file you created in the previous section.

- If necessary, open Sorted Grades.

Many instructors post their grades to a Web site for students to access. To insure privacy, grades are posted by the last six digits of the social security number. To make it easier for students to locate their grade in the list you want the numbers sorted in ascending numerical order and to add formatting to the data to make it read across the row.

- Sort the worksheet by the Last 6 SS column in ascending order.

- Apply the Colorful 1 Autoformat to the worksheet data.

- Click outside the selection to see the formatting.

You decide that you do not like how this formatting looks and want to try a different autoformat. To remove the formats applied to this range without effecting the data,

- Select the worksheet range.

- Choose Edit/Clear/Formats.

All formats are removed and the normal text style is applied to all cells in the range.

- Apply the List 1 Autoformat to the data range.

- Center the data in the Raw Score and Grade columns.

This format will make it easier for students to scroll across the row to see their grade. Now you want to save the worksheet data as an HTML document so you can post it to the class Web site.

- Choose File/Save as HTML.

Your screen should be similar to Figure A-5.

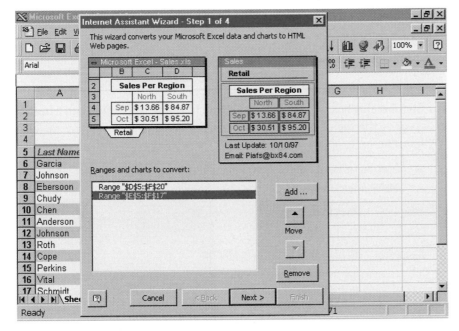

FIGURE A-5

The Internet Assistant Wizard dialog box is used to guide you through the steps to convert the worksheet to an HTML document. The first step is to specify the range of data you want to be included in the HTML document. In this case, the only information you want is the data in columns D, E, and F.

- Click Add ... .

- Select the data range including the headers in columns D, E and F.

- Click OK .

The selected range appears at the top of the list in the list box. If there are other ranges in the list box that were specified by a previous user, you need to remove them.

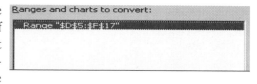

■ If necessary, select any other ranges in the list and click **Remove**.

■ Click **Next >**.

The selected default in the next step to create a new Web page is the correct selection. To continue,

■ Click **Next >**.

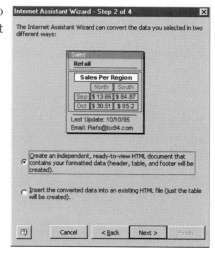

The Step 3 dialog box is used to specify a title to appear in the title bar, a header to appear at the top of the document, descriptive text to accompany the data and information to appear in a footer.

■ Enter the following information in the appropriate text boxes.

Title: **First Exam Grades**

Header: **First Exam Grades**

Description: **Grades appear in ascending numerical order by the last 6 digits of your Social Security number.**

By: **Your Name**

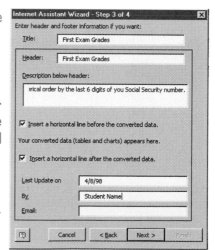

■ Turn on the two options to include horizontal lines above and below the data.

■ Click **Next >**.

The only setting you need to change in the last dialog box is to specify drive A containing your data disk as the location to save the file and a file name.

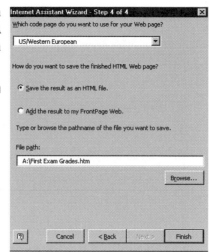

- Type **A:\ First Exam Grades.htm** in the File Path text box.

- Click   Finish .

If you have a Web browser program such as Internet Explorer, you can open the First Exam Grades.htm document to view the Web page as it would appear on the WWW. Alternatively, you can open the document in Excel and preview it.

- Close without saving the Sorted Grades file.

- Open First Exam Grades.html (change the file type to All Files).

Your screen should be similar to Figure A-6.

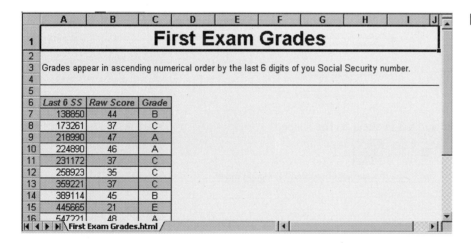

FIGURE A-6

The header, horizontal lines, data range, and footer information you specified appear similar to how they will appear if displayed in a Web browser.

- Preview, then print the document.

- Close the file.

Creating 3-D Shapes and Deleting Worksheets

In addition to the drawing features you learned about in Lab 4 you can create 3 dimensional (3-D) shapes using the Drawing toolbar. To learn about this feature, you will further enhance the Sales Chart worksheet you created in Lab 4.

■ Open the worksheet file Sales Charts from your data disk.

■ Make the Sales sheet active.

■ Copy the Increasing Sales drawing object to Sheet 3.

You will apply several different 3-D features to this object to learn about how this feature works.

■ If necessary select the object.

■ Increase the size of the object until it is approximately 4 cells high and two cells wide.

■ Display the Drawing toolbar.

Your screen should be similar to Figure A-7.

FIGURE A-7

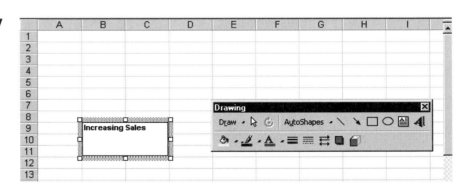

To add a 3-D effect to the shape,

■ Click  3-D

■ Select any shape from the 3-D pop-up menu.

Your screen should be similar to Figure A-8.

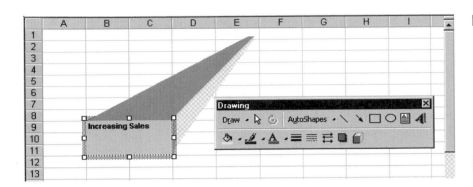

Figure A-8 shows the 3-D Style 19 shape.

- Select several other 3-D shapes to see how they look when applied to the object.

In addition, you can modify the 3-D settings using the 3-D Settings toolbar. To open this toolbar,

- Click [■] and choose 3-D Settings.

The buttons in this toolbar are used to modify the depth (the extrusion) of the object and its color, rotation, angle, direction of lighting, and surface texture.

- Use each of the 3-D settings to modify your shape.

- Select a 3-D design that you think would look good in place of the original Increasing Sales text box in the Sales sheet.

- Resize the object until it is just large enough to display the text on a single line.

- Copy the object to the Clipboard.

- Make the Sales sheet active.

- Delete the Increasing Sales text box (and arrow if necessary, depending upon the 3-D shape you created).

- Paste the new 3-D object in the worksheet and position it appropriately to point to the increasing sales section of the chart. Adjust the object as needed.

- Apply the same 3-D effect to the Decreasing Sales object.

- Preview the worksheet. Adjust the location of the charts and 3-D objects as needed so that it prints on a single page.

Your screen should be similar to Figure A-9.

FIGURE A-9

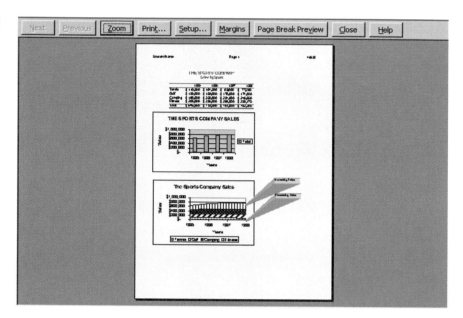

■ Print the Sales worksheet.

■ Close the 3-D Settings toolbar and the Drawing toolbar.

Since you do not need Sheet3, you will remove it.

■ Select Sheet3.

■ Choose **E**dit/Delete **S**heet/ 　　OK 　　.

■ Save the revised workbook as 3-D Effects to your data disk.

Practice Exercises

1. Open Sorted Grades. Change the sort order to descending order by Raw Score. Sort the worksheet data again by three columns: Raw Score as the primary sort, Last Name as the second, and First Name as the third. Add a 3-D text object containing text that describes the effect this sort had on the data. Print the worksheet. Save it to your data disk as Sorted Grades 3.

2. Open the 1998-1998 Summary Budget worksheet you created at the end of Lab 3. Replace the worksheet title with a 3-D colored text box containing the same information. Print the worksheet. Save the worksheet as Summary Budget Revised on your data disk.

    Save the worksheet a second time as an HTML file named Summary.HTM on your data disk. Because the drawing object cannot be saved in the HTML document, set the range to include the worksheet data only. Add horizontal lines. Include the following information in the HTML document:

Header:	Sports Company Budget
Description:	Below is the proposed budget for 1998 and the projected budget for 1999.
By:	Your Name

    Preview and print the first page of the HTML document.